Pelican Books

Your
MEMORY

Alan Baddeley is Director of the British Medical Research
Council's Applied Psychology Unit in Cambridge. He is the
author of **The Psychology of Memory** (1976), one of the most
comprehensive and readable specialist texts on the subject in
print today, has published over 100 papers concerned with
human memory problems and performance under stress, and
has contributed chapters to many books intended for a
non-specialist audience. Dr Baddeley serves on various
scientific committees, three of them concerned with special
skills training for army and navy personnel and one with
rehabilitation of the victims of strokes and head injuries. In
recent years his principal research interest has been short-term
working memory, and its links with visuo-spatial and
auditory imagery.

To Roland, Gavin and Barty.

Your MEMORY

A User's Guide

Alan Baddeley

Penguin Books

Penguin Books Ltd, Harmondsworth,
Middlesex, England
Viking Penguin Inc., 40 West 23rd Street,
New York, New York 10010, U.S.A.
Penguin Books Australia Ltd, Ringwood,
Victoria, Australia
Penguin Books Canada Limited, 2801 John Street,
Markham, Ontario, Canada L3R 1B4
Penguin Books (N.Z.) Ltd, 182-190 Wairau Road,
Auckland 10, New Zealand

First published by Sidgwick & Jackson 1982
Published in Pelican Books 1983
Reprinted 1986

Printed in Italy by Sagdos

**This book was devised and produced
by Multimedia Publications (UK) Limited**

Editor Anne Cope
Production Arnon Orbach
Design, layout and cover John and Orna Design
Picture research Tessa Paul, Marion Drescher
Illustration John Dawson, Perry Taylor
Indexing Anne Hardy

Introduction

We have inside our heads a system for classifying, storing and retrieving information that exceeds the best computer in capacity, flexibility and speed. At the same time we have a system that is so limited and unreliable than it cannot consistently remember a nine-figure telephone number long enough to dial it. How can human memory at the same time be so efficient and yet so inadequate? Indeed, what *is* memory? We talk of having a good memory or a terrible memory, of someone 'losing his memory', and of memory training. Such expressions suggest that memory is a single entity – something that can be good or bad, lost and perhaps found again, something that can be trained, like a muscle which gets out of condition if not used frequently. As we shall see, all of these common assumptions are false.

Human memory is not a simple unitary entity; it is rather a collection of interacting systems which have in common the job of storing and subsequently retrieving information. A person does not lose his memory in the sense of all these systems failing simultaneously; if they did, the person would be reduced to a vegetable. Memory does however break down in many and various ways; these are an important source of information about how normal memory works. We certainly can improve the efficiency with which we use our memory systems, but it involves the development and use of strategies to make the operation of the systems more efficient. Considerable practice and hard work is needed to develop such strategies, but the hard work without the use of the strategies is unlikely to achieve very much.

Memory is a vital characteristic of the human species. Organisms evolve to adapt to their environment in many different ways. There are however two broad classes of adaptation. The first of these involves preprogramming the organism to cope with its environment, so that it is born with all the necessary instincts and equipment to operate efficiently and effectively with virtually no learning. This is clearly a very successful means of adaptation and has enabled an enormous range of organisms, from plants, bacteria, and insects to 'simple' vertebrates, to continue to flourish for millions of years. Such organisms have their mode of adaptation 'wired in' and, as such, have minimal need for learning or memory. The second involves the production of an organism which is adaptable. Here, there is much less preprogramming, and the organism is left to modify its behaviour in response to its environment. This allows for considerably greater complexity and variability of behaviour; it also demands a larger brain and is heavily dependent on the capacity to learn and remember. The human race is the obvious example of this form of evolution – our ability to learn and to remember has allowed us to develop tools and language, technologies which have in turn vastly increased our ability to store and communicate yet more information through writing, and subsequently films and television, all of which can be regarded as an extension of the memory. However, without the individual's memory, the vast information stored in the libraries of the world would be incomprehensible. As such, the ability to learn and remember, allowing as it does the development of language, is perhaps our most crucial characteristic.

This book presents an overview of what we know at present about human memory. It is described as a 'guide' and its aims are analogous to those of a guidebook describing a country. It is written for the general reader, not the expert, and it attempts to convey both information and enthusiasm for what its author regards as a fascinating and important area. A good guidebook should give reliable and up-to-date information on the most salient and important features of a country (its major cities, roads, railways and ports for example), some indication of its history, and some economic and cultural background. On top of this broad framework however, a good guide ought also to try to convey the 'feel' of the country, to describe the interesting byways as well as referring to the motorways, to cover picturesque villages as well as important towns, to include legends as well as history. In just the same way, this book aims to provide information both about the central and important characteristics of human memory and about some of its more intriguing byways. Human memory is clearly a country that in one sense we all know. As I hope the book will convince you, however, human memory is vastly more complex, varied and fascinating than most of us ever realize.

'Education is what survives when what has been learnt has been forgotten'.
B. F. Skinner

This guidebook to human memory is concerned almost exclusively with the psychology of memory, but, just as a guidebook of a country might contain some reference to the geology of the area discussed, we shall from time to time touch on the physiology of memory. However, although the physiological basis of learning and memory is an important and fascinating topic in its own right, my own view is that its current state of development is such that it has as yet very little to contribute to the psychological understanding of memory.

As I suspect most guidebooks are, this book was written primarily from memory, although the facts were of course checked subsequently. A few years ago I attempted to write a brief survey of human memory, but re-read everything available before I began to write, with the result that, instead of producing an efficiently compiled overview, I emerged five years later with a specialist text. This time I have taken advantage of the fact that memory is a great abstracter; it is one of the best means I know of sorting out what is important from a mass of detail, an approach that has allowed me to complete this book in considerably less than five years. However, memory is very subject to personal bias, and for that reason I should perhaps conclude by saying a little about my aims in writing this book.

I set out with two aims in view. The first was to communicate some of my own enthusiasm for what I regard as a fascinating subject, and to try to make more generally available the results of some of the intensive research on human memory that has been carried out in recent years. As an experimental psychologist who has devoted a large part of his time to the study of memory, I am naturally an enthusiast, but then I suspect I might have been equally enthusiastic had I instead devoted the last 20 years to the sex life of the Australian wombat! I am however encouraged by the fact that friends and colleagues from outside the field of psychology seem to find the workings of the human memory intriguing; we are most of us interested in ourselves, and our memories are a very important part of us. I hope this book will help you appreciate both the richness of your memory, and its limitations, and thereby encourage you to make full use of its strengths while guarding against its weaknesses.

My second interest in writing this book stems from the fact that, as an applied psychologist, I am interested in using my scientific skills to help solve practical problems. The job has the great attraction of allowing me to collaborate at different times with a wide range of people working in a wide variety of jobs: from the postman to the soldier, the neurosurgeon to the deep-sea diver. However, this type of work also makes it clear how many applied problems there are, and how poor is the typical communication betweeen the person with the problem and the applied scientist who might be able to advise on the answer. This is particularly frustrating when the answer is already known, but through lack of communication is ignored.

I also wish as an applied psychologist to gain the maximum from the work that psychologists have carried out; to do this I need to inform as many people as possible. Ideally, if we have found something out which is of general importance, then I would like it to be so well known that it becomes regarded as 'common sense'. I think in some aspects of ergonomics, for example, this has been achieved. These days if a car is designed with the speedometer dial obscured by the steering wheel, it would be pointed out by newspaper motoring correspondents, who quite rightly consider the ergonomic design of cars as an appropriate area of comment, and who would regard such blatant errors as obscuring the instrument panel as contrary to common sense. As an applied psychologist who works, among other things, on human memory, I therefore have the additional subversive interest of trying in this book to take some of the many things we have found out about human memory in the last 20 years and move them a little nearer to being accepted as 'common sense'. My main purpose remains, however, that of an enthusiast trying to convey some of the intriguing and important things that psychologists have discovered about the elegant and powerful, but very fallible, system we call memory.

Author's acknowledgements _____

In writing this book I inevitably stood upon the shoulders of previous authors. The books I found particularly helpful were, first of all, Ian Hunter's deservedly popular book entitled *Memory*[1], which is particularly strong on some of the more colourful aspects of human memory. I found its case histories and information on mnemonic systems particularly stimulating, and although it is somewhat dated, having been written more than 20 years ago, it is still very well worth reading. I also found *Cognitive Psychology* by Robert Solso[2] a well-written and useful overview of current concerns in that area. John Bransford's *Human Cognition*[3] was particularly helpful in formulating the chapter on semantic memory, while the chapter on eyewitness testimony is obviously strongly influenced by Elizabeth Loftus's excellent book, *Eyewitness Testimony*[4]. Traces of all these, and of course of my previous more specialized book *The Psychology of Memory*[5], permeate my treatment of many aspects of memory.

I would also like to thank Olive Fowles for turning my sometimes barely audible monologue into typescript, and Charlotte Parry-Crooke and Anne Cope for their sympathetic editing. Finally I would like to thank my wife Hilary and my three sons for their forbearance during the various holidays over which this book was written.

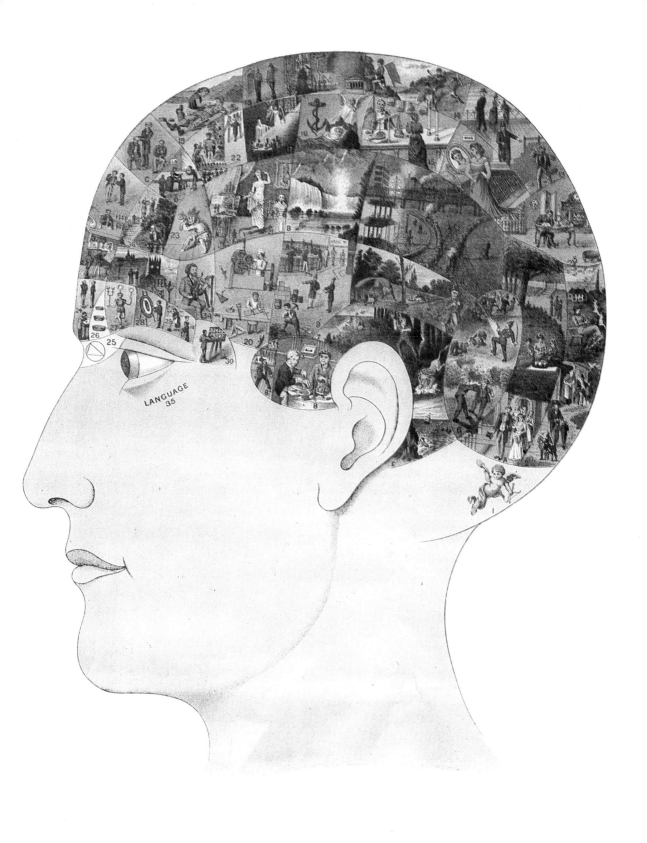

1

What is your memory? _____

Memory is the capacity for storing and retrieving information. Without it we would be unable to see, hear or think. We would have no language to express our plight, and indeed no sense of personal identity. In short, without memory we would be vegetables, intellectually dead. This may seem paradoxical since one hears of people losing their memory who, although incapacitated, are nevertheless quite capable of perceiving, thinking and talking. Why is this possible if they have lost their memory? The reason is simple. Human memory is not a single unitary function like the heart or the liver. It consists rather of a whole series of complex interconnected systems which serve different purposes and behave in very different ways. The one function that these systems have in common is that of storing information for future use. In short, you do not have *a* memory, you have many *memories*. Consequently someone who is said to have lost their memory is someone who has a malfunction in one or more of these systems. Had all of them been lost, the person would be unconscious and probably dead.

How many kinds of memory?

An obvious next question is how many memories does a human being have? Unfortunately, as with most questions regarding human memory, there is no simple answer. Once we begin to categorize the human memory system we enter the realm of theory, an area in which there are no true answers, merely those which provide a more complete and satisfactory interpretation of the available evidence. That is not of course to say that what follows is simply personal opinion; the bulk of what I shall describe is verifiable evidence about human memory. Such evidence places considerable constraints on any theory, and the theories in turn suggest where one should look for further evidence.

The structure of human memory

Throughout this book, I assume human memory to be broadly divisible into three major systems. The systems interact with each other, and can each be split into sub-systems. These are shown on page 12 and labelled *long-term memory*, *short-term memory* and *sensory memory*. In this diagram they are represented as boxes, but they could equally well have been shown as circles, clouds, or purely words. Their purpose is to provide an analogy, and the exact representation is a matter of convenience. As with a map, the theory or model should not be regarded as a realistic picture of the area it is attempting to represent. We are not trying to say that there are three separate physiological structures within the head representing the three aspects of memory. We are simply expressing the fact that the three types of memory differ in certain important ways and that it is useful to express this fact by representing the three memory systems as separate boxes. This apparently straightforward point is not always appreciated by psychologists themselves, some of whom tend to talk about 'boxology' or 'boxes in the head theories', as though the person expressing a theory in this way literally assumes that the head must contain a series of physiologically separate components that map on to the conceptual distinctions made.

The phrenological approach to memory and other mental functions assumed that everything had its place. In fact, no single area of the brain is responsible for memory.

Theories, like maps, are aids to understanding. Like maps, their usefulness depends on shared assumptions.

A theory is like a map, and the most useful map is often not an exact and realistic representation of the terrain. The well-known map of the London underground system is a good illustration of this point. It provides an elegant way of summarizing essential information about the London underground system. It sacrifices realism but given its purpose is a better map for doing so. Scientific theories are to some extent like the tube map; they represent certain aspects of the world in a simplified way. They are not meant to be taken literally, and to object to a theory because it expresses its concept in terms of labelled boxes is no more sensible than to criticize the London tube map because the colours used to represent the various lines do not correspond to the colours of the trains that run on those lines.

If we are not sure whether human memory represents one, two or many systems, how is it possible to write sensibly about it? Fortunately, if you were to compare the views of someone like myself with those of someone who argued for a single unitary memory system, you would find that we agreed on far more than we disagreed about. We would however naturally tend to discuss the areas of disagreement, and it would be easy to form the conclusion that we had no ground in common. A more accurate interpretation would be that we are arguing about the best way of thinking about the considerable evidence on which we both agree. The categorization we each adopt is to some extent arbitrary, but will only be maintained as long as we find that it helps us to understand what we already know, and successfully promote further discoveries. If one way of looking at the situation consistently appears to be fruitful, whereas the other does not, then there will be a gradual tendency for people to adopt the first view and relinquish the second. Such changes tend not to be the sudden result of a single experiment, but occur gradually as the evidence builds up, making one or other view easier to defend, or more exciting.

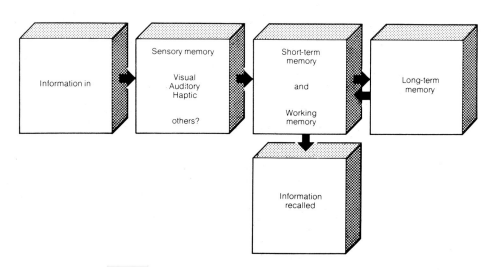

The flow of information through the memory system. (Adapted from Atkinson and Shiffrin, 1971)

Long-term memory

Of the three types of memory illustrated opposite, that which would correspond most closely to the layman's view of memory is long-term memory. This represents information that is stored for considerable periods of time. Indeed, as we shall see later, some would claim that information in memory never disappears, but simply becomes less and less accessible. Remembering your own name, how to speak, where you lived as a child, or where you were last year or indeed five minutes ago are all assumed to depend on long-term memory. Such memory is primarily concerned with storing information, unlike sensory memory and short-term memory where the storage is an incidental feature of other aspects of the system.

To an experimental psychologist the phrase 'long-term memory' refers to information which is stored sufficiently durably to be accessible over a period of anything more than a few *seconds*. The reason for this is that, on the whole, memory tested after one or two minutes seems to behave in much the same way as memory tested after one or two days, or years. The same does not apply, as we shall see in due course, to memory tested after one or two seconds, or milliseconds. Is long-term memory a unitary system? This is still a controversial question. Distinctions of at least two types are, however, commonly made.

Same location – different memories? No two people remember the same thing in the same way.

Episodic and semantic long-term memory

A few years ago the Canadian psychologist, Endel Tulving[1], pointed out a useful distinction between two types of long-term memory: *episodic memory*, which involves remembering particular incidents such as having breakfast this morning, and *semantic memory*, which essentially concerns knowledge about the world. Knowing the meaning of a word or the chemical formula for salt or the capital of France would all be examples of semantic memory. There is no doubt that there are differences between specific personal memories of individual incidents and generalized knowledge of the world, which has often been acquired over a considerable period of time. Whether these represent separate memory systems or different aspects of a single system is still uncertain. The distinction is however a convenient and useful one, as is indicated by the treatment of semantic memory in a separate chapter.

Long-term perceptual memory

A great deal of research on human memory has used verbal materials, since words are easy to present and the subject's responses easy to record and score. In recent years researchers have increasingly asked whether memory for verbal materials is characteristic of all memory, and in particular whether memory for non-verbalizable sensory experiences relies on quite different memory systems. Undoubtedly we can remember the taste of cheese or the smell of burning rubber or the sound of the sea breaking on a rocky shore without using verbal descriptions of these experiences. Are there separate auditory and visual memory systems, or an all-embracing memory system which is capable of encoding all our experiences? Taking this latter view much verbal learning is verbal only in as much as the material is presented verbally and the subject responds verbally; what is stored is the experience conjured up by the verbal material. Fortunately the general rules which apply to the learning of verbal material also seem to apply at least broadly to remembering pictures or sounds, so the overall conclusions drawn in the chapters that follow are still likely to hold whether we finish up with the conclusion that long-term memory is a unitary system, or a dual or multiple one.

An aid to working memory: a Chinese abacus. A recent study showed that a skilled abacus user can do calculations just as quickly as someone using an electronic calculator. Extremely skilled users can even dispense with the real thing and operate on an imaginary abacus instead!

Short-term memory

If you are to understand this sentence, you need to remember the beginning of the sentence until you get to the end. Without some kind of memory for the words and the order in which they occur, language would be incomprehensible.

Suppose I ask you to multiply 23 by 7 in your head. Try looking away from the page and doing this. Presumably in order to come up with the answer you first of all need to remember the number, you then need to multiply 3 by 7, and note that the answer is 21. You then need to remember the 1 and carry the 2, another task which involves remembering. You next multiply the 2 by 7, retrieve the 2 that you carried, making 16, retrieve the original 1 and come up with the answer 161. All of this involves a good deal of temporary storage of numbers, all of which need to be retrieved accurately and at the appropriate time. Having completed the sum there is no further need to retrieve information such as which number was carried, and it seems unlikely that after a couple of similar sums you would be able to remember this information.

In both the language comprehension and the arithmetic case therefore there is a need for the temporary storage of information in order to perform some other task—in these cases, understanding or calculating. Once the task has been achieved, the information stored is no longer required. Short-term memory is the name given to the system or, perhaps more appropriately, set of systems which allow this temporary storage of information which is essential for a brief period of time, and subsequently quite irrelevant.

To what extent does short-term memory represent a system which is quite different from long-term memory? Here again there has been considerable controversy over recent years. One view is that short-term memory represents the same system as long-term memory, but is used under rather special conditions which lead to very little long-term retention. The alternative view,

'Now, I wonder why he did that?' Evaluating alternative strategies depends on working memory.

which I myself support, is that long- and short-term memory involve separate systems, although they are very closely integrated in operation. I myself would further argue that short-term memory represents not one but a complex set of interacting sub-systems.

Sensory memory

When you go to the cinema, you see what appears to be a continuous scene with people moving in it apparently quite normally. What in fact is presented to your eyes is a series of still pictures interspersed with brief periods of darkness. In order to see it in the way that we do, it is necessary for the visual system to store the information from one frame until the arrival of the next, and subsequently to put them together in a way that makes them appear as a single scene with continuous movement. The visual store responsible for this is one of a whole series of sensory memory systems that are intimately involved in our perception of the world.

Even within visual memory there is probably a whole series of components which are capable of storing visual information for a brief period of time. If you move the end of a brightly glowing cigarette in a darkened room you will find that a trace is left behind, so that you can write a letter with it and have someone recognize it. This effect was used to measure the duration of the visual sensory memory trace as long ago as 1740 by a Swedish investigator, Segner, who attached a glowing ember to a rotating wheel. When the wheel was rotated rapidly, a complete circle could be perceived, since the trace left at the beginning of the circle would still be glowing brightly by the time the coal got back to its starting point. If the wheel was moved slowly, only a partial circle would be seen, since the trace of the first part would have faded before the ember reached it again. By rotating the wheel at a speed which just allowed a complete circle to be drawn and then measuring the time for one revolution, Segner was able to estimate the duration of this brief sensory store. He found it to be approximately one-tenth of a second.

This phenomenon, known as persistence of vision, can be demonstrated even more simply. Spread out the fingers of your hand and pass them in front of your eyes. Do so slowly at first, and you will notice that the scene seems unstable and tends to jump about. Now move them to and fro rapidly. You will then see what appears to be the normal scene, possibly with a slight blur in front of it. In the rapid movement condition, the scene is interrupted only briefly, hence allowing the information on your eye to be refreshed before it has faded away.

There are at least two and probably more components to sensory visual or *iconic memory* as it is sometimes called. One of these appears to depend on the retina of the eye and is primarily influenced by the brightness of the stimulus presented. The second one occurs at a point in the brain after the information from the two eyes has been coordinated. It is much more sensitive to pattern than to brightness, and represents the operation of a system involved in shape recognition.

An analogous series of sensory memories occurs in hearing. If I were to present an extremely brief click in one corner of the room, you would be very

The smell of security. Recent research on pheromones suggests that body odour plays a more subtle and positive role in life than deodorant advertisers would like us to think.

How good is your memory for tastes? Are you salivating?

good at deciding from what direction the click came. In order to do this, you would use the tiny difference in the time of arrival of the click at your two ears, performing a task analogous to the use of sonar to locate the position of a ship. However, in order to make use of this discrepancy in time of arrival of the click at the two ears, it is necessary to have a system which will store the first click until the arrival of the second, allowing this difference to be estimated extremely accurately. While one would not term this a memory system in the usual sense, it certainly is a system for storing and retrieving information and as such can legitimately be described as a very brief sensory memory system.

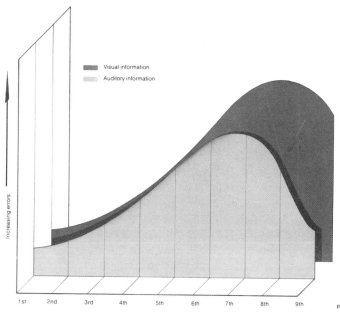

Legend:
- Visual information
- Auditory information

y-axis: Increasing errors

x-axis: 1st 2nd 3rd 4th 5th 6th 7th 8th 9th — Position of items in series

Auditory information lingers longer in one's sensory memory than visual information. This explains why the later words in a series of words are better remembered if they are heard rather than read.

The eye 'remembers'. Although the sparkler has moved on, a trace is left, allowing the single point of light to be seen as a circle.

The existence of a rather more durable auditory memory system can be shown as follows. Suppose I were to read out to you a series of nine-figure telephone numbers. The chances are that you would get most figures of each number right, but would tend to make errors. If I then switched to a system of presenting the numbers visually, one figure at a time, you would find that you made rather more errors, particularly towards the end of the sequence. The graph above shows a typical error pattern for nine-figure sequences both for those that are read and those which are heard. The higher the graph, the greater the number of errors.

The most striking feature of the graph above is the discrepancy between the two modes of presentation in the case of the last item presented. When it is spoken, it is almost always correctly recalled, whereas when it is presented visually, errors are very numerous. The reason for this appears to be that when the sequence is spoken, the last item can still be recovered from a brief auditory memory. The system is sometimes referred to as *echoic memory* since it is rather like an echo lingering on after the item has been spoken. The echo is limited to one or possibly two items. Consequently it can be wiped out by presenting a further irrelevant item afterwards. Echoic memory is left holding the irrelevant suffix instead of the last number. Hence if I had spoken the sequence of digits to you, and then followed it with the spoken instruction

Haptic memory.
Professional musicians,
who have to commit many
hours of music to memory,
use finger memory as well
as visuo-spatial and sound
memory.

'Recall', the advantage of the last item would have disappeared. The system involved in echoic memory of this type seems to be particularly geared to speech, since a simple but meaningless spoken sound such as 'bah' will disrupt performance whereas a pure tone of similar loudness and duration will not. A sequence of spoken numbers is better remembered than a sequence of numbers presented visually because auditory sensory memory appears to be more durable than visual.

Auditory sensory memory is not however limited to speech sounds. Suppose you are dubious about some component in your car engine and you listen to it while driving. What you will be trying to perceive is a repeated sound amidst the relatively random engine noise. In order to perceive the repetition you need to be able to store a long enough period of sound to be able to detect that one feature is recurring. This effect has been used to study auditory memory as follows: the listener is presented with a tape which recycles a sample of randomly fluctuating noise. The size of the sample is then systematically varied. Hence if the sample were half a second long, he would be required to perceive features that were recurring every half second. For the subject to be able to detect this, he would need an auditory memory system that stored at least half a second's worth of sound. If the sequence was repeated only every second, then a more durable memory store would be needed in order to detect the rhythmic fluctuation. When faced with this task, subjects vary somewhat in their capabilities, but on average can detect repetitions separated by up to three seconds, indicating an auditory memory system of at least this duration.

Although we have touched only briefly on sensory memory, we shall not be returning to it. It is an important component of our overall memory systems, but it is probably best seen as part of the process of perception. To explore it further would demand far more detailed analysis of perception than is possible within the limits of the present book.

Bats use echolocation
rather than sight to find their
way around. Presumably
their auditory memory is
superior to their visual
memory.

Learning to lip read. A deaf person must learn to make associations between what he sees and what he feels his own mouth and throat doing.

The physiological basis of memory

It is often assumed by non-psychologists, and indeed by a few psychologists, that psychological theories should have the final aim of giving a physiological account of psychological facts. This view, which is sometimes called *reductionism*, sees a continuous chain of explanation, extending down from psychology through physiology, which should in turn be explained in terms of biochemistry, which in its turn should be given a biophysical explanation, ultimately in terms of the sub-atomic particles studied by the physicist.

Suppose I were an architect and interested in finding out about St Paul's Cathedral, London. I could pursue my enquiries at a range of different levels. I could ask about its history, how it came to be built following the Great Fire. I could ask about the style, and the influence of classical architecture on Sir Christopher Wren, who built it. I could ask about its function, and I could ask about the details of the material from which it is built. The viewpoint that a study of memory must begin with its biochemistry would be somewhat analogous to advocating that anyone interested in St Paul's Cathedral should begin by studying the atomic structure of brick and stone. There is no doubt that such a study would be relevant, and indeed if the atomic structure of the bricks had been inappropriate, the cathedral would never have stood up. However one could know everything about the atomic structure of brick and yet know virtually nothing of interest about the cathedral. On the other hand one could know a great deal about the cathedral, while knowing nothing about the physico-chemical properties of brick.

The structure of material does of course at some point constrain the architect, and can obviously have an important bearing on the creation of a building. Similarly, in principle, a number of aspects of human memory could be importantly influenced by physiological or biochemical findings. However, many of the claims for an understanding of the molecular basis of memory that were being made a few years ago have since been shown to be premature. The neurochemistry of memory is proving to be much more complex than was previously suspected. There is no doubt that progress is being made in this important area, and that one day there may be a very fruitful collaboration between the human experimental psychologist and the neurochemist. There is at present however little area of overlap, and I therefore make no apology for not considering the biochemical basis of memory in greater detail at this time.

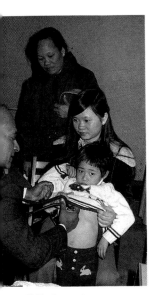

Skilled use of a stethoscope depends on a memory for rhythm.

How psychologists study memory

If psychologists do not study memory by examining its physical or biochemical characteristics, how do they arrive at their findings? Do they simply ask people how they remember things? On the whole they do not. While it is unwise to ignore people's comments on how they learn or remember, experience has shown that this kind of information is an unreliable source of evidence.

Consider for example the question of visual imagery. In the 19th century Sir Francis Galton[2] did a classic study which involved writing to a large number of eminent men and asking them to try to conjure up an image of their breakfast tables on the morning they received this unusual request. They were asked to comment at length on the richness, detail and vividness of the image they created, and enormously wide differences were observed, some respondents reporting that their remembered breakfast table was almost as vivid as their direct perception of it, others reporting no imagery at all. Subsequent work has confirmed that people differ extremely in the reported vividness of their imagery. Yet attempts to relate this to their memory abilities have proved universally disappointing. For example Sir Frederick Bartlett[3] had his subjects try to recall stories, and noted that those who claimed to have vivid visual imagery were on the whole more confident than those without such imagery, but were no more accurate in their recall. A much later study by three American investigators, di Vesta, Ingersoll and Sunshine[4], looked at the relationship between stated vividness of imagery and a range of other tests. Memory performance was not related to vividness of imagery and indeed the only measure that did show any relationship to imagery was a measure called 'social desirability', claimed to be an indicator of the extent to which subjects attempt to be obliging and give socially acceptable answers! Hence, although large differences in the reported use of visual imagery exist, they do not seem to tell us very much about the functioning of human memory.

Listening for the recurrent sound of trouble.

If people's comments on their own memory are so unreliable, how does one investigate memory? The answer is, by setting subjects various memory tasks and scoring how well or badly they do them. Sometimes experiments take advantage of participants' differential memory abilities, but more frequently they take advantage of the difficulties people have and the mistakes they make when asked to remember certain types of material. If I were to present you with a string of consonants, say *l r p f q h*, and ask you to repeat them back to me, you would probably get most of them right, but your occasional errors would be revealing; you would tend to substitute *b* for *p* or *s* for *f*. The errors are similar in sound or articulation to the correct item, and I would conclude from this, as Conrad and Hull[5] did, that you use spoken rehearsal rather than visual rehearsal, sound memory rather than visual memory, in your attempt to remember verbal information.

Another way of exploring human memory is to use a method known as 'selective interference'. I might for example test the idea that people remember addresses or telephone numbers by repeating them under their breath by preventing such repetition and seeing if it impairs their ability to remember. Ask someone to articulate some irrelevant word such as 'the' while they are trying to rehearse and write down a telephone number and their performance drops dramatically.

The chapters that follow are concerned with human memory for a wide range of material, but you will no doubt notice a bias in favour of memory for verbal material. The reasons for this are twofold. First, there is no doubt that verbal coding plays an extremely important part in human memory. Even where one is remembering visually presented pictures, or recalling actions or incidents, there is a strong tendency to supplement other aspects of memory by verbalizing, hence turning what may be initially purely a visual task into a combined visual and verbal one. The second reason for a predominance of verbal material is more practical. It is on the whole much easier to select and control verbal material than it is to manipulate visual, tactile or auditory stimuli. Suppose for example one wants to study the effects of the familiarity of the material one is using. Information exists on the frequency with which every word in the English language is used, allowing us to quantify the familiarity variable very simply. Similarly, information exists on the age at which people tend to first encounter particular words, on the tendency of a word to evoke a visual image, and so on, making verbal material by far the easiest to manipulate in experimental settings.

Another advantage of using words and letters as text materials is that they can be presented in the spoken or written mode, and can be recalled in either. With visual material, however, we are limited to one mode of presentation, and typically to testing recall by recognition.

As will become clear from the chapters that follow, psychologists investigating memory are largely in the position of someone trying to understand the functioning of a machine without being able to look inside it. Consequently they have to rely on manipulating the tasks that the machine must carry out, and carefully observe its behaviour under the various conditions. Such an approach demands considerable patience and ingenuity but, as I hope you will agree by the end of this book, can produce important insights.

A PCB or printed circuit board. The 11 million or so nerve cells in the human brain, and the connections between them, can be imagined as a PCB of enormous three-dimensional complexity.

How good is your memory?

The self-scoring exercise on the next page tests memory lapses rather than memory successes – it may alert you to your memory black spots but it will not tell you how brilliant you are in other areas! But I have included it because it demonstrates how researchers, including myself, set about exploring those aspects of memory involved in everyday living.

Self-rating questionnaires are of course highly subjective. To answer the questions you must be able to remember forgetting to remember something! And they are subjective in another way too: if you lead a highly organized life, structuring your activities so that few demands are placed on your memory, you will tend to report fewer memory lapses. That is not the same thing as having a good or bad memory in all or some of the departments discussed in this book. Older people, for example, often report fewer memory lapses than younger people, despite objective evidence that memory performance declines with age. This is because they are generally more reliant on routine and on memory aids such as diaries or notebooks – these do their remembering for them.

Listed on page 22 are some of the memory lapses that happen to all of us from time to time. Some of them may happen frequently and some may happen very rarely. How often do they happen to you? Write the appropriate number in the box beside each item.

		Question	Self-scoring	Independent scoring	Average scores*

1   Not at all in the last six months
2   About once in the last six months
3   More than once in the last six months but less than once a month
4   About once a month
5   More than once a month but less than once a week
6   About once a week
7   More than once a week but less than once a day
8   About once a day
9   More than once a day

Question	Self-scoring	Independent scoring	Average scores*
1			5
2			1
3			2
4			2
5			4
6			3
7			3
8			3
9			1
10			2
11			1
12			1
13			4
14			2
15			1
16			3
17			1
18			2

1   Forgetting where you have put something. Losing things around the house.

2   Failing to recognize places that you are told you have often been to before.

3   Finding a television story difficult to follow.

4   Not remembering a change in your daily routine, such as a change in the place where something is kept, or a change in the time something happens. Following your old routine by mistake.

5   Having to go back to check whether you have done something that you meant to do.

6   Forgetting when something happened; for example, forgetting whether something happened yesterday or last week.

7   Completely forgetting to take things with you, or leaving things behind and having to go back and fetch them.

8   Forgetting that you were told something yesterday or a few days ago, and maybe having to be reminded about it.

9   Starting to read something (a book or an article in a newspaper, or a magazine) without realizing you have already read it before.

10   Letting yourself ramble on to speak about unimportant or irrelevant things.

11   Failing to recognize, by sight, close relatives or friends that you meet frequently.

12   Having difficulty picking up a new skill. For example, having difficulty in learning a new game or in working some new gadget after you have practised once or twice.

13   Finding that a word is 'on the tip of your tongue'. You know what it is but cannot quite find it.

14   Completely forgetting to do things you said you would do, and things you planned to do.

15   Forgetting important details of what you did or what happened to you the day before.

16   When talking to someone, forgetting what you have just said. Maybe saying, 'What was I talking about?'

17   When reading a newspaper or magazine being unable to follow the thread of a story; losing track of what it is about.

18   Forgetting to tell somebody something important. Perhaps forgetting to pass on a message or remind someone of something.

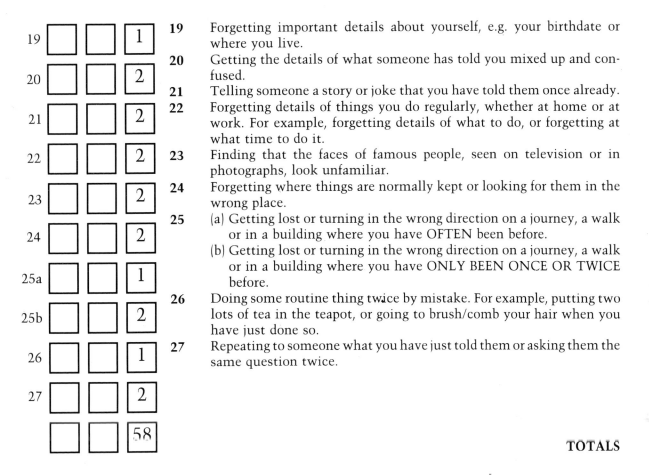

19 Forgetting important details about yourself, e.g. your birthdate or where you live.

20 Getting the details of what someone has told you mixed up and confused.

21 Telling someone a story or joke that you have told them once already.

22 Forgetting details of things you do regularly, whether at home or at work. For example, forgetting details of what to do, or forgetting at what time to do it.

23 Finding that the faces of famous people, seen on television or in photographs, look unfamiliar.

24 Forgetting where things are normally kept or looking for them in the wrong place.

25 (a) Getting lost or turning in the wrong direction on a journey, a walk or in a building where you have OFTEN been before.

(b) Getting lost or turning in the wrong direction on a journey, a walk or in a building where you have ONLY BEEN ONCE OR TWICE before.

26 Doing some routine thing twice by mistake. For example, putting two lots of tea in the teapot, or going to brush/comb your hair when you have just done so.

27 Repeating to someone what you have just told them or asking them the same question twice.

TOTALS

Now, to gain a somewhat more objective idea of your everyday memory performance ask a close friend, preferably someone who lives with you, to make his or her independent assessment of how well you remember things. Then compare the scores you gave yourself with those given to you by your friend. Alternatively you can compare the scores you gave yourself with those obtained by Harris and Sunderland when they gave the same questionnaire to a small sample of people of both sexes and all ages at the MRC Applied Psychology Unit in Cambridge. A total score of 27–58 means that your memory is generally good, 58–116 that it is average and 116–243 rather below average.

However, do not be alarmed if your score is below average. This may simply mean that you lead a very busy life which puts considerable demands on your memory. Statistically the greater the number of situations in which lapses are possible, the greater the number of lapses you will report overall.

* These averages are not necessarily representative of the population at large.

2 Feeding your memory: learning

Hermann Ebbinghaus, 1850-1909, the first psychologist to study memory experimentally. He invented nonsense syllables, which he regarded as 'uniformly unassociated'.

The scientific study of memory began in the early 1870s when a German philosopher, Hermann Ebbinghaus, came up with the revolutionary idea that memory could be studied experimentally. In doing so he broke away from a 2000-year-old tradition that firmly assigned the study of memory to the philosopher rather than to the scientist. He argued that the philosophers had come up with a wide range of possible interpretations of memory but had produced no way of deciding which amongst these theories offered the best explanation of memory. He aimed to collect objective experimental evidence of the way in which memory worked in the hope that this would allow him to choose between the various theories.

Ebbinghaus decided that the only way to tackle the complex question of human memory was to simplify the problem. He tested only one person, himself, and since he wished to study the learning of new information and to minimize any effects of previous knowledge, he invented some entirely new material to be learned. This material consisted of nonsense syllables, word-like 'consonant-vowel-consonant' sequences, such as *WUX, CAZ, BIJ* and *ZOL*, which could be pronounced but had no meaning. He taught himself sequences of such words by reciting them aloud at a rapid rate, and carefully scored the number of recitations required to learn each list, or to re-learn it after a delay had caused him to forget it. During his learning, he carefully avoided using any associations with real words that might be suggested; he always tested himself at the same time of day under carefully controlled conditions, discontinuing the tests whenever 'too great changes in the outer or inner life occurred'. Despite or perhaps because of using this rather unpromising material, he was able to demonstrate to the world that memory can be scientifically investigated, and in the short period of two years to show some of the fundamental characteristics of human memory.[1]

If you want to assess any system for storing information, three basic questions must be answered: how rapidly can information be fed into the system, how much information can be stored, and how rapidly is information lost? In the case of human memory, the capacity is clearly enormous, so Ebbinghaus concentrated on assessing the rate of input and, as we shall see in Chapter 4, of forgetting.

Rate of learning

Consider the rate at which information can be registered in memory. If you spend twice as much time learning, do you remember twice as much information? Or is there perhaps a law of diminishing returns such that each additional learning trial acquires you a little less than the previous one? Or perhaps the relationship is the other way round; the more you have acquired, the greater the probability of new information being added, rather as with a snowball being rolled by a child, with each successive revolution picking up more snow. Ebbinghaus investigated this problem very simply by creating a number of lists each containing 16 nonsense syllables. On a given day he would select a fresh list which he had not learned before, and recite it at a rate of 2½ syllables per second for 8, 16, 24, 32, 42, 53 or 64 repetitions. Twenty-four hours later he would find out how much of the list he had remembered by seeing how many

Following in father's footsteps. Boys tend to be marginally better at spatial learning than girls, though whether this stems from innate differences in aptitude or from social convention or both remains controversial.

additional trials he needed to relearn the list by heart. To get some idea of what his experiment was like, try reading the following list of nonsense syllables as rapidly as you can for four successive trials: *JIH, BAZ, FUB, YOX, SUJ, XIR, DAX, LEQ, VUM, PID, KEL, WAB, TUV, ZOF, GEK, HIW.*

The results that Ebbinghaus found are shown in the graph below which indicates a straight-line relationship between the number of learning trials on Day 1 and the amount retained on Day 2. This means that the process of learning shows neither diminishing returns, nor the snowballing effect, but obeys the simple rule that the amount learned depends on time spent learning; if you double the learning time, you double the amount of information stored. In short, as far as learning is concerned, you get what you pay for. This relationship has been explored extensively in the 100 years since it was discovered by Ebbinghaus and is known as the *total time hypothesis*. It is the basic relationship that underlies the whole of human learning. The generalization that 'you get what you pay for' is probably quite a reasonable rule of thumb when shopping. It is unlikely however that those who subscribe to it would therefore assume that the only thing to worry about is the amount of money they can afford; within this broad framework there are good buys and bad ones, items which are not worth the asking price, and bargains. Similarly in learning, despite the general relationship between practice and the amount retained, there are ways in which you can get better value for time spent, and the rest of this chapter will be concerned with these ways of beating the total time hypothesis.

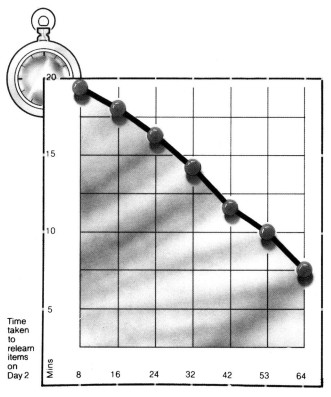

Ebbinghaus discovered that the relationship between the amount learned and the time devoted to learning is fairly simple. Here, in graph form, are the results of one of his early experiments.

Time taken to relearn items on Day 2

Mins

20

15

10

5

8   16   24   32   42   53   64

Number of repetitions on Day 1

Distributed practice: a little and often

If you examine the Ebbinghaus learning graph closely, bearing in mind the amount of time spent in practice on Day 1, you will notice that total time for learning is not in fact constant, since time spent on Day 1 gives a disproportionate saving on relearning the next day. For example 64 trials on Day 1 take about 7.5 minutes; a similar time is needed to learn the list completely on Day 2, making a total of 15 minutes. If only 8 trials are given on Day 1 however (about 1 minute), then it takes nearly 20 minutes to learn the list on Day 2. Dividing practice fairly evenly over the two days, therefore, led to more efficient learning than cramming most of the practice into the second day. This is an instance of a very widespread phenomenon, known as the *distribution of practice effect*, which simply says that it is better to distribute your learning trials across a period of time than to mass them together in a single block of learning. In so far as learning is concerned, little and often is an excellent precept.

A quick study. A little and often is a good precept in learning; even brief spells of learning are helpful.

A good example of this precept arose a few years ago when my colleagues and I were asked to advise the British Post Office on a program that aimed to teach a very large number of postmen to type.[2] Postal coding was being introduced, and the operation of the code involved a stage where the postman doing the sorting was required to type out the code on a keyboard resembling that of a typewriter. The Post Office had the option of either taking their postmen off their regular job and giving them intensive keyboard training, or of combining the training with their regular job by giving them a little practice each day. There were four feasible schedules: an intensive schedule of two two-hour sessions per day, intermediate schedules involving either one two-hour or two one-hour sessions per day, or a more gradual approach involving one one-hour session of typing per day. We therefore assigned each of our postmen at random into one of the four groups and began the training. The graph below shows the rate at which our four groups acquired typing skill; the point at which each curve starts reflects the time it took for them to learn the location of the individual keys.

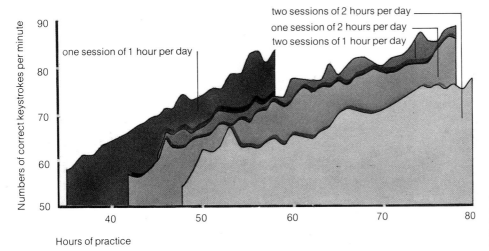

Varying rates of acquisition of typing skills under four different training regimes. (Adapted from Baddeley and Longman, 1978)

The traditional way of sorting letters. The number of sortings is limited by the length of the sorter's arm. When sorting was automated, British postmen had to learn to type.

It should be clear that the time taken to learn the keyboard and the subsequent rate of improvement were both strongly affected by the particular training schedule. The postmen who worked for only one hour a day learned the keyboard on fewer hours of training and improved their performance more rapidly than those who spent two hours a day in learning, and they in turn learnt more rapidly than those who spent four hours per day on the task. Indeed, the one hour per day group had learnt as much in 55 hours as the four hours per day group had in 80. Furthermore they appeared to be continuing to improve at a faster rate, and when tested after several months without further practice they proved to have retained their skill better than the four hours per day group.

This result did not stem from fatigue and discontent of the four hours per day group; indeed, when questioned afterwards, the one hour group was the least contented with their training schedule since, when measured in terms of the number of days required to acquire the skill, they appeared to be progressing less rapidly than their four hours per day colleagues. In drawing practical conclusions of course this should be borne in mind; four hours per day may be a relatively inefficient way of learning to type when measured on an hourly basis, but it did mean that that group had reached the standard in four weeks that it took the one hour a day group 11 weeks to achieve. Distributed practice is more efficient, but may not always be practicable.

The effect we have just described essentially says that a little every day is the optimal way of learning; but what about the distribution of practice over shorter intervals? There has in recent years been a good deal of interest in what might be called the *micro-distribution practice*. Suppose you are trying to learn French vocabulary and have the following list of words to master: *stable = l'écurie; horse = le cheval; grass = l'herbe; church = l'église.*

If we present a single item on two occasions, do you remember more if it is presented twice in rapid succession, or is recall better if the two presentations are spaced? Fortunately the answer is clear; spaced presentation enhances memory. On that basis we should go through the whole list before re-presenting and testing the first item, since that will maximize the space between two successive presentations. Unfortunately, however, life is not so simple, since it is also the case that if you succeed in remembering an item for yourself, this strengthens the memory more effectively than having it pro-

Curiosity. It may have killed the cat, but it provides an excellent stimulus for learning.

vided for you. The implications of that result are exactly the opposite to the distribution of practice effect. The sooner the item is tested, the greater the probability that it will be correctly recalled, and hence the greater the probability that it will be strengthened. The solution to this dilemma is to use a flexible strategy in which a new item is initially tested after a short delay. Then, as the item becomes better learnt, the practice interval is gradually extended, the aim being to test each item at the longest interval at which it can reliably be recalled. Hence a learning sequence for the small vocabulary list above might be as follows:

Teacher	Learner
stable – l'écurie	
stable?	*l'écurie*
horse – le cheval	
horse?	*le cheval*
stable?	*l'écurie*
horse?	*le cheval*
grass – l'herbe	
grass?	*l'herbe*
stable?	*l'écurie*
horse?	*le cheval*
grass?	*l'herbe*
church – l'église	
church?	*l'église*
grass?	*l'herbe*
church?	*l'église*
stable?	*l'écurie*
grass?	*l'herbe*
horse?	*le cheval*

Learn to write your telephone number in Chinese. Try to memorize the various characters above using the 'spaced presentation' technique used for the French vocabulary opposite.

If the learner fails an item in the vocabulary list it should be presented after a shorter delay; whenever he is correct the delay should be increased. Having used this technique, invented by Tom Landauer and Robert Bjork[3], to teach my son French vocabulary I can vouch that it does work, and furthermore that it has the advantage of ensuring that the rate of failure during learning is low so the learner does not become too discouraged.

Motivation to learn

One important factor which has not been mentioned at all so far is that of motivation. This may seem strange in the light of most studies of animal learning, where motivation is regarded as of paramount importance. This is probably because rewarding or punishing the animal is the only way the experimenter can be sure that the animal will attend to the experimental conditions and will exhibit what he has learnt. Fortunately experimental human subjects are in general rather more cooperative. Most subjects in memory experiments want to do well, whether to please the experimenter or to convince themselves that they have good memories, or perhaps because it is simply more interesting to attempt to do well than to be completely disinterested. Provided subjects give their full attention to the task then level of motivation is not an important factor.

A Swedish colleague, Lars Gören Nilsson[4], found his subjects very reluctant to accept this view, and he set up the following experiment to prove his point. He had groups of students learn lists of words under various conditions. In one condition, no pressure was put on any student to do well; they were simply told that they were taking part in an experiment on memory. In a second condition the students were not given motivating instructions during learning, but at the time of recall were told that a substantial cash prize would be given to whomever recalled the greatest number of words; a third group was told about the cash prize before they began learning. The learning performance of the three groups did not differ. A subsequent experiment included social competition as a means of increasing motivation yet further; it produced exactly the same result: no effect of motivation level on learning.

Does it then mean that motivation is quite irrelevant to learning? As any schoolteacher can tell you, this is certainly not the case. The effect of motivation is however indirect; it will determine the amount of time spent attending to the material to be learned, and this in turn will affect the amount of learning. Hence, if I were to ask you to learn a list of words comprising ten animal names and ten flower names, and I were to offer you a penny for each animal name recalled and a pound for each flower, there is little doubt that you would remember more flowers than animals. The reason would be that you would simply spend more time on the flowers, producing a result which would be equivalent to my presenting the flowers for a longer time. In a classroom situation motivation is likely to affect learning because it will affect the amount of attention a child gives to the material he is being taught; if he is interested he will devote his attention to it, whereas if he is bored, he is likely to spend time thinking about other things.

A language laboratory. As travel and communications increase, more and more people find the need to learn a second language. Learning in a laboratory allows you to learn at the speed which is most efficient for you.

Repetition and learning

If motivation is not essential to learning, what is? Some theories of learning have suggested that all that is required is repetition of the material to be learnt. Such a view would probably have appealed to Victorian educators with their emphasis on learning by heart. A number of experiments have recently suggested, however, that rote repetition, with no attempt on behalf of the subject to organize the material, may not lead to learning. A colleague, Debra Bekerian, and I were able to explore this question recently in connection with a saturation advertising campaign[5].

A couple of years ago, a new international agreement among European radio stations made it necessary for the BBC to re-assign some of the British wavelengths. In order to acquaint the public with this fact, and to familiarize them with the changes, the BBC embarked on a saturation advertising campaign. Over a period of two months, radio programs were regularly interrupted by detailed information about the new wavelengths, supplemented by slogans and complex jingles.

Debra Bekerian and I decided to test the effectiveness of the campaign by questioning about 50 members of our panel of subjects. These are people who volunteer to come along to the Applied Psychology Unit in Cambridge to take part in experiments on functions such as memory, perception and hearing. In the present case they were largely Cambridge housewives. We asked them how much time they spent listening to each radio channel, and on the basis of this and information kindly provided by the BBC about the frequency of announcements we estimated that most had heard the announcements about the new wavelengths well over a thousand times. We asked them to recall both by writing the numerical wavelength, and by marking a visual display resembling the dial of a radio.

How much had our subjects learnt? The BBC had been successful in conveying the fact that the change was about to occur since virtually every subject was aware of it. There was also considerable knowledge about the exact date of the change, with 84 per cent of our subjects reporting it correctly. Memory for details of the new wavelengths was, however, appalling. Only 25 per cent, on average, would even attempt to give the numerical wavelength, and while more people were prepared to attempt to represent the wavelength by marking the representation on the dial, most of these were little better than one would have expected on the basis of pure guessing.

Why should performance be so poor? Surely a thousand trials would be enough to teach anyone the necessary numerical information? In fact there are very good reasons for believing that this is not the case. First of all, mere repetition of information does not ensure that it is well remembered; the way in which information is processed by the learner is crucial. A second reason for suspecting that the campaign would be ineffective stems from the probability that people would simply not attend to the message. When it is first presented it is describing an event that is not likely to happen for two months and hence one which can be at least temporarily ignored. Towards the end of the two months the message has become so repetitious and tedious that it would automatically be ignored. There is very good evidence to suggest that auditory messages which we try to ignore leave very little impression on our memory. Finally, the approach basically assumed that listeners were tuning their radios on the basis of the numerical frequency of the wavelength of the station required. If that assumption was incorrect then the new frequency was likely to mean little to them, just as giving weather forecast temperatures in degrees

Practice makes perfect.
Well, sometimes!

'Put a tiger in your tank', one of the most successful advertising campaigns ever. In this case, repetition did lead to learning, and to buying. What makes a good slogan?

centigrade would mean little to someone who was quite unfamiliar with quantitative measures of temperature. We found evidence that this last point was certainly relevant since our subjects were very little better at indicating the correct current wavelengths for the radio stations which they tuned into every day. Presumably they relied on visual cues like the markings on the dial.

Fortunately, in addition to their £500 000 advertising campaign, the BBC also circulated every household by mail with information about the new wavelengths together with adhesive stickers. When we conducted a follow-up survey shortly after the changeover we found that it was these stickers that had saved the day for most people. Seventy per cent of our follow-up group had indeed had difficulty learning the new wavelengths, but for the most part they coped successfully by waiting until the changeover had taken place, then hunting for the new wavelength and marking it with the stickers which the BBC had so sensibly provided.

What conclusions can we draw from this experiment? It suggests that saturation advertising is not particularly suitable for conveying complex information. If one simply wants the listener to remember 'Botto washes whitest' it may well be that telling him so a thousand times will cause the message to be retained, though not necessarily believed. In the case of complex information which does not map onto one's existing way of thinking, however, the total effect appears to be minimal learning and maximum frustration.

Meaning and memory

As the results of the BBC study suggest, a crucial factor in deciding whether something will be learnt and remembered is its meaningfulness to the learner. Ebbinghaus explicitly tried to avoid the complicating effects of meaning by adopting a strategy of rattling through his nonsense material at a rapid rate, and sternly refusing to think about any meaningful associations. He was probably justified in believing that he had at least reduced the role of meaning in his memory experiments. Those who followed him were however rather less zealous in dissuading their subjects from using whatever meaning they could find in the material. A little thought about the list of nonsense syllables previously discussed will I think convince you that even though they were selected as being peculiarly devoid of meaningful content, nevertheless they do have associations.

By the 1930s, all the available nonsense syllables had been classified on the basis of how likely they were to give rise to meaningful associations, and it was shown that the greater the probability of an association, the greater the probability of learning a given syllable.

It can be argued that very little of our learning in real life involves meaningless material, and that the psychology of memory for nonsense might be of limited value. Consequently in recent years, there has been much more interest in using words rather than nonsense syllables for experiments on memory. Needless to say, not all words are equally easy to remember. Words that refer to concrete objects of which the memorizer can form a visual image are on the whole more easily remembered than abstract words for which imagery is difficult. Try for yourself the following two lists:

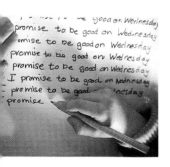

Mere repetition does not guarantee learning.

List A *virtue, history, silence, life, hope, value, mathematics, dissent, idea.*
List B *Church, beggar, carpet, arm, hat, teapot, dragon, cannon, apple.*
Now count how many you got right from each list. Most people find the words in List B more memorable than the abstract words in List A. Although the lists were made up of words which were themselves highly meaningful, the lists as a whole were meaningless, merely comprising a random selection of words. As such, they are much less meaningful than a list made up of the following sequence of words: *large, grey, elephants, terrified, by, roaring, flames, trampled, tiny, defenceless, rabbits.* Such a list would obviously be even easier to remember than the random sequence of highly imageable words that made up List B.

Learning and predictability

Wherein lies the difference between sentences and unrelated word strings? One obvious difference stems from the fact that strong relationships exist between the words in a sentence whereas they do not within a list. The structure of English is highly constrained and during the 1950s there was great interest in attempting to measure and understand this constraint. The theoretical underpinning of this analysis of language was *information theory*, a statistical approach to the understanding of language. Its influence on psychology was primarily through its emphasis on the importance of *redundancy* (synonymous with predictability). Language is redundant in the sense that successive words are not equally probable and not independent; adjectives tend to precede nouns and pronouns to be followed by verbs. The topic of the passage further constrains the selection of words. All these constraints are reflected in the tendency for each word in a sentence to be predictable on the basis of surrounding words. Hence, if I were to ask you to play a guessing game whereby I presented a sentence and asked you to guess the next word, you would do reasonably well.

It is possible to produce sequences of words that more or less approximate English prose by playing a guessing game of this sort. Suppose for example I give you a single word *the* and ask you to create a sentence incorporating it. You might produce 'The cats sat on the mat'. Suppose I then take *cats* and give it to a second person, who might produce 'Cats catch mice'. *Catch* would then be passed on to a further person who might produce the sentence 'If you are not careful you will catch a cold'. *A* could then be presented to a further person who might produce the sentence 'A stitch in time saves nine'. If we put all the words together we then get a sequence 'The cats catch a' and so on.

If instead of giving you only one word I had given you two, then the message would have been somewhat more constrained and more prose-like. If I had given four or five words, the sequence generated would have been extremely constrained. Using this procedure one can generate passages that range from random selections from a dictionary, through words selected according to their frequency in English, to passages in which relationships extend over quite long sequences of words, giving a much higher degree of constraint. Some examples of such passages generated by University of Sussex students during the 1960s are given below.[6]

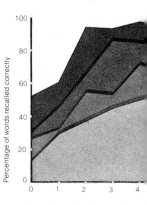

In remembering a sequence of words, the more closely the sequence resembles the structure of ordinary English the easier it is to remember. (Adapted from Miller and Selfridge, 1962)

First order
Pomegranates mouthful handle man superhero perhaps hippopotamus amazing sex stored fircones plausible happy twinkle underestimated sun boggling joint beard mauve axolotl lewd freak-out exhausted

Second order
would that although children like groovy scene one for goldilocks bears like werewolf virgins ten tickles hairy nostrils flapping voluptuously trailing walruses tusks emancipated suffragettes suffer little bogs oozing cataclysmic climax came cunningly consummated

Third order
was growing beyond hope and glory hallelujah to unnerve destroy people is groovy mind-blowing freak-out unfortunately ending hysterically bubbling bath giggling hysterically underneath sparsely populated wasteland escalating into doom irretrievably obnoxious and placated

Fifth order
by their example incalculable risks degradation for Xerxes while grovelling horribly amid decaying garbage was heaped disgustingly sideways beside bulging perverted earthworms lay mouldering silently in acid putrified thoughts Henriette fainted through excitement

If subjects are given such passages to remember, they find that the closer the approximation to normal English, the more words are recalled correctly. Results of such an experiment are shown in the graph opposite. Redundancy affects a range of other tasks in a similar way. Hence if you attempt to read out the various passages you will find that it takes less time to read the higher order approximations to English than the lower, and if you were to try to type them you would find a similar advantage.

Even within textual material, quite marked differences occur in the degree of redundancy or predictability. One way of measuring this is the *Cloze technique*[7] whereby a group of people are presented with a passage from which every fifth word has been deleted. Their task is to guess the missing words. Try it yourself on the two passages shown below.

'The sly young fox ––––– to eat the little ––––– hen for his dinner. ––––– made all sorts of ––––– to catch her. He ––––– many times to ––––– her. But she was ––––– little hen. Not ––––– of the sly fox's ––––– worked. He grew quite ––––– trying to catch the ––––– red hen. One day ––––– sly young fox said ––––– his mother, 'Today I ––––– catch the little red ––––– . I have made the ––––– plan of all.' He ––––– up a bag and ––––– it over his back. '––––– shall put the little ––––– hen in this bag,' ––––– said to his mother.'

(Extract from *The Sly Fox*, a Ladybird Easy Reading Book by Vera Southgate, 1968, pages 8–14)

The nonsense botany drawings of poet and humorist Edward Lear. They are, from left to right, *Shebootia utilis*, *Piggiawiggia pyramidalis*, *Manypeeplia upsidownia* and *Bottleforkia spoonifolia*. If only all botanical names were as easy to remember!

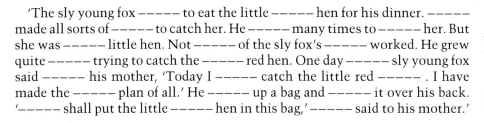

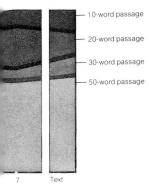

— 10-word passage
— 20-word passage
— 30-word passage
— 50-word passage

7   Text

glish

In the first place, ––––– had by that time, ––––– the benefit of his ––––– education: continual hard work, ––––– soon and concluded late, ––––– extinguished any curiosity he ––––– possessed in pursuit of –––––, and any love for ––––– or learning. His childhood's ––––– of superiority, instilled into ––––– by the favours of ––––– Mr. Earnshaw, was faded –––––. He struggled long to ––––– up an equality with ––––– in her studies, and ––––– with a poignant though silent –––––: but he yielded completely; ––––– there was no prevailing ––––– him to take a ––––– in the way of ––––– upward, when he found ––––– must, necessarily, sink beneath ––––– former level.'

(Extract from Emily Brontë's *Wuthering Heights*, Penguin Books, 1965, page 108)

The missing words from the first passage were *wanted, red, he, plans, tried, catch, a, one, plans, thin, little, the, to, will, hen, best, picked, slung, I, red, he;* and from the second passage the words omitted are *he, lost, early, begun, had, once, knowledge, books, sense, him, old, away, keep, Catherine, yielded, regret, and, on, step, moving, he, his.* Most people find the children's text rather more predictable and fill in considerably more words. Redundancy as measured by the Cloze technique is a reasonably good predictor of the rated readability of material and of its memorability. The more redundant and predictable a piece of prose, the easier it is to recall.

We have by now come some distance from the original Ebbinghaus experiments, limited as they were to the learning under rigidly controlled conditions of material stripped of all meaning. Using such unpromising material, Ebbinghaus made the enormously important discovery that human memory can be studied systematically and objectively. By throwing out meaning however he left out what is probably the most significant feature of all human memory. The importance of meaning is the main interest of the second great pioneer of the study of human memory, Sir Frederick Bartlett, whose work is discussed in the next chapter.

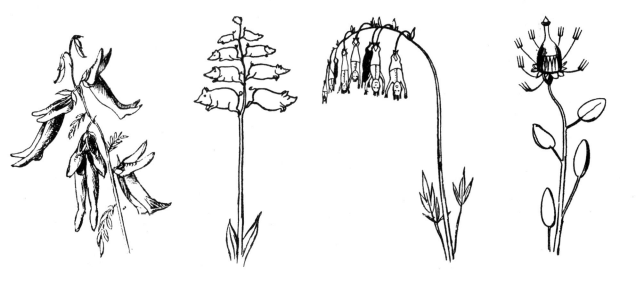

Chapter 3

Organizing and remembering

Sir Frederick Bartlett, 1886-1969. His emphasis on the importance of meaning in memory and his willingness to take the study of memory out of the laboratory provided an alternative to the more rigid Ebbinghaus tradition.

The psychological study of human memory has, over the last 100 years, been dominated by two distinct traditions. One of these stems from the work of Ebbinghaus who emphasized careful measurement of a simplified memory task under rigorously controlled conditions. The great advantage of such an approach is that it reduces the problem of understanding the enormously complex and subtle human memory system to a series of sub-problems of manageable size. This was essential for the start of the empirical study of memory, and it continues to be an important feature of the scientific study of memory; without the willingness to concentrate on tractable questions about human memory, we are unlikely to make progress. The danger that always underlies such an approach however is that we may be keeping out of experiments just those aspects of human memory which are most important and most characteristic. If we understood everything about remembering lists of nonsense syllables, it could be argued that we still would know very little about human memory as it functions outside the laboratory. This was the view argued by the founder of the second great tradition, Sir Frederick Bartlett.

In his book *Remembering*, published in 1932[1], Bartlett attacked the Ebbinghaus approach to memory which at that time had dominated psychology for 50 years. He argued that the study of nonsense syllable learning told one merely about repetition habits; by excluding meaning, Ebbinghaus had excluded the most central and characteristic feature of human memory.

Bartlett reacted against the nonsense syllable tradition by studying rich and meaningful material, learned and recalled under relatively naturalistic conditions. His subjects were asked to remember pictures and stories of which the following is a well-known example.[2] If you had been one of Bartlett's subjects you would have been asked to read the story to yourself, and then to recall it later. Try it for yourself.

The War of the Ghosts

One night two young men from Egulac went down to the river to hunt seals, and while they were there it became foggy and calm. Then they heard war-cries, and they thought: 'Maybe this is a war-party.' They escaped to the shore, and hid behind a log. Now canoes came up, and they heard the noise of paddles, and saw one canoe coming up to them. There were five men in the canoe, and they said:

'What do you think? We wish to take you along. We are going up the river to make war on the people.'

One of the young men said: 'I have no arrows.'

'Arrows are in the canoe' they said.

'I will not go along. I might be killed. My relatives do not know where I have gone. But you' he said, turning to the other, 'may go with them'.

So one of the young men went, but the other returned home.

And the warriors went on up the river to a town on the other side of Kalama. The people came down to the water, and they began to fight, and many were killed. But presently the young man heard one of the warriors say: 'Quick, let us go home: that Indian has been hit.' Now he thought: 'Oh, they are ghosts.' He did not feel sick, but they said he had been shot.

So the canoes went back to Egulac, and the young man went ashore to his house, and made a fire. And he told everybody and said:

The taste and smell of fine cognac. To the connoisseur they conjure up images related to other senses as well. Synaesthesia, the capacity to make rich associations between images from the different senses, generally enhances perception and recall.

POR TRAIT D'HOMME

POR TRAIT D'HOMME

PORTRAIT D'UN HOMME

Portrait d'un homme.

Portrait d'un homme.

Portrait d'un homme!

'Behold I accompanied the ghosts, and we went to fight. Many of our fellows were killed, and many of those who attacked us were killed. They said I was hit, and I did not feel sick.'
He told it all, and then he became quiet. When the sun rose he fell down. Something black came out of his mouth. His face became contorted. The people jumped up and cried.
He was dead.

Now close the book and attempt to recall the story as accurately as possible.

While different subjects recalled the passage in their own characteristic way, Bartlett was able to detect a number of consistent tendencies. The passages always became shorter and tended to become more coherent and to fit in more closely with the subject's own viewpoint. This shows up particularly clearly with material like *The War of the Ghosts* where a number of features of the Indian story were incompatible with European expectations. Hence, the supernatural aspect of the story was often omitted. Alternatively, puzzling features might be rationalized so as to fit into the rememberer's expectations. Hence 'something black came out of his mouth' becomes 'foamed at the mouth'. The rememberer often selects certain features of the passage and uses these to anchor the whole story. In *The War of the Ghosts* the death scene often serves this role. Detail is often changed so as to become more familiar, for example 'canoes' may often become 'boats'.

Bartlett observed that in the process of remembering a passage, the first thing the subject tends to recall is his attitude towards it: 'The recall is then a construction made largely on the basis of this attitude, and its general effect is that of a justification of the attitude'. In short, what you remember is driven to some extent by your emotional commitment and response to the event; in a laboratory experiment this may not be too important, but it may be a crucial feature of much remembering outside the laboratory. Try for example asking two participants in a quarrel for an objective account of the dispute, or even ask the supporters of two opposing football teams for a summary of the game. Under such conditions we would probably not be too surprised at having two different versions emerge.

The classic study on this effect was carried out by two American social psychologists[3] following a very violent college football game between Dartmouth and Princeton. Princeton had had a particularly successful season and one of their players, Kazmaier, had appeared on the cover of *Time* magazine. Within minutes of the start, the game was already getting very rough with the Dartmouth players concentrating on Kazmaier, who left the field with a broken nose at the beginning of the second quarter. During the third quarter a Dartmouth player was carried off with a broken leg, and there were fights, lost tempers and injuries on both sides. The accounts given by the Princeton and Dartmouth newspapers are given below. It is not hard to guess which was which!

'This observer has never seen quite such a disgusting exhibit of so-called "sport". Both teams were guilty but the blame must be laid primarily on Dartmouth's doorstep. Princeton, obviously the better team, had no reason to

Left:
A case of the unfamiliar suffering a transformation in the direction of the familiar. This happens with both picture material and verbal material. No doubt the title of the original drawing 'Portrait d'homme' (man's portrait) dictated the direction of the transformation. (Redrawn from Bartlett's *Remembering* 1932)

Anatoly Karpov, Russian Grand Master, considers his next move. The computer program has not yet been designed that can beat the world's top twenty players. Perfect memory is the computer's strong point, but at the moment the strategy of the world's top players is superior to that of the computer. But for how long?

rough up Dartmouth. Looking at the situation rationally, we don't see why the Indians should make a deliberate attempt to cripple Dick Kazmaier or any other Princeton player. The Dartmouth psychology, however, is not rational itself.'

'However, the Dartmouth–Princeton game set the stage for the other type of dirty football. A type which may be termed as an unjustifiable accusation. Dick Kazmaier was injured early in the game . . . after this incident (the coach) instilled the old see-what-they-did-go-get-them attitude into his players. His talk got results. Gene Howard and Jim Millar (from Dartmouth) were both injured. Both had dropped back to pass, had passed, and were standing unprotected in the back field. Result: one bad leg and one leg broken. The game was rough and did get a bit out of hand in the third quarter. Yet most of the roughing penalties were called against Princeton.'

Newspaper reports are of course unlikely to give the most unbiased view, and do not necessarily reflect even the writer's actual opinions. The investigators therefore decided to show a film of the game to Dartmouth and Princeton students, instructing them to be as objective as possible and to note any infringements of rules, and to classify such infringements as 'mild' or 'flagrant'. The two groups of students were roughly in agreement as to how many infringements were made by Princeton, with Princeton students judging 4.2 infringements and Dartmouth students 4.4. In the case of Dartmouth infringements however there was a huge difference with the Dartmouth students reporting a mean of 4.3 infringements while the Princeton students reported 9.8. Both sets of students rated the violations made by the opposing team as more flagrant than those made by their own.

If an observer's perception and memory of a football game can be as distorted as this, what about the case of a witness to a frightening crime where a judgement of guilty or innocent may hang on its reliability? To what extent will the witness recall what happened, and to what extent will his recall be determined by his attitude to the accused and to the crime? We shall be returning to this important question in Chapter 8.

The essence of Bartlett's approach is its emphasis on our struggle to impose meaning on what we observe and what we recall of our experience. While this can lead to error, the fact that the world is on the whole a lawful and structured environment makes such a strategy a useful one, as we shall see.

The role of organization

It is not uncommon for certain chess masters not only to play a large number of amateur players simultaneously, but to do so while blindfolded. This would seem to imply an amazing feat of memory since the master must simultaneously keep accurate track of several complex and ever changing patterns of pieces. A few years ago a Dutch psychologist with an interest in chess, Adriaan de Groot[4], decided to study the memory of chess masters, comparing their performance with that of average club players. In one experiment he set out a chess board in a position selected from a game. He allowed his chess players a series of five-second glimpses of the board, and after each glimpse required them to attempt to reproduce the position on another board. The performance of the two groups of players is shown below, from which it can be seen that the masters were correctly placing 90 per cent of the pieces after a single five-second glance, whereas the weak players were able to position only 40 per cent of the pieces correctly after one glimpse, and needed eight glimpses before they could equal the initial performance of the masters. De Groot argued from this and a number of other experiments that the advantage enjoyed by the masters stemmed from their ability to perceive the chess board as an organized whole, rather than as a collection of individual pieces.

Percentage of chess pieces remembered in their correct position

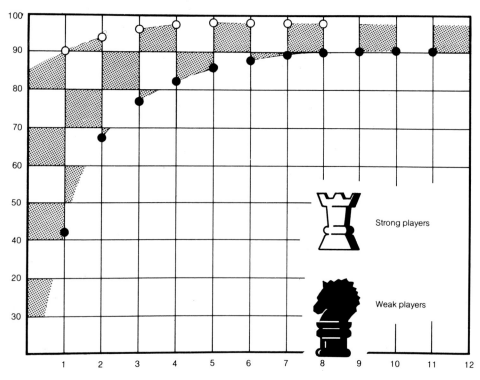

After only one five-second glimpse of a game in progress, expert chess players can remember the position of 90 per cent of the pieces on the board. Weaker players take eight glimpses to reach this level. (Adapted from de Groot, 1966)

Number of presentations

Similar effects have been shown when expert bridge players attempt to recall bridge hands, or when electronics experts are shown and asked to remember well-designed circuits. In each case the expert is able to organize the material into a meaningful and lawful pattern. In order to do so the chess player, bridge player or electronics expert brings to bear a rich background of experience.

There have of course been many laboratory demonstrations of the importance of organization for memory. In some of these, memory for relatively unstructured material is compared with the recall of material with built-in structure. Try to remember the items in the two boxes opposite. In each case read the material through at a steady rate twice and then look away and write down as many words as you can remember in any order you like.

Most people find that the items organized as a hierarchy are much easier to remember than the others, although it is in fact quite possible to organize the second collection of items in the same way as the first.

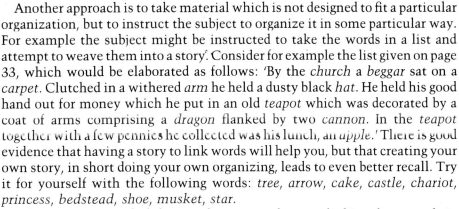

	minerals			
metals			stones	
rare	common	alloys	precious	masonry
platinum	aluminium	bronze	sapphire	limestone
silver	copper	steel	emerald	granite
gold	lead	brass	diamond	marble
	iron		ruby	

pine   elm   pansy   garden   wild   banyan   plants
delphinium   conifers   dandelion   redwood   palm   ash
violet   daisy   tropical   chestnut   flowers   spruce   lupin
buttercup   trees   deciduous   mango   willow   rose

Orderly storage leads to easy retrieval.

Another approach is to take material which is not designed to fit a particular organization, but to instruct the subject to organize it in some particular way. For example the subject might be instructed to take the words in a list and attempt to weave them into a story. Consider for example the list given on page 33, which would be elaborated as follows: 'By the *church* a *beggar* sat on a *carpet*. Clutched in a withered *arm* he held a dusty black *hat*. He held his good hand out for money which he put in an old *teapot* which was decorated by a coat of arms comprising a *dragon* flanked by two *cannon*. In the *teapot* together with a few pennies he collected was his lunch, an *apple*.' There is good evidence that having a story to link words will help you, but that creating your own story, in short doing your own organizing, leads to even better recall. Try it for yourself with the following words: *tree, arrow, cake, castle, chariot, princess, bedstead, shoe, musket, star.*

When you are satisfied that you have created a story linking these words in the appropriate order, read on. One of the most common techniques for organizing material is that of *visual imagery*. Suppose you were trying to associate two unrelated words like *rabbit* and *steeple*, so that whenever one of the words is given you can come up with the other. A good strategy to achieve this is to imagine a rabbit and a steeple interacting in some way; you might for example imagine a rabbit clinging to the top of a steeple. It does not matter how unlikely or strange the image is, provided the two components interact to form a single unitary image; imagining the rabbit and the steeple side by side will not be very helpful for example. Having created an interactive image you will find that if you are prompted with one word of the pair the other will pop up.

Visual imagery

You will no doubt have come across invitations to improve your memory either in the small advertisement section of magazines or perhaps on station bookstands. Such memory training courses involve a number of techniques, but visual imagery almost invariably plays an important role. One popular

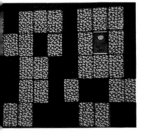

Pelmanism. Many games involve memory plus skill, but this involves memory only.

mnemonic system is a technique for allowing you to remember sequences of 10 unrelated items in the appropriate order. It requires you first to remember 10 pegwords. Since each of these rhymes with one of the numbers from 1 to 10 it is not a particularly onerous task. Try it for yourself.

One = *bun*	Two = *shoe*	Three = *tree*
Four = *door*	Five = *hive*	Six = *sticks*
Seven = *heaven*	Eight = *gate*	Nine = *wine*
Ten = *hen*		

Having mastered this you are ready to go; suppose the ten words you are trying to remember are the following: *battleship, pig, chair, sheep, castle, rug, grass, beach, milkmaid, binoculars.*

Take the first pegword which is *bun* (rhyming with one), and form an image of a bun interacting in some way with *battleship*; you might for example imagine a battleship sailing into an enormous floating bun. Now take the second pegword, *shoe*, and imagine it interacting with *pig*, perhaps a large shoe with a pig sitting in it. Pegword three is *tree*, and the third item is *chair*, so you might imagine a chair wedged in among the branches of a tree. Pegword four is *door* and that has to be associated with *sheep* so you might imagine a sheep on its hind legs tapping at the door with its hooves. Number five is *hive*, and this has to be associated with *castle* so you might imagine a beehive shaped like a medieval castle. Pegword six is *sticks* and has to be associated with *rug*. You might imagine a bundle of sticks with a rug wrapped around. Seven is *heaven*, to which you are to associate *grass*, perhaps the long lush grass of the Elysian fields might be one associate. Pegword eight is *gate*, and you want to associate this with *beach*, so a gateway opening on to a beach would be a possible associate. Nine is *wine* and here you need to form an association with a *milkmaid*, perhaps a milkmaid milking a cow and getting wine rather than milk? Finally ten is *hen* which needs to be associated with *binoculars*, perhaps by just imagining the hen peering through the binoculars. Having generated these images I should be able to come up with an accurate list of the ten words, as should you. See if you can.

Somewhat to my relief I was successful and I hope you were too. If you were not, it may in part be because it is much more effective to create your own images than to accept those created by someone else. If you remain to be convinced, try creating your own images using the same 10 pegwords for the following 10 words: *saddle, bullet, table, cigar, pylon, window, ostrich, crossbow, jacket, cloud.* Now look away and test yourself.

There are a number of other mnemonics based on imagery of which perhaps the most common are location mnemonics where the objects to be remembered are imaged at some specified location such as in particular parts of a room or particular points along a walk through a familiar city. However we shall return to this technique.

4	9	2
3	5	7
8	1	6

A magic square. However you add the numbers – across, down or diagonally – they come to 15. There are at least half a dozen ways of remembering the correct positions of the numbers. One, depending on verbal, visual and auditory memory, would be: 'For nine to free five, seven ate one six.' How many other ways can you think of?

Burgundy, Claret, Chianti, Champagne and Loire. Five bottles for five different wines. Commit the shapes and the tastes to memory.

Supernormal imagery

One should not leave the topic of mental imagery without some reference to the Russian mnemonist, Shereshevskii, who had a truly remarkable memory which relied heavily on imagery. This remarkable man was studied over a period of years by the Russian psychologist, A. R. Luria, who has written a fascinating book about him, *The Mind of a Mnemonist*[5]. Shereshevskii was first discovered when, as a journalist, his editor noticed that however complex the briefing instructions before he went out on a story, Shereshevskii never took notes. Despite this he could repeat anything that was said to him word for word, a feat which he simply took for granted. His editor, realizing that he was a somewhat unusual case, sent him along to see Luria, who gave him a series of increasingly demanding memory tests. There appeared to be no limit to the amount he could commit to memory – lists of more than a hundred digits, long strings of nonsense syllables, poetry in unknown languages, complex figures or elaborate scientific formulae. Not only could he repeat this material back perfectly, he could do so in reverse order and proved able to recall it without difficulty even years later.

What was the secret of Shereshevskii's amazing memory? He proved to be someone who had quite remarkable imagery. Not only could he rapidly and easily create a wealth of visual images, but he had an amazing capacity for synaesthesia. This is the term used to describe the capacity for a stimulus in one sense to evoke an image in another. A mild degree of synaesthesia is very common; most people have a slight tendency to associate high-pitched sounds with bright colours and low-pitched sounds with more sombre hues. It is not uncommon for people to associate days of the week with colours. However, for most people any tendency for one modality to spill over into the other is slight and of little practical significance. In the case of Shereshevskii the amount of overlap was quite enormous. For example when presented with a tone with a pitch of 2,000 cycles per second, he said: 'It looks something like fireworks tinged with a pink-red hue. The strip of colour feels rough and unpleasant, and it has an ugly taste – rather like that of a briny pickle . . . you could hurt your hand on this'. In talking to a colleague of Luria's he commented: 'What a crumbly yellow voice you have.' For him numbers tended to have shapes and colours: 'One is a pointed number – which has nothing to do with the way it's written. It's because it's somehow firm and complete. Two is flatter, rectangular, whitish in colour, sometimes almost a grey.' Numbers also resembled people, with one being 'a proud well built man' and two 'a high spirited woman'. Anything presented to him to remember was immediately encoded in this very rich and elaborate way. In general this meant that even the dryest and most unpromising material created a vivid experience which was represented not only visually but in terms of sound and touch and smell.

Shereshevskii became a professional mnemonist, giving demonstrations of his extraordinary memory on the stage. He would supplement his amazing synaesthesia by means of a number of mnemonic techniques including imagining objects located along a familiar route, and constructing stories to link them together. An example of his skill in creating a story is given by his way of tackling an extremely complex meaningless formula, part of which was as follows:

$$N. \sqrt{d^2 . x \frac{85.}{vx}} \qquad \sqrt{\frac{276^2 . 86x. n^2b}{n^2v . \pi 264}}$$

Alexander Romanovich Luria, the Russian neuropsychologist who gave the classic account of the amazing memory of the mnemonist 'S'.

He created the following story around the content of the formula: 'Neiman (N) came out and poked with his stick (.). He looked at a dried-up tree which reminded him of a root ($\sqrt{\ }$) and he thought: "It is no wonder that this tree withered and that its roots were lain bare, seeing that it was already standing when I built these houses, these two here (d^2)", and again he poked with his stick (.). He said "The houses are old, a cross (x) should be placed on them." This gives a great return on his original capital, he invested 85 000 roubles in building them. The roof finishes off the building (—), and down below a man is standing and playing a harmonica (the x). He is standing near the Post Office and at the corner is a large stone (.) to stop carts bashing the corner of the house . . .' This bizarre and lengthy anecdote not only allowed him to recall the formula perfectly then, but he was still able to recall it accurately when re-tested 15 years later!

Although this remarkable synaesthesia was obviously extremely advantageous for Shereshevskii, it did also present problems. For example if someone coughed while the material to be remembered was being read out, the cough would impress itself on his memory as a blur or a puff of steam which might well get in the way of subsequent recall. His synaesthesia also created difficulties when remembering material that had been spoken to him, since a slight difference in inflection of the speaker's voice would completely change the image and this could get in the way of his understanding even relatively simple prose. 'Each word calls up images; they collide with one another, and the result is chaos. I can't make anything out of this. And then there's also your voice . . . another blur . . . then everything's muddled'. His rich capacity for association also made reading difficult: he gave the following account of his attempt to understand the phrase "the work got under way normally": 'As for *work*, I see that work is going on . . . there's a factory . . . but there's that word *normally*. What I see is a big, ruddy-cheeked woman, a *normal* woman . . . Then the expression *get under way*. Who? What is all this? You have industry . . . that is a factory, and this normal woman – but how does all this fit together? How much have I to get rid of just to get the simple idea of the thing!'

As a professional performer Shereshevskii was very successful. However he had enormous difficulty in forgetting and consequently would find that his memory was cluttered up with all sorts of information which he did not wish to recall. Eventually he hit on a very simple solution; he imagined the information he wished to remember written on a blackboard and he then imagined himself rubbing it out. Strange to relate, this worked perfectly.

4 Forgetting: the loss of information _____

What did you do yesterday? What did you do on the same day last week? And a year ago? And ten years ago? For whatever reason, it is highly unlikely that you can recall much of what you were doing on a specific date ten years ago. You have presumably forgotten. If we wish to understand our memories, clearly we need to know not only how to get information in, but the factors which govern the forgetting of information.

The forgetting curve

The present is life-size and rich in sensation. But many people have difficulty putting space and sound and colour into their images of the past.

Once again the classic study was done by Ebbinghaus[1] using lists of nonsense syllables. This dedicated investigator had himself learnt 169 separate lists of 13 nonsense syllables, and in each case re-learned the list after an interval ranging from 21 minutes to 31 days. He always found some forgetting had occurred and used the amount of time required to learn the list again as a measure of how much had been forgotten. He found a clear relationship.

You will recall that the relationship between learning and memory was more or less linear (see page 26), with the long-term memory store being like a bath being filled by a tap running at a constant rate. But how about forgetting? Is it simply like pulling out a plug leading to a constant rate of loss, or is the relationship less straightforward? The results obtained by Ebbinghaus are shown below. Forgetting is rapid at first but gradually slows down; the rate of forgetting is logarithmic, not linear. As with Ebbinghaus's other work, this function has stood the test of time, and has been shown to apply across a very wide range of material and learning conditions. Another way of describing the relationship is in terms of Jost's Law, named after a 19th-century psychologist, which states that if two memory traces are equally strong at a given time, then the older of the two will be more durable and forgotten less rapidly. It is as if in addition to decaying, memory traces become resistant to further decay.

This is the dramatic curve that Ebbinghaus obtained when he plotted the results of one of his forgetting experiments on himself. His finding, that information loss is very rapid at first and then levels off, holds good for many types of learned material.

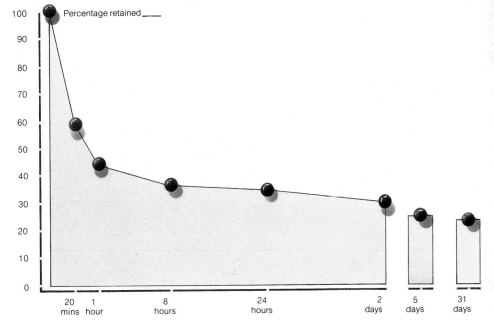

Retention interval

Memory for events

Most studies of forgetting have, like Ebbinghaus's, concerned themselves with highly constrained sets of material such as lists of nonsense syllables or unrelated words, and have rarely studied retention intervals extending much beyond a month. What happens when more realistic material is studied over longer intervals?

Answering such a question presents a major problem. Consider my question about what you were doing ten years ago. Suppose you were to produce an answer, how could I tell whether it was correct or not? It is extremely unlikely that the necessary information would be available. How then can one get around this problem? One solution is to question respondents about events which were sufficiently prominent that one can be reasonably certain that virtually everyone would have heard about them at the time they occurred. This strategy was followed by Warrington and Sanders[2] who selected items that were headline news in Britain for each of a series of years extending from the previous year to more than 30 years before. They then tested their respondents' memory for these events either by recall or recognition. We shall not include their original questionnaire since this is still used for clinical purposes, but a selection from an equivalent questionnaire designed by Muriel Woodhead[3] to cover the year 1973 appears opposite. Try it yourself, and then score how many you get right. Answers on page 51.

Does this jog your memory for the answer to question 6? (For answer see page 50)

Memory for events of 1973–Questions

1   In which European country was Sunday driving banned because of the oil crisis?

2   Naples had an epidemic of what?

3   A mini-submarine was trapped for three days off the coast of which country?

4   What incident occurred in the grounds of Government House in Bermuda?

5   What was the Siege of Wounded Knee?

6   Where did the Dona Marika oil tanker go aground?

7   What unlawful act occurred at the Old Bailey?

8   Which European country formally abolished the monarchy?

9   Which plane crashed at the Paris Air Show?

10   In which South American country was there a major earthquake?

11   What was the special reason for the Queen visiting Australia?

12   Who took part in the Cod War?

13   To what position did Gerald Ford succeed Spiro Agnew?

14   Who won the Nobel Peace Prize?

15   What was Kohoutek?

16   What revolutionary event occurred in Chile?

17   King Gustaf of Sweden was succeeded by which member of his family?

18   In which northern country did a volcano cover a small town?

19   Which French action aroused world protests?

20   What happened to the Pietà sculpture of Michelangelo?

21   Which Spanish painter died?

22   In which month did Britain join the EEC?

23   What record was broken by Skylab?

24   Which countries were involved in the October War?

The results obtained by Warrington and Sanders showed that substantial forgetting of public events of this type does occur but that contrary to popular belief younger people have a better memory than the elderly for both recent and distant events. Broadly similar conclusions were arrived at by Squire[4] in the United States, using memory for the winners of classic US horse races or the names of TV programs presented for only a single run.

The forgetting curves we have discussed so far have been concerned mainly with memory for relatively poorly learned material; what of information which was much more thoroughly learned? Light was thrown on this by an intriguing study by Bahrick, Bahrick and Wittlinger[5] who traced 392 American high school graduates and tested their memory for the names and portraits of classmates in high school. Their study showed that the ability to *recognize* a face or a name from among a set of unfamiliar names and faces, and the capacity for matching up a name and a face remained at a remarkably high level for over 30 years. In contrast to this recognition score however the ability to *recall* a name either unprompted or in response to a person's picture was at a rather lower level and showed much more extensive forgetting. In both conditions, performance of those tested after nearly 50 years was impaired, implying that there may be an aging effect possibly associated with more general intellectual impairment.

Although recall of information from many years before is generally poor, clearly people are able to recall some incidents, particularly if they are especially unusual or vivid. A particularly good example of this comes from a study[6] of an East Anglian fishing community. In June 1901 the following report appeared in the press (see opposite).

The Liberia-registered tanker, Dona Marika, ran aground on the Pembrokeshire coast of Wales in August 1973, spilling 5 000 tons of aviation fuel.

Only one of these faces is famous, but which? Can you put a name to him? Answer on page 52.

Memory for events of 1973—Answers

1 Holland
2 Cholera
3 Ireland (or Eire)
4 Governor shot (murdered/killed/ also his aide
5 American Indians' protest to Government
6 Milford Haven (South Wales/Welsh coast)
7 Bomb explosion
8 Greece
9 Russian (Soviet) supersonic airliner (or TU 144)
10 Nicaragua
11 To open the Sydney Opera House
12 Iceland and Britain
13 Vice-presidency of the United States of America
14 Kissinger *or* Le Duc Tho (it was shared)
15 A comet
16 President Allende killed *or* military Junta overthrew Government
17 Grandson
18 Iceland
19 Nuclear tests (in Pacific)
20 Attacked by a man with a hammer
21 Picasso
22 January
23 The number of days spent in space (57)
24 Egypt, Israel and Syria

STRANGE TRAGEDY AT WINTERTON
Body found in the Sandhills

Late on Tuesday, a gruesome find was made on the sandhills at Winterton, a large fishing village eight miles north of Yarmouth. It appears that a fisherman with his dog, accompanied by a Yarmouth gentleman, was walking along the cliff, when they came across the body of a man hanging from a post driven high up in the sandhills and partially covered with the sand. The body was hanging by a piece of stout cord, which had been neatly fastened to the post, evidently driven into the sands by the deceased's own hand. The features were quite unrecognizable, and covered with fungus. From the clothing the body was believed to be that of a fisherman named Gislam, who had been missing from home about five weeks, and who was supposed either to have been drowned or to have gone to sea. So it was subsequently identified. The spot is a very wild and lonely one, and very rarely visited by Winterton people, and the body would probably not have been discovered now had it not been that the dog in question called the attention of his master to it . . .

The inquest was held the next day and local newspaper readers were given the following account of it.

The inquest was held on Wednesday afternoon by Mr Coroner Chaston, acting as deputy for the liberty of the Duke of Norfolk . . .
   The first witness called was deceased's brother-in-law, Albert Robert George, also a fisherman, living at Winterton. Deceased, he said, was thirty-six years of age. He was at times very strange in his manner, and witness could not say whether on those occasions he was wholly responsible for his actions. He last saw him alive on the 8th of May near his own home. Deceased then put his arms round his little three-year-old son Stanley, said 'Good-bye' and walked away. Witness supposed he was going to sea. He did not know that anything had occurred to upset him.
   The deceased's widow, Susannah Boulton Gislam, concurred with the evidence given by the previous witness, her brother. Her late husband's life,

she said, was insured in the Prudential. There was no quarrel between him and her before he left home on May 8th, which was the last occasion on which she saw him alive; but he had been upset by being served with a County Court summons. She did not think that he fully knew what he was doing at times, though she had never heard him threaten to commit suicide, or even mention such a thing.

 . . . The Coroner having summed up, the jury retired to consider their verdict. After a few minutes the Foreman announced that they could not agree as to whether it should be *felo de se* or temporary insanity. The Coroner further addressed them and pointed out that it might be his duty, in case they could not agree, to bind them over to the Assizes. On this they retired again, and returned in a few minutes with a verdict 'That deceased committed suicide whilst temporarily insane'.

Then, in 1973, one man's memories of the events of that distant summer were revived by an interviewer.

Interviewer   We've been told that in some villages years ago if someone did something which the rest of the village disapproved of, a man might be a wife beater or a wife might be unfaithful to her husband?
Respondent   Yes. Uh huh.
Interviewer   That people would gather round at night and bang tins and this sort of thing?
Respondent   Not for that reason, not for that reason, but they'd – yes, they'd do it, yes. I know one.
Interviewer   What was that, could you tell me about that?
Respondent   Well – long story, 1910 this was. This woman wanted her husband to get away to sea or be earning some money – they'd none. Well, you could understand the woman a' being – getting on to him about getting of a – at the same time, if he couldn't he couldn't. He went on the beach one day, and he was last seen at a – at an angle – and he went – as people saw him, to the south. But – he was artful. When he knew people were all down – on the – down home after their dinners – he turned and went north. They – ransacked the hills – they went to Yarmouth to see if he went on a boat. And nobody found him. No one. And they gave it up. Well, his poor wife – didn't – hardly get – well she didn't go out of doors . . . The result was – a man one evening – this happened in May, and six weeks following, so that'd be in June – perhaps the fore-part of July, I won't say exactly – a man was – well, like – they used to go walking along the water's edge . . . He had a dog with him, perhaps he'd got – come out to give this dog a good run. And this dog would not leave this place. That got up on the hills. And he kept barking and yapping, barking and yapping, good way from Winterton, toward the north. And he thought to himself, whatever on the earth's that – he called him several time. The result was he had to go see – and there was this here man – tied to a post, about that high. And he – well – he was picked by the birds. Awful. Weren't fit to look at. Of course he – got the dog away . . . Well he had to come home to Winterton and got the coastguard and – report it. And of course that was – soon a – well – hullaballoo. There was some people – were against her, so much as if they – dressed up – an effigy, lit it up – didn't do it 'til it got dark at night, ten or eleven o'clock, and went round – against where they lived. I don't know what they sung now, I was only – ten. I forget . . . But – that poor old girl went – well she didn't go mad but she had to – go to the – hospital, so she died there.

Interviewer   People felt she'd driven, nagged him into it?
Respondent   Yes. Yes.
Interviewer   You said it happened in 1910 and you just said you were ten years old?
Respondent   Well, I was ten years old.

The famous face is the one at the top on the right: golfer Gary Player.

Interviewer You were born?
Respondent 1890.
Interviewer If you were ten that would be 1900.
Respondent Well, didn't I tell you 1900?
Interviewer I think you said 1910.
Respondent Ah well 1900 might be. Just into the – just into the – 19 – twentieth century. That was June, that – May when he – he done it and – I can't tell you the exact date but – he was buried – in Winterton churchyard.

Bearing in mind that the event had occurred over 70 years before, the account is surprisingly accurate, even to the date, given the appropriate prompting by the interviewer. The remembered account provides a good deal of additional detail, the barking of a dog, what the man thought, and so forth, which may or may not be an accurate memory of the man's account. It seems likely that the excellent recall stems from the very striking and macabre nature of the incident, which might well of course have made it into the sort of local story that would be recounted from time to time over the years, hence helping to preserve the memory.

THE YARMOUTH HERRING FISHERY.—RETURN OF THE BOATS.

Herring boats land their catch in Yarmouth at the turn of the century. The stormy East Coast of England was the scene of the Winterton tragedy.

It is tempting to assume that because we remember an incident that happened 20 years ago, we are accessing a 20-year-old memory. That can only be concluded if we have not recalled the event in the meantime; if we have, then at the very least we will have practised and rehearsed that event, and at worst we may be remembering not the event itself but our later reconstruction of it.

The importance of this factor shows up very clearly in a study by Marigold Linton[7] using herself as a subject. Every day for a five-year period, she would note down in her diary two events that had occurred on that day. At predetermined intervals she would randomly select events from her diary and judge whether she could in fact recall the event in question. Given the fact that she was sampling in this way, a particular event could crop up on a number of occasions, so that she was able to re-analyze her results to find out what effects such earlier recalls had on the later memorability of an event. Her results are shown below; the items that were not re-tested showed quite dramatic forgetting over a four-year period (65 per cent forgotten). Even a single test was enough to reduce the amount of forgetting, while items which had been tested on four other occasions showed a probability of forgetting after four years of only about 12 per cent. When this factor is taken into account, the forgetting curves look broadly similar to what one might expect from the original Ebbinghaus experiments.

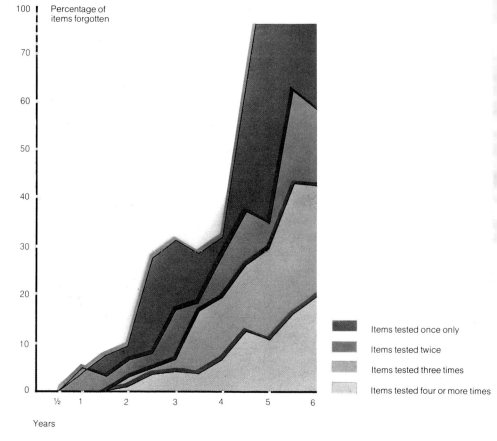

The probability of forgetting something depends on the number of times it is 'rehearsed' or called to mind. In the long term, the chances of forgetting something only called to mind once are very high indeed. (Adapted from Linton, 1978)

Items tested once only
Items tested twice
Items tested three times
Items tested four or more times

Theories of forgetting

There are two traditional theories of forgetting. One argues that the memory trace simply *fades* or decays away rather as a notice that is exposed to sun and rain will gradually fade until it becomes quite illegible. The second suggests that forgetting occurs because memory traces are disrupted or obscured by subsequent learning, or in other words that forgetting occurs because of *interference*. How can one decide between these two interpretations of forgetting? If the memory trace decays spontaneously, then the crucial factor determining how much is recalled should simply be elapsed time. The longer the delay, the greater the forgetting. If forgetting results from interference however then the

Do memory traces fade or do they get overlaid?

crucial factor should be the events that occur within that time, with more interpolated events resulting in more forgetting.

It is often difficult to separate the importance of time from the importance of events, but it is occasionally possible. In one study by Graham Hitch and myself[8], rugby football players were asked to recall the names of the teams they had played against earlier in the season. The graph on page 56 shows the probability of their recalling the last team they played, the one before that, and so forth. It proved to be the case that most players missed some games either due to injury or other commitments so that, for one player, the game before last might have taken place a week ago, for another it might have been two weeks or even a month before. Consequently it was possible to ask whether forgetting depended on elapsed time or number of intervening games. The result was clear. Time was relatively unimportant, whereas number of games was a critical factor, suggesting that for this situation at least, forgetting was due to interference rather than to trace decay.

If forgetting only occurs when some similar event intervenes, it presumably means that if one asks only about the last time a given event has occurred, and one avoids the occurrence of any intervening events which might interfere with the memory trace, then no forgetting should be observed. A number of attempts have been made to test this prediction, some of them using animals and attempting to immobilize the animal during the interval. For example, one study used cockroaches[9], taking advantage of the fact that if induced to crawl into a cone lined with tissue paper, a cockroach will apparently lie quite inert, just as if asleep. The experimenters therefore taught their cockroaches to avoid turning into a previously attractive darkened compartment by giving them an electric shock whenever they did so. They then retested their cockroaches after varying intervals of time ranging from 10 minutes to 24 hours. The immobilized cockroaches showed relatively little forgetting (25 per cent) in contrast to their colleagues who had been allowed to crawl about and do whatever cockroaches like to do in the intervening time, and who showed forgetting of 70 per cent.

Immobilizing human subjects is rather more difficult, but a number of experiments have attempted to study forgetting under conditions of reduced interference. It has been shown for example that subjects who learn material immediately before going to bed will show better retention 24 hours later than those who learn in the morning, and then indulge in a normal day's activities. However, although lack of interference may be one factor here, it is almost certainly not the only one, since subjects who learn a list of words in the morning and then sleep before recalling it later in the day show as much forgetting as those who remain awake and active during the interval.[10] One possible reason why learning in the evening might lead to better retention than learning earlier in the day is because the physiological process of consolidating the memory trace may operate more effectively at night. The human body has a number of cyclic rhythms that vary through a 24-hour period. The most obvious one is the sleep/wake cycle, but associated with it are a number of others including body temperature which rises during the day and drops at night, and the production of a range of hormones, some of which may possibly be important in allowing the development and consolidation of the physiological trace that presumably underlies learning.

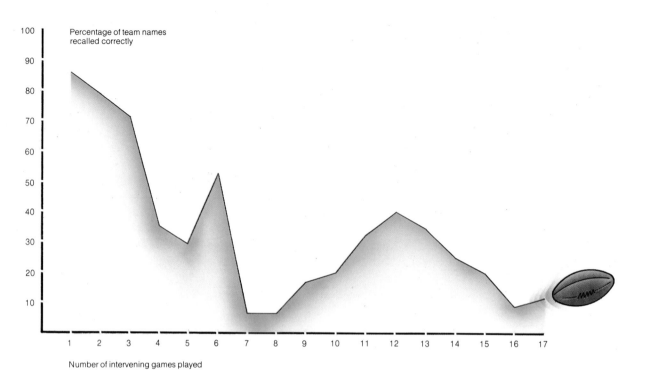

Percentage of team names
recalled correctly

Number of intervening games played

This graph, showing rugby players' memory of the teams they have recently played, is a particular instance of the general tendency for recent events to interfere with memory of similar but less recent events. Perhaps Game 6 was sufficiently memorable to interfere markedly with players' recall of the names of the teams they played in Games 7 and 8! (Adapted from Baddeley and Hitch, 1977)

Another of Bartlett's experiments, similar to a favourite Victorian parlour game. The drawings here and on pages 58 and 59 were done by different people on the same day, each person seeing the drawing done by the person before them. Note how the hieroglyphic owl progressively degrades, then develops a tail and then builds up into a cat. Then the cat begins to degrade. (Bartlett, *Remembering*, 1932)

Sleep and memory

A number of people have suggested that sleep may be important in learning, not because of its direct biochemical effect on the memory trace, but rather because of some form of reorganization that goes on while we are dreaming. It has been suggested that the process of dreaming serves the purpose of organizing the events experienced the previous day, relating them to what has gone before and discarding what is irrelevant. While this is an intriguing idea, there is little evidence to support it. One can identify the period during which a sleeper is dreaming by recording the electrical impulses put out by his brain during sleep, and by monitoring the movement of the sleeper's eyes. From time to time, the eyes move rapidly around beneath the closed lids. This can be monitored through the electrical potential given off by the eye muscles, and it is found to be associated with a particular brain rhythm. If the sleeper is woken up during this period he will report that he was dreaming. Such rapid eye

We dream several times a night yet remember little or nothing of what we dream. Why? There is no accepted answer. Perhaps our low level of arousal during sleep means that our dreams never consolidate. Or perhaps Freud was right when he suggested that dreams are the fears and desires we repress in the waking state. Or is waking so different from sleeping that when we are awake we cannot retrieve the memories laid down in sleep? In which case sleep would be the ideal time to remember dreams.

movement (or REM) sleep occurs throughout the night but predominantly towards morning. By presenting material at different times during the night, it is possible to ensure a greater or smaller amount of dreaming between the presentation and subsequent test of the material, and hence ask the question whether dreaming enhances subsequent memory or causes it to be poorer. The same question can also be asked when drugs which are known to inhibit dreaming are used on the sleeper.

There have been a number of experiments conducted in this area and the results are frankly disappointing. Some results show a slight tendency for dream sleep to be more helpful than deep sleep without dreams, whereas some show the opposite; the result seems to depend not only on the method of manipulating sleep but also on the type of material the person is learning.

Despite their differing results most workers in the area seem to interpret their results in terms of consolidation rather than referring to some process of sorting out the previous day's experiences. Whatever interpretation is made of these results, the observed effects are small and give little support to the view that dreaming plays a central role in the process of learning, attractive though this idea might seem.

Interference and forgetting

A more fruitful way of investigating the effect of interference in forgetting is to abandon the idea of producing a forgetting interval that is completely devoid of interfering activity, and instead to study the effect of different types of interfering material on recall. A good example of this is a study carried out 50 years ago by McGeoch and MacDonald[11] in which they had their subjects learn and re-learn a list of adjectives. They studied the effects of interference by varying the activity between the original learning and the subsequent recall. They found that the amount of forgetting was least when the subjects merely rested during the interval, and was somewhat more when they learned unrelated material in it such as three-figure numbers or nonsense syllables. It increased when the subjects were required to learn other adjectives, being greatest when the interpolated learning involved adjectives that were similar in meaning to those originally learned. This result shows the characteristic feature of interference, that the more similar the interfering material, the greater the amount of forgetting.

Some idea of the importance the role of similarity plays in producing interference can be gained from the material below. This comprises two lists, A and B. In each case there are five nouns: each is the name of an occupation such as 'doctor', and each is accompanied by an adjective such as 'wealthy' that might describe it. Start with List A and read through it, trying to commit to memory the adjective associated with each noun. When you have done so, cover up the list and test yourself by attempting to produce the adjective associated with each of the five nouns which are listed again beneath. Repeat the procedure until you get all five right and note the number of learning trials required. Then go on to List B and repeat the process.

List A	**List B**
sailor – tipsy	*vicar – cheery*
actor – pompous	*curate – merry*
politician — crafty	*paison – happy*
lawyer – noisy	*rector – jovial*
singer – doleful	*priest – jaunty*

Test	**Test**
politician ?	*parson* ?
sailor ?	*priest* ?
singer ?	*vicar* ?
lawyer ?	*curate* ?
actor ?	*rector* ?

You will presumably have found that it was much easier to learn List A, where the five nouns and the associated adjectives were fairly dissimilar, than List B where they were virtually synonymous. This particular exercise looks at the effects of similarity within a list. Very comparable effects occur if you learn one item and then try to learn something else that is highly similar. You will be slower in acquiring the second item, and in doing so will tend to forget the first to a much greater extent than would have been the case if the two items were quite unrelated.

There are of course few situations where the amount of potential confusion between initial and later learning is as great as this. Indeed, in general, the learning of one set of facts will help the learning of another; the world is a structured and coherent place, not a collection of purely arbitrary relationships, so although interference can certainly be demonstrated, there is some disagreement as to how important it is outside the laboratory.

In one study[12] two groups of subjects were given a piece about Buddhism; for one group this was followed by a passage on another form of Buddhism, for the other by a neutral passage about libraries. Both groups were then required to recall the original piece of prose. There was little difference between the two groups, indicating that no serious interference had taken place. Since that time more carefully designed passages have shown that interference can however be demonstrated in prose recall. For example, a study by Crouse[13] required his subjects to learn a passage concerning the life of a fictitious poet, John Payton. The passage began with the following sentences: *Payton was born in Liverpool at the end of October 1810. When he was only five years of age his father, who*

This photograph was taken in South Africa in the early years of this century. If you suspect that much of what you have 'forgotten' still lurks in your memory, have a look at your old school photographs.

Places which seemed large to us as children look very small and ordinary when we return to them as adults.

was a servant, was killed by a robber. It continued in this vein, finally concluding: *Soon after this, however, he began to suffer haemorrhages in the lungs and after much misery, he died in Geneva on April 12th 1859.* After studying and recalling such a passage, subjects went on to learn two further passages of a similar nature, each based on the same biographical framework and containing detailed 'facts'. One such passage concerned an imaginary poet, Samuel Hughes: *Hughes was born in Paddington at the end of October, 1805. When he was only nine years of age, his father, who was a weaver, was killed in a swimming accident.* It eventually concluded: *Soon after this, however, he began to suffer haemorrhages of the lungs, and after much misery he died in Paris on March 18th 1846.*

Subjects were then asked for individual pieces of information about the first passage, such as where John Payton was born, how his father died and so on. They proved able to recall only 54 per cent as much as subjects who, instead of reading other similar biographical passages, had been given unrelated material to read, indicating that substantial interference effects had occurred.

It must be admitted that such experiments go to extreme lengths to maximize interference, and to my mind at least, the remarkable feature of this area is just how well the memory system manages to cope with a continuous stream of often similar information without becoming clogged by interference. Perhaps a good illustration of this is given by the case of a car driver who changes from driving in Britain to driving in the United States or vice versa. In my own case, having spent all my driving life on the left-hand side of the road, I found remarkably little difficulty in switching to driving on the right. One would clearly be unwise to assume that no interference occurs in this situation, yet the amount of interference is remarkably small.

Retroactive interference

The forgetting of old information caused by new is normally termed *retroactive interference* (RI). The term 'retroactive' implies that the interference works backwards, which is of course not strictly true. What does happen is that the new material somehow supersedes the old. In general this type of interference increases as the amount of new learning increases, and is most dramatic when it is interfering with a relatively weak older memory trace.

Retroactive interference was very extensively studied during the 1940s and 1950s, when a whole range of experimental means of producing interference effects were explored; these typically used the technique of *paired-associate learning* whereby one item, the stimulus, is associated with another, the response. Hence if you have learnt to associate the word *tipsy* with *sailor*, and you are then required to learn a second word, for example *cautious* with *sailor*, then the learning of this will tend to weaken the initial response (*tipsy*). It is as if two competing associations are being set up, in which the stronger the initial association is, the more resistant it will be to interference from later learning. Similarly, the greater the degree of later learning there is, the greater the amount of interference there will be with the initial association. There has been a good deal of controversy as to whether forming the second association (*sailor – cautious*) actually weakens the first, or simply overshadows it by its greater strength. Whichever occurs, there is no doubt that the two do tend to conflict so that whatever strengthens one will minimize the probability of recalling the other.

Proactive inhibition

We have so far concentrated on the case where the later learning interferes with the earlier. What about the case, however, where the old response suddenly breaks through and wins out against the new? This phenomenon is termed *proactive inhibition*. It is as if the old trace, having been displaced and suppressed by the new one, strikes back, often when you least expect it. An example of this occurred to me recently. One of my local pubs sells beer brewed by a company called Wells, who used to make a very strong beer called Fargo. They subsequently replaced it with a weaker beer which they called Bombadier to which I reluctantly converted. About a year later, on returning to my local after a month's absence I went in and ordered a pint of Fargo, and it was only after being asked where I had been for the last twelve months that it dawned on me that I was the victim of proactive inhibition (or should it be called 'inactive prohibition'?).

The first person to suggest that proactive inhibition, or PI as it is often known, might be a major source of forgetting was the American psychologist Benton J. Underwood[14]. He was interested in explaining why subjects who had learned a list of nonsense syllables should show so much forgetting when tested 24 hours later. It was assumed at the time that most forgetting was the result of retroactive interference, and that substantial interference would depend on the subject learning similar material in the intervening period. Since it seemed unlikely that Underwood's subjects went home and swotted up yet more nonsense syllables, it was far from clear where the interference might come from. It occurred to Underwood that while retroactive interference from similar material might be implausible, proactive interference was a real possibility. The reason for this was that almost all work on human learning at the time was done in a relatively small number of laboratories, all of which traditionally used undergraduate subjects. If you happened to be a student at one of these departments then you were likely to be required to serve a substantial number of hours in the verbal learning laboratory as part of your course. It occurred to Underwood that it might be interference from the many *previous* lists of nonsense syllables that his long-suffering subjects had learned that was causing forgetting. Fortunately it was possible to find out how many previous lists each subject had learnt and to plot the amount of forgetting in a 24-hour period as a function of this prior experience. He was able to obtain similar data from a range of other studies and, putting it together, concluded that the more lists of nonsense syllables one has learned previously, the more likely one is to forget the most recent list!

In essence, PI and RI reflect the fact that our experiences tend to interact, to run into one another, with the result that our memory for one experience is unlikely to be completely isolated from our memory of others. The more similar two experiences are, the greater the probability that they will interact. In many cases this interaction is helpful, since the new learning builds on to the old. However, when it is important to separate the two memories, problems occur, exaggerating the amount of forgetting that would otherwise have occurred. We should be aware of the potential dangers of such forgetting. For instance, designers of surveys and questionnaires may be tempted to rely on our memories to a greater extent than is wise, asking about the frequency and incidence of events and expecting us to respond with a degree of detail that is totally unrealistic. Perhaps more seriously, the eyewitness to a crime may be assumed to have a much better recall of the incident than is at all reasonable.

Accessing the memory trace

The very fact that PI occurs, with earlier memories supplanting more recent ones, implies that the effect of interference is to make earlier traces less accessible, not to destroy them. If intervening material can disrupt access to earlier memory traces, are there ways in which access can be regained? The general problem of access to a memory trace, or retrieval, will be discussed in further detail in Chapter 7.

Knowing something, but not being able to access it, is a very common experience. This occurred to me recently when my wife referred to a visit we had made to the town of Aldeburgh on the Suffolk coast before we were married. I simply could not recall the incident, although I was sure that I had been to Aldeburgh, and could conjure up a vivid visual image of a long-sweeping, rather grey pebbly beach with strong associations of Benjamin Britten and his gloomy and romantic opera *Peter Grimes*. To what extent I was actually remembering something I had experienced or something that had been conjured up by reading or watching television, I found it hard to judge. And I confessed no, I could not remember the visit. 'You remember, it was when you sat in the seagull dung!' my wife said. Immediately the memories came flooding back – not at all like the mournful romantic image of Aldeburgh I had previously been scanning!

Clearly, we store far more information than we can retrieve at any given time. Some indeed would claim that we store every piece of information we have ever experienced, and that it is all lying there in our memory banks simply waiting for the appropriate key to be turned that will release it to come flooding back. One piece of evidence that is often cited in favour of this view is the report by the eminent neurosurgeon, Wilder Penfield[15], of memories evoked by direct electrical stimulation of the brain. Penfield performed over a thousand brain operations in which a portion of the skull was lifted and part of the cortex removed. The purpose of this operation was to reduce epilepsy by removing from the brain areas of scar tissue which can act to facilitate seizures. In carrying out these operations it was routine for the patient to be conscious, and before removing the portion of the brain, the neurosurgeon would stimulate the brain electrically in order to plot the function of that area. The purpose of this process was to avoid removing certain crucial portions of the brain, in particular those involved in language and speech where a comparatively small brain lesion may dramatically impair the ability to speak.

When Penfield stimulated the patient's temporal lobes, a total of 40 reported 'flashbacks', which appeared to be memories of previous incidents and often

Memories tend to merge into one another the farther back one tries to go.

occurred in great detail. Blakemore[16] gives the following account: 'One of Penfield's patients was a young woman. As the stimulating electrode touched a spot on her temporal lobe, she cried out: "I think I heard a mother calling her little boy somewhere. It seemed to be something that happened years ago . . . in the neighbourhood where I live." Then the electrode was moved a little and she said: "I hear voices. It is late at night, around the carnival somewhere – some sort of travelling circus. I just saw lots of big wagons that they use to haul animals in"'. Both Blakemore and Penfield seem to assume that what was being evoked were accurate memories of real events 'with no loss of detail, as though a tape recorder had been receiving it all.'

Taken at face value these observations seem to suggest that all experience is stored in great detail somewhere in the brain. Such an interpretation of Penfield's results is however open to a number of objections. First, the incidence of reported flashbacks is extremely low, less than 4 per cent of the patients tested, and to my knowledge no other neurosurgeon has reported similar findings. That is not to say that Penfield's results are not genuine, but simply that further investigation is made difficult when the phenomenon is so hard to reproduce.

A more fundamental objection comes from the fact that no evidence is given that what was being reported were indeed actual events. As we shall see later on, even under normal conditions it is possible to have a clear image of an incident you were sure you experienced, and of which you can produce plenty of detail, which turns out subsequently never to have occurred. There is no doubt that Penfield's electrode did cause items to be retrieved from memory, and that they were associated in the patient's mind with a feeling of familiarity. There is however no evidence that the feeling of familiarity was justified; it could have been an artificially induced *déjà vu* sensation, an unjustified feeling of familiarity. As we shall see in Chapter 9 on amnesia, the areas stimulated in these cases, in the region of the temporal lobe and hippocampus, are certainly implicated in long-term memory, but there is considerable evidence to suggest that damage to them produces a memory disturbance, which may itself be based on a disruption of the patient's ability to judge the familiarity of material he has learnt. In short, intriguing though they are, the flashbacks reported by Penfield's patients do not represent very strong evidence for the proposition that nothing is ever forgotten.

Chapter 5   Emotional factors in forgetting

Sigmund Freud, the originator of psychoanalysis, put forward an interpretation of forgetting which has been popular for many years. In his book *The Psychopathology of Everyday Life*[1], Freud suggested that many of the processes he had identified in the mental life of his neurotic patients could also be detected in normal behaviour. The best example of his claims is the occurrence of what are known as 'Freudian slips' whereby a slip of the tongue or of the pen results in the speaker or writer making an error which reflects his true opinions, which he was trying to hide; for instance the President of the Austrian House of Deputies, who when opening a session of which he expected very little, mistakenly declared the session closed. Freud's views have over the years evoked a great deal of controversy and opposition, and he would have been unsurprised, although perhaps unamused, by the typographical error that occurred in a recent British Psychological Society Bulletin, where a list of forthcoming events referred to 'the Fraud Memorial Professorship'.

Freud suggested that a good deal of everyday forgetting might have its origin in the repression of events associated with anxiety. He gives an example of a man who, when attempting to recall a poem, blocked on a line describing a snowy pine tree as covered 'with the white sheet'. When asked to free associate to this phrase, the man remarked that it reminded him of the sheet that would be used to cover a corpse, and through this it was associated with the recent death of his brother from a congenital heart condition which he feared would eventually cause his own death. While such cases do have plausibility, most of the examples given by Freud are much more tortuous and questionable. A sceptic could argue that, given enough flexibility, one can link virtually any word with any experience.

There have therefore been a number of attempts to produce repression in the laboratory. Some experimenters have tried to teach subjects lists of nonsense syllables and then been thoroughly nasty to them with the purpose of causing them to repress anything associated with the experiment.[2] Sure enough, they perform badly at recalling the previous items, and do much better in subsequent sessions when the 'repression' is removed by telling them that the nastiness was all part of the experiment! Unfortunately, apart from being ethically dubious, the results of such experiments might just as plausibly be ascribed to subjects' natural reluctance to try very hard in response to an unpleasant and rude experimenter.

Sigmund Freud, 1856-1939. The psychoanalytic view of forgetting is that it is a symptom of repression, a mechanism we use to exclude unacceptable thoughts and recollections from consciousness.

Freud's consulting room at 19 Berggasse, Vienna. Freud sat in the armchair at the head of the couch, out of sight of his patients. He attributed their neuroses to forgotten and unresolved childhood conflicts.

Another experiment[3] required subjects to produce associations to a series of words, some of which were neutral like *tree*, *cow* and *window*, while others had emotional overtones, such as *fear*, *angry* and *quarrel*. Immediately afterwards subjects were given the same words over again and asked to recall the association they had given. There was a clear tendency for them to remember fewer emotional associations than neutral ones. On the surface this appeared to support the Freudian view of repression; presumably the words associated with anxiety would produce responses which were themselves associated with anxiety, and hence they would be repressed. The situation is however more complex since there is a good deal of evidence to suggest that a highly arousing word will be poorly remembered when tested after a short delay, but well remembered after a longer period.

John Dean testifying during the Watergate hearings. He 'remembered' conversations with President Nixon in such detail that he became known as 'the man with the tape recorder memory'. But his testimony turned out to be inaccurate when compared with the actual tapes of those conversations. Did the pressure of a public hearing cause him to elaborate on facts only half remembered?

Memory and arousal

We are clearly not always equally alert. Our mood and general level of physiological arousal will tend to range from deep sleep through drowsiness to a normal waking state, a state of high agitation or excitement and, under extreme conditions, to terror and panic. High arousal tends to be accompanied by changes in the electrical activity of the brain as recorded by the electroencephalogram (EEG), and by an increase in heart rate, palm sweating and in the electrical conductivity of the skin. Arousal can also be altered either by manipulating the environment or through drugs. Hence loud noises will tend to increase arousal, whereas deprivation of sleep will tend to cause it to decrease. Amphetamine or the caffeine contained in a cup of coffee will tend to lead to a higher arousal, while a tranquilliser will tend to reduce it. Other drugs such as alcohol have more complex effects, initially increasing but then decreasing arousal level.

To what extent does arousal influence performance? Clearly in an extreme case it has a massive effect since a subject who is asleep has a very limited performance repertoire. It has in fact been suggested that when sleeping we are able to learn, and there have been a number of attempts to market sleep-teaching systems. These offer the unwary purchaser the attractive prospect of being able to learn easily and painlessly by simply presenting a tape recording of the material to be mastered while the purchaser sleeps. Unfortunately, objective measures of the effectiveness of sleep-teaching suggest that nothing is learned save the few scraps of information that are presented during the occasional periods during the night when we approach wakefulness, in between the long periods of deeper sleep. It appears then that if you wish to learn, it is advisable to be conscious at the time.

A very wide range of levels of arousal occur in the fully conscious individual, and there is no doubt that performance is sensitive to arousal level. In general, performance improves as arousal increases up to some peak, beyond which it deteriorates, a relationship known as the Yerkes-Dodson Law, after the two people who first pointed it out.[4] At one level some form of inverted U-shaped relationship is obvious; neither somnolence nor blind panic are likely to be particularly efficient states of mind for the performance of any task. Different tasks reach optimal performance at different levels of arousal; the level at which you are likely to run fastest or hit hardest will be higher than that which is best for threading a needle or solving a complex intellectual puzzle.

What is the optimal arousal level for memory? Like much else in human memory, this proves to be a complex question. It depends crucially on when the material learned is subsequently recalled. If recall is immediate, then performance is best under a relatively low level of arousal; higher levels of arousal lead to poor initial performance but in the long run they produce better learning.

This was shown most clearly in a series of experiments conducted by Kleinsmith and Kaplan[5] in 1963 in which subjects were presented with the task of learning to associate numbers with words. The words were selected as being either relatively neutral such as *swim* and *dance* or as having emotional overtones such as *rape* and *vomit*. Three groups of subjects were tested, the first recalling after a delay of two minutes, the second after a 20-minute delay and the third after a delay of one week. The results of this study are shown on page 68, from which it is clear that the low-arousal words were initially well recalled but showed marked forgetting. Recall of the high-arousal words in contrast actually improved over the delay in time. Kleinsmith and Kaplan argue that high levels of arousal help the memory trace to consolidate, but during the early stages of consolidation make retrieval difficult. The high arousal items therefore have a short-term penalty by being difficult to retrieve, but in the long term they benefit from good consolidation. While I must confess I do not find this interpretation particularly compelling, there is no doubt that something approaching this phenomenon does exist, although it rarely presents itself as clearly as in the original study.

Arousal level fluctuates systematically throughout the day, being relatively low shortly after waking up and then gradually increasing throughout the day

Emotions running high. Does emotional arousal lead to better memory or worse?

Things pleasant and unpleasant. Most people's memories seem to contain more of the former.

up to the evening when it begins to drop again. It has been known since the time of Ebbinghaus that learning ability varies with time of day. However it has recently been shown by Folkard and his collaborators[6] at the University of Sussex that the optimal time for learning depends crucially on whether you test recall immediately or after a delay. Folkard presented schoolchildren with a story either in the morning or in the afternoon. They were then tested either immediately or several days later. Folkard found that on immediate test, the children who had learned in the morning did better, but when tested after a delay there was a consistent advantage to having learned in the afternoon. He points out that the traditional school timetable tends to place most of the more demanding subjects in the morning, a state of affairs which might appear to be justified if the children are tested straight away, but which is not likely to lead to the best long-term learning.

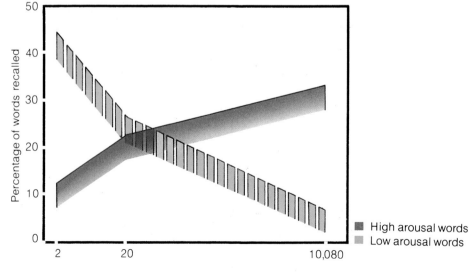

This graph shows the effect of arousal levels on memory. Arousing words are less well recalled initially than non-arousing ones, but better remembered later. (Adapted from Kleinsmith and Kaplan, 1963)

■ High arousal words
■ Low arousal words

Percentage of words recalled

50
40
30
20
10
0

2   20   10,080

Log time in minutes

Forgetting what is unpleasant

You will recall that the evidence of repression in the word-association study described on page 66 was based on the fact that people were poorer at recalling the associations to emotional words than to the more neutral words. Since testing was immediate, this could either reflect repression or else the tendency for high arousal to lead to poorer immediate recall just discussed. A crucial test would be to repeat this experiment, but include a delayed recall exercise.

Two University of Cambridge undergraduates, Brendan Bradley and Beverley Morris, and I decided to test this interpretation.[7] We therefore had our subjects produce associations to the neutral or emotional words, but whereas half of the learners were tested immediately, the other half were not tested until 28 days later. As in the original study, we found that associations to emotional words were poorly recalled initially, but that after 28 days they were consistently better remembered than those to neutral words. If the case of the initial poor retention had been repression, then one would expect the emotional words to continue being difficult to recall; exactly the opposite happened, indicating that arousal rather than the repression of anxiety was the true cause.

Freudian repression, therefore, has not proved at all easy to demonstrate under laboratory conditions. However, one area in which it has been claimed that it can be easily demonstrated is in the recall of life events. Try it for yourself; I want you to try to write down as many events as you can from the first eight years of your life. Give yourself a few minutes to dig them up since they are unlikely to spring to mind at all easily. When you have written down as many as you can move on to the next paragraph.

Now try to categorize your memories as pleasant, unpleasant or neutral. According to a study carried out by Waldfogel and cited by Hunter[8], pleasant memories should total about 50 per cent, unpleasant about 30 per cent and neutral about 20 per cent. This preponderance of pleasant over unpleasant memories is also characteristic of memories from later life and can be attributed to repression, though it is always possible that one simply has more pleasant than unpleasant experiences.

The Freudian theory suggests that incidents associated with pain and anxiety will be forgotten more readily than pleasant incidents. A related question is whether pain is remembered as being less intense than it really was. Some interesting information on this point came from a recent study by Robinson and his colleagues[10], who were investigating the effectiveness of analgesics in childbirth. They had their patients rate the pain experienced during childbirth using a line with the ends defined as 'no pain' and 'as much pain as you can possibly imagine'. Their patients indicated the amount of pain they were experiencing during childbirth by marking the line, and on subsequent occasions indicated the amount of pain remembered after delays of 24 hours, 5 days and 3 months.

Robinson and his colleagues were interested in comparing three methods of pain relief given during childbirth. The graph below shows the pain ratings obtained under the three conditions at the time of childbirth, and when rated from memory. Note however that in all three conditions, memory for the pain seemed to fade over time. This raises the interesting question of whether this tendency to forget just how intense a pain has been is characteristic of all pain, or whether it is limited to the pain experienced during childbirth. One can certainly imagine good biological reasons why a species which forgot how painful childbirth was might be more likely to flourish than a species in which the memory of the pain persisted.

However the evidence which supports the Freudian view of forgetting most convincingly comes not from normal forgetting, but from the pathological forgetting associated with neurosis. This shows up particularly clearly in cases of hysterical amnesia.

Anxiety, by Edvard Munch.

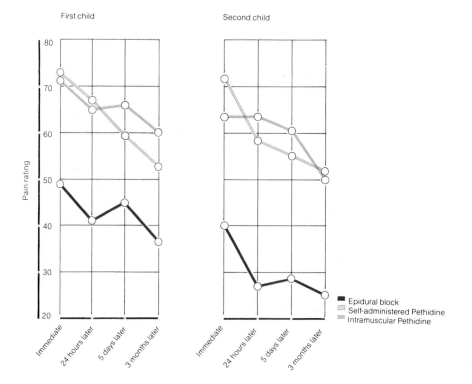

This graph not only shows the relative efficacity of two different analgesics administered to women in childbirth, but also how quickly and substantially memory for pain fades. (Adapted from Robinson et al., 1980)

Hysterical amnesia

Occasionally one hears of people who have 'lost their memory' and are found wandering around apparently totally unaware of who they are, where they come from or how they got there. With a little care and attention memory usually comes back within a few days, although cases exist of much longer amnesias. Almost invariably such people are undergoing an emotional crisis in their life. It is as if life has become intolerable, and the only way of coping is temporarily to cease to be themselves (see Chapter 9).

The term *fugue* is used to describe this pathological forgetting. The pattern demonstrated varies, and seems to depend more on the amnesic's assumptions about the way in which memory works than on the actual working of memory. In this respect one is reminded of glove anaesthesia[11] whereby a hysteric will lose all sensation in a hand, the pattern of numbness following the shape of the hand and bearing no relation whatsoever to the underlying nerve distribution. The cause is psychogenic and not based on dysfunction of the nerves themselves. While hysterical symptoms clearly differ from straightforward physical symptoms, they are not necessarily any less genuine to the patient, or any more under conscious voluntary control.

In general a patient suffering from fugue is likely to recover relatively rapidly, confront the source of the anxiety and not be very likely to relapse. There are however cases where hysterical patients alternate between states of mind, with the patient in one state being completely unaware of their personality and actions when in the other. The French psychiatrist Pierre Janet[11], who was a contemporary of Freud, gives the following case history.

Two events which etched themselves in the memories of millions of people. Can you remember where you were or what you were doing when President Kennedy or Pope John Paul was shot? Sudden, amazing events can give rise to 'flashbulb' memory; memories of this kind often contain peculiarly static and vivid images.

'Irene was a girl of 20 years, who was greatly disturbed by the long illness and death of her mother. Her mother had reached the last stage of tuberculosis, and lived alone in abject poverty with her daughter, in an attic. The girl watched her mother during 60 days and nights, working at her sewing machine to earn a few pennies to sustain their lives. When finally her mother did die, Irene became very much disturbed emotionally. She tried to revive the corpse, to call the breath back again. In her attempts at placing the limbs in an upright position, the mother's body fell to the floor, whereupon she went through the strain of lifting her back into bed, alone.

'Certainly, such experiences cannot be forgotten in the ordinary course of things. Yet in a little while Irene seemed to have grown forgetful of her mother's death. She would say, "I know very well my mother must be dead, since I have been told so several times, since I see her no more, and since I am in mourning; but I really feel astonished at it all. When did she die? What did she die from? Was I not by her to take care of her? There is something I do not understand. Why, loving her as I did, do I not feel more sorrow for her death? I can't grieve; I feel as if her absence was nothing to me, as if she were travelling and would soon come back."

'The same thing happened if you put to her questions about any of the events that happened during those two months before her mother's death. If you asked her about the illness, the mishaps, the nightly staying up, anxieties about money, the quarrels with her drunken father – all these things seemed to have quite vanished from her mind.

'What had happened to her? Had something happened to her nervous system?

wipe away all traces of the horrible events she had experienced? Was she simply pretending she did not remember? Or, did she remember without being able to recall, owing to some powerful inhibitions?

'Some light is thrown on this question by a study of the crises (or fits) which she began to experience some time after her mother's death. These would last for hours at a time, and during them she would lose contact with her immediate surroundings and perform scenes with the skill of an actress. She would re-enact all the events that took place at her mother's death, as well as other unpleasanter episodes in her life, all with the greatest detail. She would carry out with words and acts different events, and when death finally came to her mother would prepare for her own suicide. She would discuss it aloud, seem to speak to her mother, and to receive advice from her. She fancied that she would try to be run over by a locomotive. She acted as though she were on the way, and stretched herself out on the floor of the room, waiting with dread and impatience for death to come. Finally, when it came, she would utter a terrible shriek, and fall back motionless, as if she were dead. Then she would get up and begin acting over again one of the previous scenes. After a time the agitation would seem to die down and she came back to normal consciousness, took up her ordinary business, seemingly quite undisturbed about what had happened, and with a concomitant loss of memory for the events she had so faithfully dramatized.'

Childhood memories. Do most people have more pleasant than unpleasant childhood memories because they forget what is unpleasant or because they generally have pleasant childhoods?

Multiple personality

An even more extreme example of repression occurs in the case of multiple personality when one person will on different occasions adopt two, and sometimes even more, mutually exclusive personalities. The situation is that dramatized by Robert Louis Stevenson in *Dr Jekyll and Mr Hyde*. While such cases are relatively rare, well over 100 have been reported, and some 20 or more of them have possessed more than two distinct personalities. The best-known case is that reported in the book *The Three Faces of Eve* by Thigpen and Cleckley published in 1957[12]. The patient originally had two contrasting personalities – Eve White, who was modest, gentle, hardworking and kind, and Eve Black, who was irresponsible, flashy and selfish. Eve Black was aware of Eve White but the reverse was not the case. During the course of treatment a third and much more balanced personality emerged, Jane, who was aware of both Eves, and who eventually succeeded in producing a balanced amalgam of the two.

We continue to be fascinated by the bizarre phenomenon of multiple porconality, whoro ono body is inhabited by two minds, each appearing to 'forget' about the other.

There is no doubt that repression does occur in cases such as this. It probably also plays an important role in neurotic behaviour of a less flamboyant kind. How could it work? At a crude level, a patient may simply refuse to report what he does not wish the listener to know about. At a more subtle level, it is likely that when he is thinking about certain events or people that are remotely related to the source of his anxiety, he will find this unpleasant and direct his memory search elsewhere. Such a simple expedient is likely to keep the source of anxiety well away from the focus of attention. Freudian psychoanalysis claims to use techniques such as free association and dream interpretation to uncover the hidden sources of anxiety and help the patient learn to cope with them. The question of how successfully it does so is beyond the limits of the present account.

6

Storing knowledge: semantic memory ____

What is the capital of Italy? How many months are there in a year? Who is the current President of the United States? Do rats have wings? What is the chemical formula for water? Is *umplitude* an English word? Is New York south of Washington?

I am sure that you found all those questions relatively easy to answer, and furthermore did so very rapidly. I could of course have gone on asking such questions and could indeed without much difficulty fill the whole of this book with them, since there is an enormous amount of general knowledge of the world which all of us possess but tend to take for granted. Consider our knowledge of the meaning of English words. If you were to stop the first adult you encountered and test his vocabulary, you would discover that he knew the meaning of anywhere between 20 000 and 100 000 English words. Add to this any foreign languages he might know, then his knowledge of the world, both in terms of international geography and also in terms of his own neighbourhood. Simply to function in a society he must know a great deal about social customs – how to set about buying a hamburger or making a telephone call or perhaps finding a room in a hotel for the night. Then take into account all the specialist knowledge he has probably acquired in connection with his work and with hobbies and pastimes, details of football teams or television shows, pop music or the arts, or indeed any other areas of a mass of information that we all carry around in our heads. It is only when we start to think of how we could provide an equivalent source of knowledge that is as extensive and can be interrogated as quickly and accurately that we begin to realize what a phenomenal memory system we do possess.

One alternative source might seem to be a straightforward matter of simply having a computer with a very large store and entering in all the necessary information. When a question was produced one could simply scan the store until the answer appeared. But how would the store be searched? Early computer models used a serial search strategy, systematically examining each potential storage location in turn. Using such a system, if one wished to retrieve the meaning of a word, one would presumably go through all the words in one's brain serially until one came up with the right one. Suppose that one had a rather small vocabulary, a mere 20 000 words. With a serial search system the understanding of each word would require the searching of an average 10 000 memory locations. Understanding fluent speech in this way would seem to require the sort of speed of search that is well beyond our current skills in computer science.

Clearly however the human memory system does not operate simply by scanning all possible memory locations. It takes advantage of the fact that language is predictable first at the level of the individual word, where 'the' is almost always followed by an adjective or a noun, and secondly in terms of meaning, where a sentence like 'The boy was bitten by the . . .' allows one to narrow down the range of things that might plausibly have bitten the boy to a relatively small number, and thirdly in terms of our general knowledge of the world. This knowledge is structured, just as the world is itself structured and organized. In general, the more we know the more complete our organization of that knowledge will be, and the easier it will be to incorporate new information. The expert chess players we discussed in Chapter 3 found it easy to take in information about a new chess position because they could map it onto an

Hieroglyphics from a pyramid at Sakkara, Egypt. If you knew that these ancient symbols were an inventory of weapons or the story of a hunting expedition you would be much better equipped to translate them than if you knew nothing at all about their context.

already existing knowledge of chess that was rich and flexible. At a simpler level, the avid soccer supporter is likely to have a much more complex and rich perception of the current strengths and weaknesses of the various teams, and because of this is likely to be very much better at remembering the football results than someone who has only a slight interest.

Storing simple concepts

Before going on to read this section try the two sets of questions set out below, timing yourself on both sets.

Set 1

Name a fruit beginning with the letter	p	_____
Name an animal	d	_____
Name a metal	i	_____
Name a bird	b	_____
Name a country	F	_____
Name a boy's name	H	_____
Name a girl's name	M	_____
Name a vegetable	p	_____
Name a weapon	s	_____
Name a flower	p	_____

Time _____

Two ways of storing knowledge: a set of encyclopedias, with all entries alphabetically arranged; and a map, with streets and buildings locatable by grid references.

Set 2

Name a fruit ending with the letter	h	_____
Name an animal	w	_____
Name a metal	r	_____
Name a bird	n	_____
Name a country	y	_____
Name a boy's name	D	_____
Name a girl's name	N	_____
Name a vegetable	t	_____
Name a weapon	w	_____
Name a flower	t	_____

Time _____

The Reading Room of the British Museum, the hub of a great data storage system.

You probably found that it was considerably quicker to complete Set 1 than Set 2. What does this imply? It tells us simply that the initial letter is a much more effective cue than the terminal letter of a word. This in turn tells us something about the way in which names are stored, since there is no necessary reason why the above should be the case; logically one could design a system where items were retrievable either by the first, last, second, fourth or any other letter.

Elizabeth Loftus[1] and her colleagues[2] have carried out a number of experiments exploring the task of coming up with a particular word, given a category and a first letter. She found that giving the category (*fruit* for example) first, and the initial letter afterwards led to faster responding than the reverse. It is as if subjects can start to activate the category *fruit* in preparation for searching for the appropriate letter, but cannot activate all words beginning with, say, *p*. This is probably because the category *fruit* is a reasonably coherent and manageable one, whereas words beginning with *p* represent far too large and diffuse a category to be useful. Evidence of this view comes from a study in which the category used was *type of psychologist*, and the initial letter was that representing the name of the people in question. Hence a typical question might be 'Give me a development psychologist whose name begins with *P*' (Piaget) versus 'initial letter *P* – a developmental psychologist'. Students who were just beginning to specialize in psychology showed no difference between the two orders of presentation, but those who had already specialized were faster when the category was given first. Presumably they had already developed categories such as 'developmental psychologist', and hence were able to use them whereas the novices simply searched all psychologists and then checked afterwards, not having sufficiently developed their categories to operate otherwise.

An early 17th century engraving of the library at the University of Leyden. Note the simple classification system. Note too the chains, suggesting that books were rare and expensive.

Inference in semantic memory

Did Aristotle have feet? Was George Washington at the Battle of Hastings? What is Beethoven's telephone number? A support system that merely recorded and accessed information previously presented would be likely to respond 'don't know' to all three of these questions. It is highly unlikely that you have ever specifically been told that Aristotle had feet, but nevertheless it seems a reasonable assumption that he did. Indeed had he not possessed feet it is something that one would almost certainly be aware of, so one can infer that Aristotle had feet and respond 'yes'. In the case of the George Washington question, while there were large numbers of people at the Battle of Hastings whose names we do not know, the fact that George Washington lived several hundred years later allows us to conclude reasonably confidently that he was not present. In the case of Beethoven's telephone number, a simple computer memory would search diligently through lists of telephone numbers and come up with the information that he either does not possess a telephone or is perhaps a recent subscriber whose number has not yet been added to the directory. Once again, knowledge of the approximate date when Beethoven died and the probable date when the telephone was invented allows one to come to the conclusion that he did not possess a telephone and hence had no telephone number.

Psychologists began studying the process of accessing knowledge in the last century, but then neglected the topic for virtually 70 years. The rediscovery of this important problem stemmed from the attempt to produce computer memory systems which would have some of the richness and flexibility of human memory. One of the most influential sources of modern work is a computer program devised by Ross Quillian and called *The Teachable Language Comprehender*[3]. The heart of this program is a system for representing and accessing knowledge. Knowledge is stored in terms of a network of interrelated concepts; more specifically the relationship is hierarchical, with particular instances being linked together at a more abstract level. This system is best demonstrated if you look at the diagram below which shows a sample of part of this network. Take the concept *canary*; this is linked to the more abstract concept of *bird* which in turn is linked to the concept of a *living thing*. Attached to each concept is a series of attributes, hence *canary* is associated with its characteristic colour, *yellow*, the fact that it can sing and so on. This model has a further interesting feature, namely that it economizes on the amount of information directly stored by only storing at the level of *canary* information that is not characteristic of all birds, and only storing at the level of *birds* information which is not characteristic of all living things. In order to decide that a canary can fly, the program uses a process of inference, moving from the fact that a canary is a bird to the fact that birds can fly. A statement such as 'canaries have skin' involves a further inference from 'a canary is a bird' to 'a bird is a living thing' to 'living things have skin'. On the basis of the model, a psychologist, Alan Collins, and Ross Quillian predicted that it would take longer to verify sentences that involved moving further through the network than those that could be verified more directly. Hence verifying that 'a canary is yellow' should take less time than deciding on the truth of the statement 'a canary breathes'. When people were asked to verify such simple sentences, this proved to be so

Quillian's model of semantic memory. At every level general concepts give access to more specific concepts.

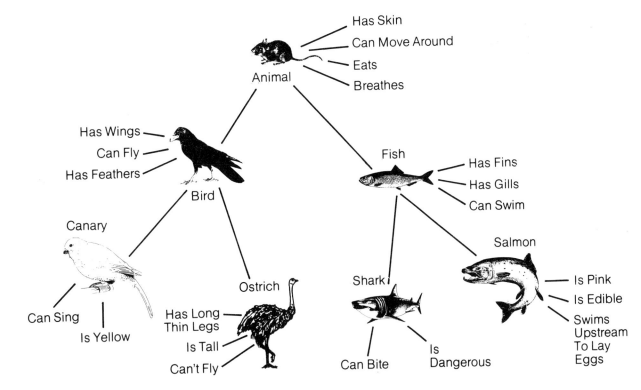

In order to get a feeling for this task try the examples below. These are not the specific examples used by Collins and Quillian but were devised by Neil Thomson and myself in order to look at the effect of various stresses on trying to access semantic memory. You may not be too surprised to learn that alcohol slows down the rate at which such sentences can be verified.

	Yes	No
Pork chops can be bought in shops.	—	—
Jamaica is edible.	—	—
Oranges drill teeth.	—	—
California is a state of America.	—	—
London is a place.	—	—
Potatoes move around searching for food.	—	—
Drills are scientists.	—	—
Aunts are relatives.	—	—
Spaghetti is a dish.	—	—
Corporals can be bought in shops.	—	—
Beer is a liquid.	—	—
Gin is sold by butchers.	—	—
Fish and chips are an alcoholic drink.	—	—
Peas are edible.	—	—
Antarctica tends the sick.	—	—
Beefsteaks are people.	—	—
Chairs are furniture.	—	—
Priests wear clothes.	—	—
Flies carry disease.	—	—
Mayors are an elected representative.	—	—
Asia has high mountains.	—	—
Paris is a living creature.	—	—
Rattlesnakes move around searching for food.	—	—
Bees treat the mentally ill.	—	—
Knives are manufactured goods.	—	—
Trout have fins.	—	—
Squirrels are fish.	—	—
Lions are four-legged animals.	—	—
Sharks have wheels.	—	—

While Collins and Quillian obtained results which supported their view, other interpretations are of course possible. One might for example argue that yellowness is something that you specifically store about canaries, since it is one of their dominant features, whereas the possession of skin and a tendency to breathe is not something particularly characteristic of them.

Consider the following two statements: (1) 'A canary is a bird, and (2) 'A penguin is a bird'. On the Collins and Quillian model both should take an equal amount of time to verify since they simply involve moving from *canary* or *penguin* to the level above, namely *bird*. In actual fact it takes longer to decide that a penguin is a bird than that a canary is a bird. Why should this be? It has been suggested that a concept like 'bird' is not a simple label attached to all instances of bird. It comprises rather a set of characteristics which birds tend to possess, but which are not possessed to the same extent by all birds. This was tested by Eleanor Rosch[4], who produced a series of sentences containing the word 'bird'. Examples might be as follows: 'Birds eat worms'; 'I heard a bird singing'; 'I watched a bird fly over the house'; 'The bird was perching on the twig'. Now try replacing the word *bird* in each case by the following instances: *robin, eagle, ostrich, penguin*. It will be obvious that whereas *robin* fits all the sentences, *eagle, ostrich,* and *penguin* fit progressively less well; in short, penguins and ostriches are less typical of birds than eagles, which in turn are less typical than robins. If you ask people to name as many birds as they can in a limited period of time, they tend to produce typical birds such as robins and blackbirds rather than atypical birds such as ostriches and penguins, even though they are in no doubt that all are birds. Similarly if asked to verify a sentence like 'an ostrich is a bird' they take reliably longer than to decide that 'a robin is a bird'.

What does this mean for the structure of our knowledge system? It implies that the concepts we use do not comprise rigidly defined categories, but are much more loosely determined. This point was made by the philosopher Wittgenstein using the category *games*. What are the defining characteristics of a game? I think you will find if you try to come up with a definition that it is very difficult to think of a single set of features that all games have in common. Wittgenstein suggests rather that members of the category *games* are like members of a family who have certain characteristics which they tend to share; some members of the family may have a number of characteristics whereas others have only one or two, often not the same one.

Sometimes an item falls on a category boundary; is *tomato* a *fruit* or a *vegetable*? The conflict here comes from its general appearance and manner of growth on the one hand, and the fact that it tends to be savoury, whereas most fruits are sweet, on the other. Another example is a *dolphin*, which has the appearance of being a *fish*, but which we have to learn specifically is a *mammal* in order to exclude it from the category *fish*. The particular boundary we might draw on a category can vary with context; we might for example refer to a spider as an insect in colloquial conversation, although knowing that strictly speaking it is an arachnid and has too many legs to be an insect.

A given concept may have quite different boundaries in different situations. The term 'repression' would suggest one set of meanings if used in a discussion of psychoanalysis and a different set when used in a discussion of dictatorship; although the two sets of meanings have a common origin they differ quite markedly. Communication in such situations depends crucially on shared assumptions about concepts.

John Bransford[5] describes an informal experiment in which the experimenter E walked into the office of a colleague C and said simply, 'Bill has a red car'. Here is his description of C's reactions.

'He looked very surprised, paused for about three seconds, and finally exclaimed "What the h—— are you talking about?" After a hasty de-briefing session C laughed and told E what had gone on in his head. First he thought that E was talking about a person named Bill that C knew. Then C realized that

E could not in all probability know that person; and besides Bill would never buy a red car. Then C thought that E may have mixed up the name and really meant to say J (a mutual friend of C and E). C knew that J had ordered a new car, but he was surprised that it was red and that it had arrived so soon. C also entertained a few additional hypotheses – all within about three seconds. After that he gave up, thereupon uttering "What the h—— are you talking about?"'

Schemata

The common ground demanded for understanding extends well beyond merely having the same interpretation of simple concepts. Consider the following passage taken from a study by Bransford and Johnson[6]:

'The procedure is actually quite simple. First you arrange items into different groups. Of course one pile might be sufficient depending on how much there is to do. If you have to go somewhere else due to lack of facilities, that is the next step; otherwise, you are pretty well set. It is important not to overdo things. That is, it is better to do too few things at once than too many. In the short run this may not seem important but complications can easily arise. A mistake can be expensive as well. At first the whole procedure will seem complicated. Soon, however, it will become just another facet of life. It is difficult to foresee any end to the necessity for this task in the immediate future, but then one never can tell. After the procedure is completed one arranges the material into different groups again. They then can be put into their appropriate places. Eventually they will be used once more and the whole cycle will then have to be repeated. However, that is part of life.'

Asked to rate the comprehensibility of this passage on a scale ranging from one to five, Bransford and Johnson's students rated it as pretty incomprehensible with a mean of 2.29. As might be expected, when asked to recall it they performed rather poorly, scoring only 2.82 out of a possible 18 ideas. A second group, *after* reading it but *before* they recalled it, was told that the topic was washing clothes. This did nothing to enhance either its comprehensibility or the amount recalled. A third group however was given the topic before they read it; their comprehension ratings averaged 4.5 out of 5 and they recalled over twice as many ideas. Try reading it again yourself bearing in mind that it is about washing clothes.

The problem in comprehending the description stemmed not from the writer and reader having different concepts, but because the reader was not keyed in to the appropriate situation. Once he was aware of the correct semantic context, the passage immediately made sense. A number of years ago the British psychologist, David Bruce[7], showed very similar effects in a task that simply involved listening to and repeating sentences spoken in a noisy background. Bruce showed that giving subjects the context made it much more likely that they would hear the sentence properly, so that if for example the subject were told 'sport' he would be much more likely to correctly report a sentence like 'our centre forward scored the winning goal'.

Cues of this kind give access to a whole complex of knowledge about a particular topic. Sir Frederick Bartlett[8] used the term *schemata* to refer to such knowledge structures, while later theories have either adopted Bartlett's terminology or occasionally devised their own, as in the case of *frames* or *scripts*. Both of these are essentially schema concepts developed by computer scientists attempting to produce computer programs which will simulate the comprehension of text.

Scripts

Essentially a script is an integrated package of information that can be brought to bear on the interpretation or understanding of a given event. For example, a story involving a restaurant brings into operation a 'restaurant' script which involves all the information the comprehender already has about restaurants: that one normally sits at a table with others, that the food is cooked and then brought by a waiter, that the waiter will get the food from a kitchen and subsequently expect to be paid and tipped, and so forth. It is such information that is brought to bear in a statement such as 'Luigi's is a nice restaurant but the waiters are slow'. If it were spelled out fully, it would involve statements to the effect that food is delivered by waiters, that one cannot order a meal until the waiter comes, that a second course is not served until the first has been cleared away and that the speed with which all these operations proceed is variable. In contrast a statement like 'Luigi's is a good gym but the waiters are slow' is baffling, because the 'gym' script and the 'waiters' script simply do not mesh, and hence one can only make sense of the statement by assuming either that the gym is the name of a restaurant or that 'waiters' refers to some role analogous to but different from that of a waiter in a restaurant, perhaps involving handing out locker keys or equipment. The programs developed by Schank[9], the originator of the 'script' concept, have built into them information about the relevant scripts, and hence are able to go beyond the information explicitly given in the text, by making inferences on the basis of previous knowledge. In this way they resemble human comprehension.

Schank has produced a number of impressive demonstrations of the phenomenon of inference, but in doing so he raises the problem of exactly what should and should not be included in a script. Should a 'waiter' script include the fact that waiters normally wear socks? Presumably not, since most men in western countries at least wear socks. If it did, would it contain information about what socks looked and felt like, and that in the case of a waiter, they were more likely to be black than red? Such information is likely to be potentially available to the human reader, but is of course unlikely to be specified or utilized unless necessary. Similarly however, the type of information specified in a Schank script is rarely explicitly used by a human. Take for example the following sentence: 'John went to New York by bus'. This is interpreted by Schank's program as 'John went to a bus stop. He waited at it a few minutes. He entered a bus. The driver got the ticket from John. He went to a seat. He sat down in it. The driver took John to New York. John got off the bus.'

It is certainly not necessarily the case that he sat down rather than stood; similarly he might have caught a bus immediately or had a long wait. The script could presumably specify that John waited for the bus door to open before entering, or that he waited for the bus to stop before he got off. On what basis did Schank decide not to include them? This unfortunately is one of the great problems of attempting to simulate a system as extensive and rich as human semantic memory. It contains such a vast amount of interrelated information, any piece of which is at least in principle usable in connection with any other. Any actual computer simulation is obviously going to leave out some of the possible links and the question therefore arises as to which should be omitted and which included. Any choice is likely to be somewhat arbitrary, and hence to leave you with the problem of deciding whether a given failure of the simulation is because your simulation is wrong in principle, or simply because being finite it has had to leave out some of the details. This problem is likely to be with us for a long time, but while it presents real difficulties for evaluating attempts to simulate human memory, such computer simulations can prove fruitful.

The nature of semantic memory: images or propositions?

We have so far discussed the semantic memory system without saying anything about its constituent units: it is for example easy to slip into the assumption that semantic memory is concerned with the associations between words. In fact the stuff of which semantic memory is made could better be regarded as concepts or ideas which are clearly in some cases *related* to words, but which are not in themselves words. However, semantics has been studied primarily by linguists or psycholinguists, and hence the greatest emphasis on meaning has been in relation to language. Perhaps the most extreme view of the importance of language in meaning is that put forward by the linguist Benjamin Lee Whorf[10], and generally known as the *linguistic relativity hypothesis*. Whorf argues that language is not simply a way of expressing your view of the world but that language itself determines this view: 'We dissect nature along lines laid down by our native language. The categories and types that we isolate from the world of phenomena we do not find there because they stare every observer in the face; on the contrary the world is presented in a kaleidoscopic flux of impressions which has to be organized in our minds – and this means largely by the linguistic system in our minds.'

An Eskimo's extensive 'snow' vocabulary is tied to his intimate knowledge of many different snow conditions.

Whorf argued on the basis of this that people who speak different languages will see and remember the world differently. He supports his view by offering examples of the difficulty of translating languages of very different cultures. One example he gives is from the Apache language of the American Indians where the sentence 'It is a dripping spring' is represented by a phrase meaning 'As water, or springs, whiteness moves downward'. Eskimo languages are said to have a large number of adjectives describing different snow conditions, and there is little doubt that an Eskimo would be better at perceiving these differences and at remembering them than would someone from the Mediterranean. However there is a chicken and egg problem here; while Whorf would argue that language structures the Eskimo's world, one could equally well argue that the Eskimo's language develops as a result of his different perception of the world. How can one separate these two views? One way might be to show that different environments give rise to different perceptual capacities in non-verbal animals. One might predict that polar bears would be better at discriminating between different types of snow than would Indian honeybears! However, while such an experiment might present an interesting challenge to the comparative psychologist, it would clearly be extremely difficult to carry out and to interpret. Fortunately there are other ways of tackling the question.

  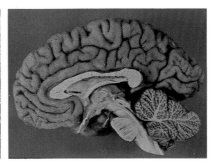

Three computers of increasing sophistication. From left to right: an early 1960s computer designed to calculate the most economical means of generating and transmitting electricity; an early 1980s home computer; an even more elegant home computer.

Many years ago, two American psychologists, Roger Brown and Eric Lenneberg[11], showed that certain colours appeared to be particularly easy to name and to remember. Such 'focal' colours tended to be named very consistently, with many subjects giving the same name. Furthermore the names tended to be short, such as red and green, in contrast to names of less focal colours such as vermilion and turquoise. These results were initially interpreted along the lines of the Whorfian hypothesis, that colours which correspond to good verbal labels are easily perceived and well remembered. However, Eleanor Rosch[12] has pointed out that the alternative interpretation, that the language followed the perception, is equally plausible, and furthermore she was able to come up with convincing evidence for this view. She did so by testing a group of speakers of Dani, a language spoken until recently by a Stone Age people living in New Guinea. Dani has the interesting characteristic of containing only two colour terms, roughly corresponding to dark and light. Rosch argued that if Whorf were correct, the Dani speakers should not show the normal tendency for focal colours to be consistently recognized and easily learned. She found that although the overall level of performance of the Dani speakers was lower than that of American subjects, they nevertheless showed exactly the same tendency to find the focal colours easy both to discriminate between and to remember. Despite having no labels for red, green and yellow, the Dani found them easy colours to handle, suggesting that language is based on perception, not the reverse.

Two men of the Dani people of New Guinea. The Dani language has no words for colours, only 'dark' and 'light'.

A less extreme linguistic argument suggests that, although the semantic system might initially be based on and driven by our perception of the world, it encodes that information in terms of a linguistic system. This of course cannot be true of all semantic information since much of it is beyond our capacity to express in words. One example of this is our knowledge of the shapes of countries. This was investigated recently by Ian Moar[13] who used a technique he terms *mental triangulation*. This technique is based on a system used by surveyors to construct maps, but whereas a surveyor would take bearings from one point to another, Moar required his subjects to indicate the relevant directions by drawing. He gave them each a piece of paper with a vertical line marked North and a dot at the bottom of the line, and asked them for example to draw a line representing the direction between pairs of British cities, such as London and Edinburgh, Edinburgh and Birmingham, Birmingham and Bristol, Bristol and London. By combining the various directions he was able to construct mental maps which represented the subject's concept of the country. Below are the results obtained by two of his groups of subjects, Cambridge housewives and Glasgow housewives. It should not prove too difficult to guess which group produced which result

Naturally the Glasgow housewives tended to exaggerate the size of Scotland; their English counterparts did the same to England, though not to quite the same extent. Britain is represented roughly by a triangle with a base that

Left: an outline of Britain with all the towns correctly located.

Centre: Britain as seen by the Cambridge housewives. Note the relative vastness of the distances in the south of England.

Right: the version produced by the Glasgow housewives. Note the great shrinkage of the distances south of Carlisle!

deviates by quite a few degrees from the horizontal. Notice that both groups 'straighten up' the triangle.

It is doubtful whether anyone would wish to argue that mental maps are represented purely verbally, and it is even more doubtful whether anyone could be found who would defend a purely verbal interpretation of our memory of Winston Churchill's face or the colour of a sunset, let alone the sound of an orchestra tuning up or the taste of Camembert cheese. It is however much easier to defend a linguistic interpretation of the types of semantic category we were discussing earlier in the chapter. Are such categories as fruit, carpenters' tools and birds basically language categories, or are they categories which happen to have a linguistic label?

One experiment by Potter and Faulconer[14] required their student subjects either to name or categorize pictures of common objects or to read or categorize their printed names. They observed that their subjects were able to

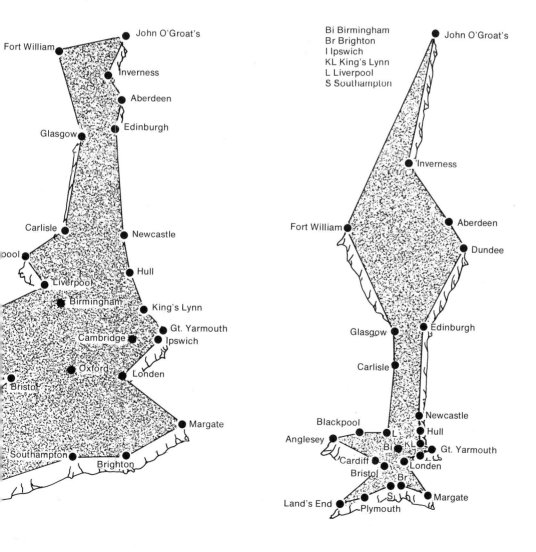

Most people would be more successful at remembering the items above and opposite than the corresponding word list *torch, bear, book,* cake, *glove, anchor* and so on. This is because visual material can be coded

categorize a picture of a dog as an animal or a picture of a saw as a carpenter's tool just as rapidly as they could categorize their names, and *more* rapidly than they could produce the name given the picture. If the categorization were to depend on first naming the picture, then there is no way in which categorization could be more rapid than naming.

Is it possible then that semantic concepts are stored as images? There is no doubt that visual or spatial characteristics can be important. One might for example have a concept of all round things or red things, but it is much less easy to argue that a concept such as justice or guilt is primarily stored in terms of its visual characteristics. Of course one can come up with visual images that might in some sense represent justice, but such images would be of very little assistance in deciding whether justice had been done in a particular court judgment. The most plausible assumption is probably that concepts are stored in some abstract code which may be translated into a verbal or linguistic form or into an image when the need arises, just as information stored in a computer may, given the appropriate command, be displayed either as a drawing on a cathode ray tube, as a printout on a teleprinter or, given, the appropriate peripheral equipment, as a series of sounds. In all three cases the information stored could be the same, but its mode of display quite different.

People vary enormously in the extent to which they claim to have vivid visual imagery. This is very rarely, if at all, reflected in what they actually recall, although, as Bartlett pointed out, those using visual imagery might recall with a greater degree of confidence than those using a verbal strategy. The reason for this lack of difference is presumably that what is recalled is determined by what is stored, not by the preferred method of display. The visual imagers may be using an equivalent of a cathode ray tube and the verbalizers the equivalent of a teleprinter, but since both draw on a single abstract store, the accuracy of what they recall will not differ.

Learning new concepts

So far we have been concerned entirely with how existing knowledge is stored and accessed, but have said nothing about the crucial question of how new concepts are formed. Since this is the question that lies at the heart of all education it is obviously a very important one, and yet it is very poorly understood. Much of the psychology of education has been concerned with episodic memory, recalling experiences, rather than semantic memory, the development of knowledge, and even now this is only gradually beginning to change.

The problem of concept formation has been of interest to psychologists for many years, but in the past the emphasis has been on concept identification rather than the acquisition of new concepts. In a concept identification study, the experimenter usually selects, on a somewhat arbitrary basis, a particular combination of features, and the subject's task is to work out what that combination is. A good example of this approach is given by experiments carried out by Heidbreder[15] in the mid-1940s. Heidbreder's subjects had to attach nonsense names, such as *RELK, FARD* and *LING*, to various categories of objects.

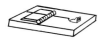

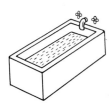

It can be argued that formation of concepts of this kind is analogous to the task confronting the child learning a language or trying to understand the world. What sort of results have emerged from such studies? As might be expected, it seems easier to learn concrete concepts such as *building, animal, face* than more abstract concepts such as *twoness* or *roundness*. A concept based on an obvious characteristic such as size or colour is more quickly acquired than one based on less obvious features, such as orientation on the page. Where two features are involved, conjunctive rules, whereby the concept demands both features (for instance green *and* square), are easier to apply than dysjunctive rules where the target need only be green *or* square.

There is an extensive literature on concept identification, often associated with relatively complex models which attempt to predict the way in which people will behave on such tasks. I myself remain to be convinced that this kind of task bears very much relation to the process whereby children learn about the world or their language, and although such tasks are occasionally of practical value, for example in deciding whether a brain-damaged patient has suffered frontal lobe damage, I think they tell us very little about the way in which our extensive and rich store of knowledge is developed and accessed.

A line of investigation which seems to be much more promising is that being developed by John Bransford and his colleagues[16] at Vanderbilt University in Tennessee. This is described in more detail in Bransford's book *Human Cognition*[17], but some of the flavour of his approach is given by the following example which comes from the doctoral dissertation of one of his students, K. E. Nitsch. Nitsch set out to teach his subjects a series of concepts which were applicable to social situations. Examples of these are:

CRINCH – to make someone angry by performing an inappropriate act.
MINGE – to gang up on a person or thing.
RELL – to rescue someone from a dangerous or problematic situation.

Nitsch was interested not only in the extent to which people could learn these definitions, but how well they could generalize them to new situations. In one experiment, Nitsch produced six such concepts, and required one group of subjects to learn the concepts so that they could come up with a definition whenever given the concept, while a second group was taught by means of examples until they could categorize each example correctly. Both groups were then tested on a series of examples which were entirely new to them. Those who had learnt the definitions did considerably worse than those who had learnt through example.

A second experiment was concerned with the range of examples used during learning. It was explained for example that the term CRINCH was originally used by waitresses, and the term MINGE by cowboys. One group was given examples taken entirely from these two contexts, while a second group was given the same information about origin, but was given a wider range of instances. Examples of these instances are given below.

Having mastered the concepts of crinching and mingeing to a point at which they were accurately able to apply them, subjects then moved on to an entirely new set of instances selected from social contexts that were different from any

verbally as well as visually. Dual coding increases one's chances of remembering something. It also helps to explain why words which conjure up strong images are more memorable than abstract words.

previously experienced by either of the two groups. The correct application rate of both groups dropped. For Group 1, trained on consistent context examples, it dropped from 89 per cent in the old context to 67 per cent in the new context. But for Group 2, trained on varied context examples, it dropped from 91 to 84 per cent. Clearly the latter were better at generalizing their learning to new situations.

Group 1 – Consistent context for new word

CRINCH – to make someone angry by performing an inappropriate act; originally used by waitresses. Usage: when a diner fails to leave a tip; when diners argue about the prices on the menu; when a diner deliberately spills ketchup; when diners complain about slow or inefficient service.

MINGE – to gang up on a person or thing; originally used by cowboys and cowhands. Usage: when three or more riders decide to converge on a single animal; when three or more work together to brand an animal; when three or more encircle a wolf or other marauder to prevent its escape; when three or more join forces against a rustler.

Group 2 – Varied context for new word

CRINCH – to make someone angry by performing an inappropriate act; originally used by waitresses. Usage: when a man does not remove his hat on entering a church; when a spectator at a public event blocks the view of those behind; when someone flicks ash over a beautifully polished table; when diners complain about slow waitress service.

MINGE – to gang up on a person or thing; originally used by cowboys and cowhands. Usage: when a band of dissatisfied sailors threaten their captain with mutiny; when an audience booes a mediocre act on stage; when someone is helpless to defend himself against attack; when a group of cowboys join forces against a rustler.

Nitsch's experiment makes the simple but important point that if one wishes to teach concepts that will generalize, then it is important to expose the learner to a wide range of examples. Unfortunately, however, there is a cost to this approach. Nitsch found that his single-context group all learnt readily within four trials, whereas people given a range of concepts during this learning phase had much more difficulty and required more training.

In his next experiment, therefore, he tried out a hybrid training scheme which aimed to obtain the generality of varied training, while avoiding the problems created during the initial learning phase by being presented with too wide a range of examples. In this study three groups were used, and all were given seven practice trials. The same-context group was trained entirely on examples drawn from the context in which the concepts were said to have originated, 'restaurant', 'cowboy', and so on. The varied-context group had examples drawn from the context of origin, followed by three trials with varied contexts. All three groups were then tested on the ability to apply their concepts to quite new social situations. Their performance is shown in the table below.

Correct application of concepts	Old content	New content
Same-context group	90%	69%
Varied-context group	92%	82%
Hybrid-context group	90%	91%

(adapted from Nitsch, 1977)

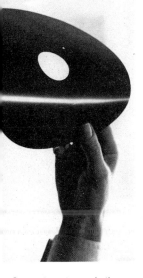

Computer memory in the form of a floppy disc. Data is stored magnetically along the circular tracks, and can be read, added to or altered by the computer. Floppy discs, which can be changed as needed, are a form of external memory. The computer's internal memory is contained on silicon chips.

As in the previous study, all groups were performing at a level of 90 per cent correct when the initial context was used. As before, subjects trained on a limited context had more difficulty applying the concepts in new situations than those who had had varied training. What of the third group? The hybrid training system appears to have been extremely successful; not only did subjects need no more training than the same-context group, but they transferred even better than the varied-context group. The conclusion is clear – that it is easier to acquire new concepts if the range of examples is limited, but if one wishes the information to generalize, then it is important to give broad experience in the training situation itself.

Such a conclusion is not of course particularly revolutionary. Most professional training courses attempt something of this kind. A medical student will begin by learning in a somewhat over-simplified way how the normal body works, and will learn about the effect of various diseases on normal function. During his clinical training he will be exposed to a range of examples within each of a number of hospital departments. Within any given department the number of possible afflictions will be constrained, so that he will be unlikely to need to be too worried about neurological factors while he is attached to a consultant gastroenterologist, or about skin diseases during his familiarization with obstetrics. As a junior doctor he will be likely to have to confront a much wider range of possible illnesses, working perhaps as a casualty officer in a hospital, and doing so with much less direct supervision. By the time he eventually emerges as, say, a general practitioner, he will have had a great deal of experience that will allow him to bridge the gap between whatever theoretical understanding he might have of a particular disease as reflected in the textbooks, and its actual manifestation in a particular patient who may well be suffering from a number of other problems at the same time.

Chapter 7

Retrieval: unlocking the storehouse _____

I would like you to begin by imagining you are a spy, required to commit to memory the following coded message:

$$
\begin{array}{ccccc}
A & A & Y & S & A \\
S & M & J & P & T & C
\end{array}
$$

Time yourself, and see how long it takes to remember it.

Memory is often likened to a vast library, full of rich information. For the library to be useful, however, the information must be accessible, and this means that it needs to be organized and catalogued. As we saw in Chapter 3, the process of organization is a crucial one, and the reason why it is crucial is that unless information is stored in an orderly and systematic way, it will not be accessible at the appropriate time. An unorganized memory would be just like a library with rooms full of books stored at random; an historian wanting to read about some aspect of the French Revolution might well have to search through thousands of books before finding anything relevant. Such a library would be relatively useless. The mode of organization is also critical. A library might store all its books with red covers in one room, all with blue covers in another, while yellow covers would be in a third room, but this would scarcely help our historian unless he happened to know that the book he was looking for had a particular cover, and preferably a rather odd one at that.

A more useful classification would be in terms of subject, with the subjects being classified in terms of initial letter; hence we would presumably look under F for French or under R for revolution. Suppose however I wanted instead to find Conrad's novel *Heart of Darkness*. Would I look under H, D or N for novel? Clearly we need a cross-classification in terms of the author. Suppose I only know the outline of the plot and that it was a book by a Polish novelist who was famous for writing in English. At that point my only recourse would be to abandon the catalogue and talk to the librarian since the human cross-classification system is so much richer and more flexible, if less reliable, than most schemes so far devised for libraries.

Is long-term memory really like a library with the vast amount of information we experience every day neatly coded and tucked away, ready to be brought out at the appropriate moment? Certainly, speaking subjectively, the amount we forget is much more impressive than how much we remember. As I wrote this passage I could hear a large number of swallows chirping outside my window, and some cars passing on the road at the bottom of the garden. It is hard to believe that every chirp and every car was stored away in my memory. Similarly, as I looked out of the window I could see a field of wheat and behind it a wood. Was every ear of wheat and every tree that I saw going to be duly stored just in case at some time, perhaps 20 years hence, I might need that information? It seems highly unlikely. And yet logically of course we can never prove that the information has not been lost. Probably it has not; probably what is stored is some representation of my memory of looking out of my window together with a representation of a cornfield and a wood based on my general knowledge of cornfields and woods, together with perhaps one or two features that are peculiar to this particular view. And if you take this line, does it not suggest that long-term memory is less like a library, accumulating information steadily through life, than like a scene where new events constantly displace old? Perhaps, when we forgot, it is genuinely because the

Orderly disorder. This old shoemaker knows exactly where to find every lace and eyelet.

memory trace has been destroyed, not that it has become inaccessible.

However, this view must also be too simple. If all forgetting represents the destruction of the memory trace, then the sum total of our memories must be what we can recall at any given time. There is abundant evidence that this is not so, and it is clear that we know more than we can retrieve in any given instance. Though it may not be possible to recall a piece of information at a particular moment, it may be possible to retrieve given a clue or cue. *Retrieval cues* allow one to locate information which is otherwise inaccessible. Read through the following list of 28 words carefully twice, then take a sheet of paper and, looking away from the list, try to write down as many of the words as you can in any order you wish.

hut, cottage, tent, hotel, cliff, river, hill, volcano, captain, corporal, sergeant, colonel, rose, violet, daffodil, peony, zinc, copper, aluminium, bronze, gin, vodka, rum, whisky, drill, saw, chisel, nail.

The 28 words came from the following seven categories: *dwellings, natural features, military ranks, flowers, metals, alcoholic drinks* and *carpenters' tools*. Now write these categories on the back of your answer sheet and see how many words from each you can recall. Now compare the number recalled under the two conditions. Most people find that the category cues enable them to retrieve words they had previously left out. It is as if the cues direct you to search in the appropriate location in memory, and as such allow access to traces which would otherwise have been missed.

While there is no doubt that both cueing and recognition can reveal information which was not accessible to memory using straightforward unaided recall it could be argued in both cases that the memory trace was present, but simply not strong enough to allow recall. The recognition item or the cue provides further information which, together with the weak trace, allows the item to be produced. Rephrased in terms of the library analogy, this is like arguing that the problem is not one of locating the book but of recognizing it once it has been located.

The bramble bush approach to retrieval – too hit and miss to be useful.

Learning to retrieve

A demonstration which is not open to this objection was made by the Canadian psychologist, Endel Tulving[1], who modified the normal procedure for learning lists of words as follows. A typical learning experiment involves presenting subjects with a list of words (36 in all), asking them to recall it, presenting it for a second time, asking for a second recall, and so on, until the list is mastered. Tulving modified this by following each learning trial with three successive attempts at recall. So subjects would read through a list of words, try to recall it, then try to recall it again, and again, and then go on to a second reading of the same list of words. This would be followed by another three recalls and then another presentation of the same words (i.e. learn, recall, recall, recall; learn, recall, recall, recall; learn, recall, recall, recall, and so on).

What effect did this procedure have on performance? Somewhat surprisingly, subjects under this regime learned just as rapidly as those who alternated learning and recall trials; it appears that the process of searching for and retrieving items actually contributes to learning – there seems to be a process of learning to retrieve.

When he looked in detail at the three successive attempts to retrieve, Tulving noticed that the total number of words retrieved did not differ within each of the three successive recalls; if the subject recalled five words on the first recall, he would recall about five on the second, and on the third. This is perhaps unsurprising in the absence of learning trials between the recalls. What was surprising however was the fact that only about half of the words were recalled consistently on all trials, the other half being made up of words which popped up and disappeared again. Suppose the list had contained the words *dog*, *cat* and *canary*, then the word *dog* might have been recalled on all three trials, whereas *cat* might have been recalled on the first trial, lost on the second, (when *canary* might have been recalled), but might have reappeared on the third. This means that the subject was clearly not revealing on any given recall trial all that he knew; it was as if he was rummaging about in a box containing the items he had stored, sometimes pulling out one and sometimes another. This effect is not of course limited to newly acquired material. If you wish to observe it in yourself, try writing down the names of as many countries in Africa as you can in three minutes. Then repeat the exercise. You will find that on the second occasion countries that were not included in the first instance pop up, but that some of the previously recalled ones are forgotten.

'On the tip of the tongue'

From a subjective viewpoint, perhaps the most convincing evidence that we possess information in our memories which we cannot access comes from the experience of being asked a question to which we are sure we know the answer, though we cannot produce it at that precise moment; we feel we have it 'on the tip of the tongue'.

A few years ago, two Harvard psychologists, Roger Brown and David McNeill[2], decided to try and see whether this feeling was based on genuine evidence or was simply an illusion. They set up a 'tip of the tongue' situation by reading out a series of definitions of relatively obscure words to their subjects and asking them to name the object being defined. Take for example 'a musical instrument comprising a frame holding a series of tubes struck by hammers'. Subjects were instructed to indicate if they were in the 'tip of the tongue' state, convinced that they knew the word, but unable to produce it. When this occurred, they were asked to guess at the number of syllables in the word and to provide any other information, such as the initial letter. They were consistently much better at providing such information than one would have expected by chance. Other studies have shown that giving the subject the initial letter, in this case *x*, frequently tends to prompt the correct name, *xylophone*.

The task of trying to remember the names of capital cities of countries is a good way of evoking this effect. If you would like to try for yourself I suggest you read rapidly through the list of countries on page 96, eliminating those for which you can immediately produce the answer or for which you are fairly convinced you do not know the answer, and concentrating on the remainder.

A better chance of finding what you want – searching in a well ordered system.

Systematic searching gives the best chance of success. A Swiss Army avalanche rescue team advances in an orderly line across the snow, prodding with search poles.

Cover up the initial letters for your first run through. Then see if the letter cues prompt recall for the difficult ones. Then look at the answers opposite and see if you were right.

	Country	First letter of capital city
1	Norway	O
2	Turkey	A
3	Kenya	N
4	Uruguay	M
5	Tibet	L
6	Australia	C
7	Portugal	L
8	Romania	B
9	Burma	R
10	Bulgaria	S
11	South Korea	S
12	Iraq	B
13	Cyprus	N
14	Philippines	M
15	Nicaragua	M
16	Yugoslavia	B
17	Colombia	B
18	Canada	O
19	Thailand	B
20	Venezuela	C

In general the feeling that you know something is a reasonably good guide that you do . . . given the right prompting. In a similar capital city recall test to that shown here, recall was over 50 per cent when cues were given for the cities people thought they knew, but only 16 per cent for those they thought they didn't.

We have established then that even if everything we experience is not stored, nevertheless our memory stores do contain more information than we can access at any given moment. What therefore determines the accessibility of information? To return to our library analogy, good retrieval depends on good encoding; the way in which a book is classified on entering the library determines the way in which it can best be accessed later. Suppose we go back to the code that you committed to memory at the beginning of this chapter. How well can you remember it? Try writing it down.

Organization is the key to efficient retrieval.

If, like the redoubtable Dr Ebbinghaus, you rehearsed it rapidly and frequently without recourse to anything as artificial as a mnemonic aid, then you can probably remember the first line moderately well but will, I suspect, have a little difficulty remembering the second. If on the other hand you have the twisted mind of a crossword puzzle addict, you might have noticed that if you start in the bottom right-hand corner and read each column of letters from bottom to top, the sequence spells the mystic word *catspyjamas*. If you noticed this, then I suspect you will have had little difficulty in reconstructing the code extremely accurately. If, however, I had asked you to reel off verbally the sequence of letters on the top row, you would have been likely to fare rather less well than if you had simply committed them to memory in a straightforward way – although given pencil and paper, you could of course have produced them reliably and reasonably quickly. In short, the method of retrieval depends on how the material is encoded during the learning.

Answers

1 Oslo	2 Ankara	3 Nairobi	4 Montevideo	5 Lhasa	6 Canberra
7 Lisbon	8 Bucharest	9 Rangoon	10 Sofia	11 Seoul	12 Baghdad
13 Nicosia	14 Manila	15 Managua	16 Belgrade		17 Bogota
18 Ottawa	19 Bangkok	20 Caracas			

Classifying incoming material

We have so far made a reasonable case for the viewpoint that our memory systems are faced with a genuine retrieval problem, and that what is retrieved depends rather crucially on the way in which the information was encoded or classified in the first place. Taking once again the library analogy, if Shakespeare's *Julius Caesar* has been categorized by the librarian under 'History', then we are likely to have difficulty retrieving it given the cue 'Drama'. Clearly, the way in which we encode incoming material is not rigidly predetermined, so does it matter how information is classified, or are all methods of encoding equally useful, provided they are systematic and logical?

There are in fact substantial variations in the after-effects of different methods of classifying material. Try categorizing the words given on page 98, ticking 'Yes' or 'No' after each (for instance, if asked whether HAT is in upper case, you would respond 'yes' since it is printed in capitals, not in small lower case letters). When you have finished, do the addition sum that follows and then read on.

Is your memory like this, a vast accumulation of fact to be rummaged through on the offchance?

		Yes	No
Is the word in lower case?	*prince*	☐	☐
Does the word rhyme with dog?	*FOG*	☑	☐
Is it the name of an animal?	*tiger*	☑	☐
Does the word rhyme with pin?	*STYLE*	☐	☑
Is it the name of a fruit?	*BOTTLE*	☐	☑
Is the word in upper case?	*SCISSORS*	☑	☐
Does the word rhyme with castle?	*battle*	☑	☐
Is it the name of a game?	*FLOOR*	☐	☑
Does the word rhyme with stump?	*skunk*	☑	☐
Is the word in upper case?	*lamp*	☐	☑
Is the word in lower case?	*TABLE*	☐	☑
Is it the name of a piece of furniture?	*desk*	☑	☐
Does the word rhyme with grave?	*SLAVE*	☑	☐
Is it the name of a unit of time?	*statue*	☐	☑
Is the word in lower case?	*oak*	☑	☐
Is it the name of a vegetable?	*carrot*	☑	☐
Is it the name of a building?	*MOUNTAIN*	☐	☑
Does the word rhyme with locket?	*rocket*	☑	☐
Is it the name of an insect?	*COCKROACH*	☑	☐
Is the word in lower case?	*GUN*	☐	☑
Does the word rhyme with wheat?	*WHEEL*	☐	☑
Is the word in upper case?	*book*	☐	☑
Does the word rhyme with wrote?	*coat*	☑	☐
Is the word in upper case?	*TOMB*	☑	☐
Does the word rhyme with hot?	*YACHT*	☐	☑
Is it the name of a disease?	*measles*	☑	☐
Is the word in lower case?	*typist*	☑	☐
Is it the name of a country?	*SHOE*	☐	☑
Is the word in upper case?	*COACH*	☑	☐
Does the word rhyme with simple?	*temple*	☐	☑

Addition sum

$4 + 6 + 3 + 7 + 9 + 1 + 5 + 8 + 3 + 2 =$

Now try to recall as many as possible of the 30 words you have just classified. Write them down in any order you like. You will have noticed that giving the answer Yes or No required three separate types of word processing: first you had to decide whether the words were written in upper or lower case; second you had to make decisions about the sound of the words when pronounced; and, third, you had to process their meanings.

Score how many of each type of word you recalled. The words classified according to case were *prince, scissors, lamp, table, oak, gun, book, tomb, typist, coach*; those classified on the basis of rhyme were *fog, style, battle, skunk, slave, rocket, wheel, coat, yacht, temple*; and those classified according to semantic category were *tiger, bottle, floor, desk, statue, carrot, mountain, cockroach, measles, shoe.*

Typically, people find that superficial processing of a word, purely in terms of its appearance, leads to very poor subsequent recall or recognition, while paying attention to its sound leads to slightly better recall. But the best processing by far comes from attending to a word's meaning. The graph below shows the results of an experiment similar to the one you have just performed. There is a very clear advantage to encoding on the basis of meaning rather than visual appearance or sound.

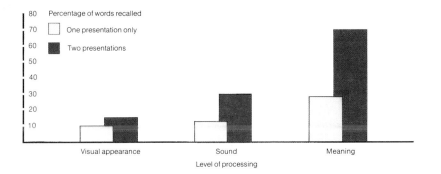

Processing incoming information according to meaning appears to leave a stronger memory trace than processing on the basis of sight or sound. (Adapted from Craik and Tulving, 1975)

Depth of processing

In an influential paper written in 1972, Fergus Craik and Robert Lockhart[3] suggested that a great deal of knowledge of human memory could be summarized very simply by assuming that the amount of information retained depended on how deeply it is processed during learning. Their concept of depth was based on a perhaps over-simplified view of the way in which we process information. It assumed that in the case of a written word it is first processed purely in terms of its visual characteristics, that these are then turned at a deeper level into a representation of the sound of the word, and that this subsequently evokes the word's meaning. In judging whether it is written in upper or lower case letters, there is no need to process information at any other than the purely visual level; such shallow processing is assumed to give rise to a relatively impoverished memory trace which will be of little assistance in the task of recalling the words. In order to decide what the word sounds like, however, it is necessary to go beyond this superficial visual analysis and to attend to the sound of the written word; this is assumed to give rise to a rather more robust and useful trace. However, processing the word in terms of its

Facts are often easier to recall if you make the effort to give them personal significance.

meaning requires one to go beyond this stage, creating a richer and more durable memory code.

Despite the importance of meaning, Craik and Lockhart do not of course claim that only meaning is stored. If that were so, we would never learn to talk or to understand speech, since both of these processes require the learning of 'shallow' auditory features of the spoken word. There is also evidence to suggest that we do, sometimes at least, remember incidental physical features of a situation; for exampe, one can sometimes remember where on a printed page one read some particular fact. There is, however, a problem in specifying exactly what is meant by 'depth'. Without a means of independently deciding how deep a given type of processing is, it is difficult to test the theory.

An alternative concept to that of depth is probably that of richness or breadth of processing. Let us go back to the librarian classifying books. He could categorize them in terms of their size, but even if we knew the size of the book we were looking for, this would not be particularly helpful. In the same way, trying to access a word on the basis of whether it was in upper or lower case letters really gives one little useful information. Most libraries of course classify books in terms of their content, classifying the content in turn on the basis of a range of dimensions which should be rich and flexible enough to allow you to track down a book on Chinese Ming pottery, or mole catching, or the sonnets of William Shakespeare, or teaching yourself Swahili. The essence of such a system is that it is structured and organized but at the same time rich and flexible. These are the characteristics which make semantic coding so widely used in long-term memory – the structure is built in through our knowledge of a structured world, and because it is so rich, containing so many different but related dimensions, semantic coding allows us to lay down very precise but nevertheless retrievable codes.

In general, information that is encoded in terms of a rich and detailed representation of the world is likely to be more accessible later than material which is processed in terms of a simpler or more impoverished scheme. What other stratagems might help to classify new material so that it can be easily retrieved? As one might expect from what has gone before, enriching and elaborating the code tends to make it more memorable. Hence a subject who is asked to make up a story about a word is more likely to remember it than one who is simply asked to decide whether it is a meaningful word or not. Similarly, if you are trying to associate the words *man* and *watch*, a simple sentence like 'the man dropped the watch' is less likely to lead to good learning than a more elaborate one like 'the old man hobbled rheumatically across the court-

Details of three famous landmarks. Can you on the basis of these visual cues predict which landmarks appear on page 102.

yard and dropped the gold watch down the castle well'. Generally, putting a lot of effort into encoding leads to better recall, so that you are therefore more likely to remember the solution to different problems than to easy ones.

Retrieval cues

Suppose that we have logged a certain piece of information in our long-term memory systems, that we have categorized it or classified it in an appropriate way; how do we access it when the time comes? One way of calling up a memory is to present all or part of the code that was laid down when it was classified. Again, going back to the library analogy, if the play *Hamlet* had been classified under 'Shakespeare', 'Drama', 'Verse', 'Prince' and 'Denmark', then some subset of these would be enough to allow us to locate a copy of the book. We use the term *retrieval cue* to refer to the information used to access a memory trace. These cues are assumed to help us access memory traces in the same way as key words help the librarian access books.

The retrieval cue concept was introduced into the current study of memory by Endel Tulving, who has contributed most to our understanding of the process of retrieval. In one experiment[4] he presented subjects with a series of words to be retained and then recalled; each word was accompanied by a cue word which had some association, but not a very strong one, with the word to be retained. An example might be the word *city* accompanied by the cue word *dirty* in one case, or *village* in another. Subjects were asked to recall the original words, either unaided or prompted by the cue word. The presence of the appropriate cue substantially increased the chance of recalling the target word. Tulving argued that for a retrieval cue to be useful, it had to be presented at the same time as the target word. A different associate of the word *city*, such as *busy*, that had not been presented during learning would not act as an effective retrieval use. If it was not presented, it would not form part of the memory trace that was classified, and it could therefore not be used to evoke that trace. Tulving has gone on to show that this effect is a very powerful one; in a series of ingenious demonstrations[5] he has shown that the learner can actually be induced to produce the target word but fail to recognize it as the word presented, and yet be quite able to recall it when given the retrieval cue.

In order to understand how this can happen it is necessary first of all to explain about *word association*. In word association, the subject is given a word and asked to respond as quickly as possible with the first word that comes to mind. Some responses are extremely common; if for example I give you the word *hot*, you are likely to respond with *cold*, *bread* is likely to evoke *butter* and *black*, *white*. Tulving began by taking a set of such common response words and presenting them as a list to be learned, each one accompanied by a low-frequency associate (one given by relatively few subjects) – for example *cold* might be accompanied by a fairly uncommon associate such as *ground*. Having learned the list, subjects were then asked to recall as many as possible of the words. Results showed that a small proportion were recalled but a good number had apparently been forgotten.

The visual cues on page 100 belong to these famous landmarks: from left to right, Big Ben in London, the Eiffel Tower in Paris, and the Statue of Liberty in New York.

The next stage was to induce the subject to produce the words himself by giving him the associates. In our case therefore the subject would be asked to give his association to the word *hot* and would duly produce *cold*. The third stage was to ask the subject to go down the responses he produced and say whether any of them were words he had originally learned. Under these circumstances recognition of the original words was very low. Our subject is very likely to produce the word *cold* in response to *hot* but deny that it had been on the learning list. Finally the retrieval cue *ground* is presented and the subject again invited to produce the response. In a substantial proportion of cases the response *cold* is produced, despite the fact that the subject has previously produced *cold* and failed to recognize it as one of the words originally learned. Since recognition is almost always easier than free or uncued recall this presents a genuine paradox. How does one explain it?

In fact such a result is mysterious only if you assume that what the subject is learning is literally the word *cold*. If you think about it, however, this is clearly not what we are asking the subject to remember; he already knows the word *cold*, so what we are asking him to do is to remember that the word *cold* occurred during a particular part of our experiment. In short, we are asking him to remember an experience, but to indicate his memory of the experience by responding with the word *cold*. If I present him with the word *cold* together with the associated word *ground* then the experience that he has conjured up is likely to be one that is a composite of these two, perhaps *burial* or *camping* and *sleeping on a cold groundsheet*. If I ask you to respond with the first word that comes to mind on giving you the word *hot* then once again the word *cold* will appear but it is very unlikely to be associated with the type of experience that has accompanied the *cold ground* encoding. It may simply be classified at a superficial level as 'the opposite', or perhaps as the labelling on the control of a shower. Consequently presenting *cold* in that context evokes an experience which has little overlap with the original experience and as such it does not serve as a good retrieval cue. When the word *ground* is presented, however, it reminds the subject of the experience, or perhaps an image generated during learning, which in turn evokes recall of *cold*.

There are other ways of showing the same effect. For example if I give you a sentence like *the man tuned the piano*, but give another person the sentence *the man lifted the piano*, then the cue *something heavy* is likely to be a very poor retrieval cue for you, but a very good one for your colleague who is in fact likely to find it an even better cue than the word *piano*. Thus we remember what we experience and we access our memory by using a fragment of that experience as a key to the whole.

Smells as retrieval cues

Smells and tastes are a particularly powerful source of recollection for many people. Probably the most famous literary example comes from the beginning of Proust's great novel *Remembrance of Things Past* where he describes how the taste and smell of a madeleine cake soaked in lime tea brings back with enormous vividness memories of his childhood: 'I had recognized the taste of the crumb of madeleine soaked in her concoction of lime-flowers which my Aunt used to give me . . . immediately the old grey house upon the street,

Fish porters at work just before the closure of Billingsgate fish market in London in 1982. The smell of fish still lingers, a pungent reminder of Old London.

where her room was, rose up like the scenery of a theatre to attach itself to the little pavilion, opening on to the garden, which had been built out behind it for my parents . . . and with the house the town, from morning to night and in all weathers, the square where I was sent before luncheon, the streets along which I used to run errands, the country roads we took when it was fine.'

It certainly seems to be the case that smells show virtually no forgetting. In one study for example Engen and his colleagues[6] had their subjects smell a cotton swab impregnated with any one of a hundred different smells. After an interval ranging from 3 to 30 seconds, they were induced to smell a second swab and decide whether the odour was the same or different. While performance was certainly not perfect, it was well above chance and showed no evidence of forgetting over the 30-second interval. A similar result was observed when a slightly different technique was used. Subjects were asked to remember five different odours, and were then presented with a sixth and asked whether it was one of the previous five or not. Again, no forgetting occurred over a 30-second delay.

Having observed no short-term forgetting, Engen and Ross went on to study long-term memory for odours.[7] In one experiment subjects were asked to remember 48 different odours, and then tested 30 days later with 21 pairs of odours (each pair comprised one odour from the original 48 and one new odour). The old odours were correctly identified on 67 per cent of the occasions, and when subjects were required to remember only 20 odours rather than 48, their recognition rate increased to 77 per cent. However, Engen and his colleagues found that performance could be reduced by pairing an old odour with a new one that was similar (onion with garlic, for example); this sent the detection rate down from 77 to 64 per cent.

In addition to all the other stresses of working underwater divers are likely to be affected by state-dependent memory; instructions given on the surface may be hard to remember underwater, and things observed underwater may well be forgotten on arrival back at the surface.

From the admittedly scanty evidence available, therefore, it seems that smells are remarkably resistant to forgetting. In this respect they resemble continuous motor skills. Why should this be? We can only speculate, but one possibility is that smells are relatively isolated from the rest of our memory experiences. The words of a verbal request or comment are repeatedly used in other language contexts, while most of the visual stimuli we perceive are followed by large numbers of similar visual experiences. Furthermore, in the case of verbal or visual information, we can imagine and recreate the experience. I suspect that our ability to imagine smells and tastes is much more limited. It is comparatively easy for me at least to evoke the visual image of a rose, but much harder to imagine its scent. That may be peculiar to me but I suspect not; try imagining both the visual appearance and odour of the following: a raw onion, white mice, scotch whisky, burning leaves. In most cases I can create some representation of the odour, but it is not nearly so vivid as the visual image I can create.

It is possible that having a durable memory for tastes and smells was once of survival value to our species. Recognizing a particular taste or smell and remembering that it was associated with sickness would have guarded us against eating poisonous or putrifying foods. A wide range of experiments involving non-humans has shown that many species are particularly good at detecting associations between taste and nausea, whereas associations between tastes and electric shocks are more difficult to learn. This particular piece of psychology has been applied to the practical problem of discouraging coyotes in the United States from attacking young sheep. The bodies of young sheep are impregnated with a substance that will make the coyote sick, and are left out. The coyote eats the sheep, becomes ill, but on recovery has developed an aversion to lamb which persists.

Memory which depends on context

So far we have been talking about the active process of categorizing or classifying our experience and the importance of this for memory. What about those features of our experience which are only incidental to our interpretation of it? Consider the case cited by the 17th-century British associationist philosopher, John Locke, who tells the story of a young gentleman who, having learnt to dance, 'and that to great perfection, there happened to stand an old trunk in the room where he had learned. His idea of this remarkable piece of household stuff had so mixed itself with the steps of all his dances, that though in that chamber he could dance excellently well yet it was only while that trunk was there; nor could he perform well in any other place, unless that or some other such trunk had its due position in the room.'[8]

The idea that reinstating the environment in which an event was experienced will bring the memory of that event flooding back has of course played an important part in detective fiction, at least since Wilkie Collins' *The Moonstone*. It was also a popular theme in detective films of the 1950s; in a typical situation, the key witness who has seen the crime while frying his breakfast on the fatal morning, fails to recall some crucial details. He is taken back to his kitchen by the artful sleuth one morning, and with the crackling of the eggs and the sizzling of the bacon, the crucial piece of evidence comes flooding back, allowing the crime to be solved and the hero saved. Is there any evidence though that reinstating the environment of learning enhances recall?

There is in fact a great deal of evidence that such effects occur. It is as if new learning is isolated from old, reducing the possibility of one interfering with the other. Take people who have lived in a foreign country for a number of years and acquired the language; they return home and after a couple of years feel that they have forgotten most of what they learned of the second language. Fortunately, on returning to the foreign country, the language rapidly comes back, suggesting that it was merely inaccessible, not lost.

A few years ago, Duncan Godden and I had the opportunity of exploring

Ancient fortifications etched in the hillside at Maiden Castle, Dorset, England. Distant experiences are often remembered by extrapolating from single, often fuzzy, clues; an archaeologist does much the same when he tries to reconstruct ancient civilizations from a few pots and coins.

context dependency, as it is called, in connection with an applied problem, namely that of training deep-sea divers.[9] Earlier experiments of my own on the effect of cold on divers had suggested quite incidentally that the underwater environment might induce strong context dependency.[10] This suggestion was supported by the observations of a friend who was in charge of a team of divers attempting to watch the behaviour of fish about to enter, or escape from, trawl nets. Initially he relied on de-briefing his divers when they surfaced, only to find that they had apparently forgotten most of the fishy behaviour they had seen. Eventually he had to send his divers down with underwater tape recorders so that they could give a running commentary on the fishes' activities; the tapes were then transcribed.

Intrigued by this, Godden and I set up an experiment in which divers listened to 40 unrelated words either on the beach, or under about 10 feet of water. After the 40 words had been heard our divers were tested either in the same environment or in the alternative one, and then asked to recall as many of the words as possible. The results we obtained are shown opposite. In a subsequent experiment, Duncan Godden trained divers in a simple manual task which involved transferring nuts and bolts from one brass plate to another. In all conditions the subject was required to work entirely by touch, a very common situation for the commercial diver who often has to operate in water so muddy that he can see nothing. One group began work under water immediately while the other was first given practice trials on land. The question that concerned Godden was the relative efficiency of land training versus underwater training. His results showed that the dry land training actually *hindered* underwater performance to the extent that the first underwater run was reliably poorer than it would have been had no prior training whatsoever been given.

What therefore are the theoretical implications of the context dependency effect? Some light was thrown on this by a later experiment[11] in which Duncan Godden and I repeated our verbal memory experiment, except that, instead of testing by free or uncued recall, we used a recognition test. Under these conditions we observed no trace of context dependency. Our subjects recognized the same number of words regardless of whether they were remembered in the environment in which they were learned. This seems to suggest that environmental cues may be important in helping to locate the relevant memory trace, but are not used in evaluating whether it is the appropriate trace or not. In a recognition test, where presenting the target word makes access to the relevant trace very probable, there is no need for the extra help of environmental cues.

State dependent memory

We have shown that reinstating the external environment in which an item was learned makes it easier to recall that item; a similar effect occurs when the learner's *internal* environment is changed by means of a drug such as alcohol. This effect is known as *state dependency*. Goodwin and colleagues[12] cite clinical evidence of this: heavy drinkers who hide alcohol or money when drunk are unable to remember where it is hidden once they are sober. On becoming drunk again they remember (and are hence able to get even more drunk). Goodwin studied this effect using a whole range of tests and found in general that what is learned when drunk is best recalled when drunk. Similar results have been shown with a wide range of other drugs including marijuana and nitrous oxide, the gas which dentists sometimes use to anaesthetise patients during tooth extraction.

In a recent review of this subject, Eich[13] convincingly showed that state dependency is only observed when memory is tested by recall, and disappears when recognition testing is used, exactly as is the case with context dependency. Once again it appears that the subject's internal state will help him access the memory trace, but that when access is made easy by presenting an item for recognition, this initial search stage is not necessary. When deciding whether or not a particular item has been presented earlier in the experiment, it does not seem to matter whether the context during testing is the same as that during learning.

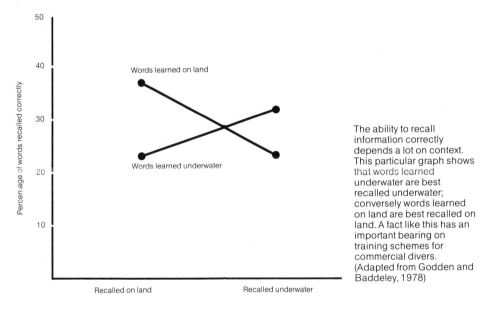

The ability to recall information correctly depends a lot on context. This particular graph shows that words learned underwater are best recalled underwater; conversely words learned on land are best recalled on land. A fact like this has an important bearing on training schemes for commercial divers. (Adapted from Godden and Baddeley, 1978)

This last conclusion suggests that retrieval must have at least two components, the first involving finding the memory trace, the second involving some form of evaluation of it. In short, retrieval is much more than a simple process of setting up the appropriate retrieval cue to guarantee the correct response.

Recollection

While much of our retrieval from long-term memory is effortless and automatic, this is clearly not always the case. In particular, when we are trying to retrieve something which is on the fringe of accessibility, we indulge in a process which is much more like searching or even problem solving. I shall use the term *recollection* to refer to this active and interactive aspect of retrieval. Some of the flavour of recollection is given by the following account which was produced a few days after the experience described had taken place.

Thursday 16 November, 1978

On Tuesday I travelled to London. On the platform I notice a vaguely familiar face. I am preoccupied and since the person in question shows no obvious signs of recognizing me I assume that it is someone I have perhaps seen on other occasions on the train or around Cambridge, and forget about it. As I get off the train I notice him again, since he has been sitting in the same carriage. Again he seems familiar. As I have been thinking about processes of memory and retrieval I decide to see if I can remember who he is.

Two associations occur, the name Sebastian and something to do with children. Sebastian seems to me to be a specific and useful cue, but unfortunately all it calls up is the name of a friend in another city, the schoolboy son of a friend in Cambridge and an association with teddy bears through Evelyn Waugh's *Brideshead Revisited*. I also sense there are some vague associations with a darkish room with books, but nothing clear enough to suggest any useful further search.

A little later, for no apparent reason, the association 'babysitting' pops up and I immediately recall that we were both members of a mutual babysitting group; that his name is indeed Sebastian, although I cannot remember his second name, that he lives in a road whose location I am quite clear about and in a house which I could visualize relatively easily. A very clear image of his sitting-room appears together with the fact that it contains a large number of very finely printed books, and that he himself is by profession a printer. I remember noticing in fact that he has a printing press in one room of his house. I have no doubt that I have successfully identified him.

Two days later, thinking about this as an illustration of a certain type of remembering, it occurs to me that I still have not remembered his name or that of the street in which he lives. I have no clues about his name, but know that he lives in either Oxford Road or Windsor Road. The two are linked, one running at right angles to the other, and I have a colleague who lives in the one that Sebastian X does not live in. If I have to guess, I would say that he lives in Oxford Road, and if I have to guess as independently as I can, I would say that my colleague lives in Windsor Road. I therefore plump for Oxford Road, though without any of the certainty which I feel about identifying him. I am however certain that he does not live in Richmond Road (since I don't *think* I know anyone who lives in Richmond Road). I also try again to remember his surname. Sebastian —, nothing, and then for no obvious reason the name 'Carter' appears. It feels right, although not overwhelmingly so. There are other Carters about! Then the association 'Penny Carter' appears as his wife's name. I am fairly sure that this is correct and it reinforces my belief that his name is Sebastian Carter. By now, about an hour later, I am quite convinced.

I go and check the babysitting list. There is no Carter. Undeterred, I go to the telephone directory. After all this effort I had better be right. 'Carter' is indeed in Oxford Road. That does not of course mean that it actually was Sebastian Carter. I resolve to ring and ask him.

November 16th, evening: I ring Sebastian Carter – was he on the 14.36 train to Liverpool Street on Tuesday, November 14th? He was.

No doubt you yourself have had similar experiences, and if so, will need no convincing that the process of recollection is an active if sometimes frustrat-

'It has long been an axiom of mine that the little things are infinitely the most important.' Sherlock Holmes, arch sleuth and master of reconstructing crucial events from tiny pieces of evidence. (A *Vanity Fair* cartoon by Spy)

ing one. There certainly is an apparent unconscious process whereby information 'pops up' for no obvious reason. The name 'Sebastian' and the association with babysitting were examples of this, and it is arguable that many, if not most, of the things we remember come to us effortlessly without apparent search. But what if the appropriate information does not spring conveniently to mind? We seem to take the fragments that are suggested and use them rather in the way that a detective might use a clue. In the case of the clue 'Sebastian' I followed up a number of plausible associations, each of which could be rejected. On what grounds did I reject them? Usually because it was obvious why that association should occur, and equally obvious that it did not lead to any further clues. In contrast, the vague association with children produced babysitting and then a clear image of the Carters' house. This in turn produced other information including the fact that Sebastian Carter is a printer and a clear visual image of seeing a printing press in his house. In short, the clue about children gave rise to a great deal of information which would not otherwise have been aroused by the simple prompt 'babysitting'; in any case the vast majority of houses in which I have babysat have not contained printing presses.

In one of the few experiments to explore directly the cues used in deciding whether we know something or not, Brown, Lewis and Monk[14] gave their student subjects lists of town names to remember. They subsequently tested their memory for the names using a recognition test in which they included, in addition to the original towns, a number of other town names, and the name of the home town of the student in question. The students were virtually always successful in reporting that the name of their home town had not been presented during learning. Presumably they argued that had it been so, they would certainly have noticed it and remembered.

Suppose I ask you your own name. I assume you will remember it rapidly and be reasonably confident that you are correct. And yet I doubt if you indulged in very much of a search for confirmatory evidence that you were correct. How do people *know* that they are right? We can only speculate; a plausible interpretation might be to suggest that any question which occasions a rapid answer, and to which there are no realistic alternative answers, will evoke a high degree of certainty. While this may be a plausible hypothesis, we really have no solid evidence on this point.

Direct access or retrieval by inference?

While it seems plausible to assume that we combine direct access to information (the phenomenon of information appearing to pop up of its own accord) with more indirect inferential techniques when recollecting events in our lives, neither of these processes is easy to study. In particular it is often impossible to confirm incidents in detail, so how do we judge whether they are being recollected accurately? Nevertheless the retrieval of information has been studied, and most recently by Camp, Lachman and Lachman.[15]

Two types of question were created in their experiment. With the first type the subject was expected to access the information either directly or not at all. Examples of this first type of question were: 'Which man's wife was turned into a pillar of salt?' (Answer: 'Lot') or 'What was the name of the flying horse of mythology?' (Answer: 'Pegasus'). In general, if such information is available, it is likely to be directly available and thus unlikely to be accessed by reasoning from other more available information. They contrasted this with a second type of question, where inference was the more likely source of information. Examples were 'What southern US city is named after an ocean?' (Answer: 'Atlanta') and 'What horror character would starve to death in Northern Sweden in the summer time?' (Answer: 'Dracula'). You will get a better feel for the two types of question if you try the two sets given below. Work as quickly as you can, marking in each case one of the four alternatives. Then move on to the following paragraph where you can check how many you got right.

Type 1 – Direct access questions

1 What was the name of the flying horse of mythology?
   (A) Pyramus, (B) Griffin, (C) Grisines, (D) Pegasus
2 Who was 'Old Hickory'?
   (A) Johnson, (B) Jackson, (C) Taylor, (D) Truman
3 Which person wrote *Uncle Tom's Cabin*?
   (A) Stowe, (B) Michaels, (C) Mitchell, (D) Stovall
4 What were the Ten Commandments kept in?
   (A) Temple of Joshua, (B) Ark of the Covenant, (C) Tent of David, (D) Aaron's Casement
5 What man's wife was turned into a pillar of salt?
   (A) Ezekiel, (B) Loca, (C) Ebenezer, (D) Lot
6 Who is responsible for the basic concept of inertia?
   (A) Newton, (B) Galton, (C) Nevell, (D) Galileo
7 What man wrote 'Pygmalion'?
   (A) Shaw, (B) Wilde, (C) Shakespeare, (D) Winthrop
8 What creature was struck dumb when his riddle was answered?
   (A) Siren, (B) Sphinx, (C) Chaos, (D) Cyclops
9 What was the name of the girl who drowned in a 1969 car accident with Senator Edward Kennedy?
   (A) Harris, (B) Harrington, (C) Kopechne, (D) Kupchek
10 Who co-starred with Bette Davis in *Whatever Happened to Baby Jane*?
   (A) De Havilland, (B) Crawford, (C) Crandall, (D) De Winter

To the direct access questions the correct answers were: D B A B D A A B C B. In the case of the questions requiring inference, the correct answers were: D A C B D D A B A B. Camp and his colleagues found that their subjects took slightly longer to answer the inference questions, as one might plausibly expect if a more elaborate search and verification procedure needed to be used. Subjects reported that the process involved in the verification was different in each case, along the lines one might expect; much more searching and hypothetic testing was needed for the indirect sentences. The two question types also produced a different pattern of errors. Camp and his colleagues divided errors into those that were phonetically similar to the correct answer (such as 'Pyramus' for 'Pegasus' or 'vermilion' for 'vanilla'), and those which were meaningfully related to the correct answer (such as 'Galileo' for 'Newton'). Inferential questions gave rise to considerably more semantically related answers than did direct access questions, whereas the two did not differ in the likelihood of making a phonetic error. It seems probable that semantic factors and semantic plausibility are much more important in the indirect retrieval of information than they are in direct retrieval.

Type 2 –Inference questions

1   Which celestial body besides the sun causes the earth's temperature to drop?
    (A) Capricorn, (B) comet, (C) Mercury, (D) moon
2   Which liquid is most often used by a nurse while treating a patient?
    (A) mercury, (B) manganese, (C) water, (D) wash soap
3   Which ingredient in gasoline does not come from plants?
    (A) lithium, (B) oil, (C) lead, (D) octane
4   What musical instrument is made only of leather and metal?
    (A) cyclephone, (B) cymbal, (C) viola, (D) violin
5   How many months of the year don't share their first letter with another month?
    (A) seven, (B) four, (C) six, (D) five
6   Which pet besides a bird lays eggs?
    (A) gerbil, (B) guppies, (C) German shepherd dog, (D) goldfish
7   Which southern city of the United States is named after an ocean?
    (A) Atlanta, (B) Ithaca, (C) Augusta, (D) Indianapolis
8   Which domestic animal continually wears man-made apparel?
    (A) hog, (B) horse, (C) cat, (D) canary
9   Which continent other than Antarctica is a natural habitat of penguins?
    (A) South America, (B) Australia, (C) North America, (D) Asia
10 What ingredient of cakes comes from beans?
    (A) coconut, (B) vanilla, (C) vermilion, (D) camomile

8 Eyewitness testimony

A few years ago I received an unexpected telephone call. A London solicitor wanted to know whether I would be prepared to testify in court that a face seen once could not possibly be recognized 11 months later. Since I knew of no evidence on the durability of memory for faces, I declined but asked for more information on the case. It turned out to be an enquiry in connection with what was to become a famous case, that of George Davis, a professional criminal from the East End of London, who was being prosecuted for a shooting incident. The evidence rested crucially on the report of a police eyewitness who claimed to have seen Davis briefly and under far from ideal conditions 11 months previously, and who subsequently identified him in a police line-up. There were in fact many dubious features to the eyewitness testimony, including the fact that a photograph of Davis had been shown to the eyewitness before the line-up. However, the solicitor seemed less interested in these aspects of the case and, since I was not prepared to testify on the question of delay, all I could do was refer him to a colleague. The case went to court and Davis was convicted.

In the following months, a vigorous and well-organized protest campaign was launched by George Davis' family and friends. They claimed that because of his previous record he had been framed for a crime of which he was entirely innocent. The campaign attracted a good deal of interest, particularly after an incident when the campaigners caused the cricket Test Match between England and Australia to be disrupted by breaking into the ground overnight and digging up the wicket.

In general, professional criminals appear to accept that they will be caught from time to time and do not make much fuss about it, so the vehemence and indignation shown by George Davis' family suggested that there might indeed be a case to answer. Eventually, the case for re-trial was conceded, the eyewitness evidence was interpreted as inadequate and George Davis was freed. Shortly afterwards he was caught taking part in a robbery, tried and convicted. On this occasion there was no protest.

Innocent or guilty?

However reliable or unreliable, there is no doubt that eyewitness testimony carries a great deal of weight. In 1976 the Devlin Committee analyzed all identification parades which had been held in England and Wales during the year 1973[1]. There were over 2 000 of them, with 45 per cent of them leading to a suspect being picked out. Of these, no less than 82 per cent were subsequently convicted. In all there were almost 350 cases in which eyewitness identification was the *only* evidence of guilt. Even here, 74 per cent were convicted, indicating the overwhelming weight given to eyewitness testimony.

Victims of violence seldom remember much about their attackers. A recent study of Loftus in which a film of a robbery did or did not include the accidental shooting of a child showed that violence markedly reduced people's memory for details.

Consider the following case, taken, as is much of this chapter, from Elizabeth Loftus' excellent survey of the issue of eyewitness testimony[2]. On 15 May 1975, the assistant manager of a department store in Monroe, North Carolina, was forced into a car by two men, one pointing a gun at him and telling him to lie down in the back of the car. He had only a brief glance at the men before they pulled stocking masks over their faces. They then drove to the store and demanded that he open the safe. He convinced them that he did not know the combination so they took 35 dollars from his wallet and let him go.

The victim, Robert Hinson, could say very little about the men other than that one of them looked Hispanic, and that their car was an off-white 1965 Dodge Dart, but he also said that one kidnapper resembled a man who had recently applied for a job in the store. On the basis of the fragmentary evidence available, a composite sketch was created of one of the suspects.

Some three days later the police stopped a 1965 white Plymouth Valiant, arresting the driver and passenger, Sandy and Lonnie Sawyer. Neither looked like the composite sketch, neither had applied for a job at the store; both denied knowing anything about the kidnapping.

At the trial, Robert Hinson positively identified the Sawyers as the men who had kidnapped him, and despite the fact that four witnesses testified that Sandy was at home at the time of the kidnapping and four vouched that Lonnie was at a printing plant visiting his girlfriend, the jury nevertheless found them guilty. As they were led from the court, Lonnie cried out: 'Momma, Daddy, appeal this. We didn't do it.'

The Sawyers were fortunate in having the support of a determined and persevering family, a tenacious private detective and a television producer who had become interested in the case. Their first real break came in 1976 when Robert Thomas, a prisoner at a youth centre, admitted to being one of Hinson's kidnappers. Encouraged by this the detective re-checked some of the earlier leads and discovered that Thomas had indeed applied for a job at the store shortly before the kidnapping. Furthermore, he had a friend whose mother owned a 1965 Dodge Dart. He went on to interview some of the jurors and a number admitted that, although the evidence did not seem very strong, they eventually became tired and simply went along with the majority.

The justification for a re-trial seemed very strong, but the judge decided that, despite the new evidence, too much time had elapsed. The Governor was petitioned for a pardon and, while awaiting the outcome of this, Thomas confessed in writing, and then on camera; he subsequently recanted, but finally withdrew his recantation. On that day the Governor of North Carolina pardoned the Sawyers. They had spent two years in jail, had narrowly escaped sentences of 28 and 32 years, and the process of freeing them had cost their impoverished family thousands of dollars. And all this was due to the jury's willingness to accept the word of the victim who admitted to seeing his assailants only briefly, and went entirely against the evidence of eight witnesses who testified to the fact that the accused could not have been present at the crime. There were clearly powerful forces at work here, sympathy for the victim, outrage at the attackers, and a feeling that someone should be brought to justice. Given a plausible candidate, it is all too easy to persuade oneself that the crime is solved, particularly when the victim is prepared to point the accusing finger.

Suspect testimony

Psychologists have been interested in the accuracy of eyewitness testimony for at least 80 years. In 1895 the psychologist J. M. Cattell[3] reported some investigations on the accuracy with which his students observed and recalled

Supporters of the 'Free George Davis' campaign, march past Westminster Abbey on their way to Scotland Yard to deliver a letter complaining of continued suppression by the police of information likely to prove Davis' innocence. At the time (1976) Davis was serving a 17-year sentence for armed robbery.

everyday events. In one question he asked them what the weather had been like a week previously; it had in fact snowed early and subsequently cleared. Of the 56 people who replied only seven reported snow. As Cattell points out, it seems that people 'cannot state much better what the weather was a week ago than what it will be a week hence'.

Cattell followed this question with a series which you might like to try.

1   *Do chestnut trees or oak trees lose their leaves earlier in the autumn?*
2   *Do horses in fields stand with head or tail to the wind?*
3   *In what direction do the seeds of an apple point?*

Cattell found that accuracy of observation was not very much better than the rate one would expect from guessing. Chestnut trees lose their leaves first (59 per cent); horses stand with tails to the wind (64 per cent); and apple pips point upwards towards the stem (39 per cent).

We also tend to be surprisingly bad at recalling details of objects we see or use daily.

American psychologists Adams and Nickerson[4] asked subjects to draw exactly what was represented on each side of a US penny piece. Some of the results they obtained are shown opposite. On average their subjects recalled only three of the eight critical features of the coin (head, In God We Trust, Liberty, date, building, United States of America, E Pluribus Unum, and One Cent), and even the features correctly recalled were more often than not mislocated.

One might plausibly suppose that an eyewitness, observing a novel event such as a crime, would notice much more and be in a much better position to remember it than when reporting on the incidental features of a coin or other 'familiar' object. However, many factors work against the witness, tending to obscure and distort his memory. Some are obvious: he sees the incident only once and is usually not expecting it; what he sees is often of very short duration; criminals are usually careful to minimize the chances of their being

The real thing, back and front. In the Adams and Nickerson study less than 30 per cent of people were able to locate the eight critical features correctly.

Look carefully at these two accident photographs and then turn to page 121.

Eight attempts at drawing a US penny piece from memory. There is of course no guarantee that what you draw is what you see in your mind's eye. People's drawing skills are notoriously poor. (Adams and Nickerson, 1979)

recognized. The influence of other factors may, however, be less obvious and straightforward.

Some of the sections which follow contain a series of questions devised by Elizabeth Loftus[5], researching common beliefs about eyewitness accounts. She questioned over 500 University of Washington students during her work. You may like to compare your replies with theirs.

Stress

'When a person is experiencing extreme stress as the victim of a crime, he will have:

(a) greater ability to perceive and recall the details of the event;
(b) the same ability to perceive and recall the details of the event as under normal conditions;
(c) reduced ability to perceive and recall the details of the event;
(d) greater ability to recall the details of the event but less ability to perceive the details of the event.'

Which answer would you choose? According to Loftus, the correct answer is (c) which was in fact chosen by 67 per cent of the students she questioned; (a) was chosen by 12 per cent, (b) by 3 per cent, and (d) by 18 per cent.

Evidence for the effect of stress in this situation is unfortunately somewhat scanty, but in general it seems likely that efficiency will follow the Yerkes-Dodson Law, described on page 67.

There is no doubt that in the heat of battle efficiency may be grossly reduced. In any given infantry engagement a large proportion of troops never fire their rifles, while tasks such as controlling missiles have been shown to degrade quite sharply when the controller is afraid.[6] There is little evidence of the effect of fear on eyewitness testimony, however; while one can ask people to recall the details of situations in which they were terrified, it is rarely possible to check the accuracy of their accounts. From what we know of the effects of milder levels of stress and arousal one might expect attention to be narrowed and perception possibly biased. High arousal might, however, be expected to lead to good consolidation of the memory trace and hence good retention of whatever was perceived, although a Freudian might argue that the stressful event would be repressed. We are sadly lacking in solid evidence on this point.

Violence

Suppose that a man and a woman both witness two crimes. One crime involves violence but the other is non-violent. Which of the following statements do you believe is true?

(a) both will remember the details of the violent crime better than the details of the non-violent crime;
(b) both will remember the details of the non-violent crime better than the details of the violent crime;
(c) the man will remember the details of the violent crime better than the details of the non-violent crime and the reverse will be true of the woman;
(d) the woman will remember the details of the violent crime better, and the man will remember the details of the non-violent crime better.'

The limited amount of existing evidence suggests that (b) is the correct answer to Loftus's question, with both men and women remembering violent events less well than non-violent events. This was chosen by only 18 per cent of Loftus's subjects, the most popular answer being (a) (66 per cent), while 6 per cent chose (c) and 10 per cent (d).

Loftus's question was directly investigated by Clifford and Scott[7] who showed 48 subjects, of whom half were men and half women, one of two videotapes. Both tapes concerned a search for a criminal by two policemen, reluctantly assisted by a third person. The beginning and end of the two tapes were identical, but the middle portion differed. In the non-violent version, the interaction between the police and the reluctant third person was almost entirely verbal, with a few mild restraining actions by one of the policemen, while in the violent version of the film, one of the policemen physically assaulted the third person. Subjects were then tested for their memory of the event using a 40-item questionnaire. Both men and women remembered consistently less of the violent version than they did of the non-violent. A single experiment is not of course enough to allow us to draw confident conclusions, but it does suggest that the 'common sense' view on this point may well be quite wrong.

An ugly incident on the football terraces. How did it start? Protagonists, bystanders and police are likely to remember the incident very differently.

Weapons

One might expect that a violent crime involving a weapon would lead the subject to concentrate much of his attention on the weapon, and hence take in much less information about the assailant or the details of the incident. Alternatively, one might assume that the presence of a gun would focus attention very strongly on the person wielding it and would brand the person and the incident indelibly on the mind of the victim. Loftus tested the views of her students using the scenario that follows.

'Consider a situation in which a person is being robbed. The robber is standing a few feet from the victim and is pointing a gun at him. The victim later reports to a police officer, "I was so frightened I'll never forget that face". Which of the following do you feel best describes what the victim experienced at the time of the robbery?

(a) the victim was so concerned about being able to identify the robber that he did not even notice the gun;
(b) the victim focused on the robber's face and only slightly noticed the gun;
(c) the victim got a good look at both the gun and the face;
(d) the victim focused on the gun which interfered with his ability to remember the robber's face.'

Which option would you choose? Opinion was evenly divided on this question between response (c), good information about both the gun and the face, and response (d), focusing on the gun, with 39 per cent of the students choosing each. Twenty per cent thought the victim would hardly notice the gun and 2 per cent felt that he would not notice it at all.

What little evidence is available seems to support the view that the presence of a weapon will distract the victim's attention away from the robber. In a study described by Loftus and carried out at the University of Michigan[8], a subject was asked to wait outside an experimental laboratory before participating in an experiment. In the 'no weapon' condition, the subject was allowed to overhear a harmless conversation about equipment failure in the experimental room, after which someone emerged from the room holding a pen and with grease on his hands, and after uttering a single statement, left. In the 'weapon' condition a different subject would hear a hostile interchange between two people ending with breaking bottles, chairs crashing and someone leaving the experimental room holding a letter opener covered with blood. Again he uttered a single line before leaving. Subjects were subsequently given an album containing 50 photographs and asked whether or not the person who had emerged from the room was represented there. In the 'no weapon' case subjects located the correct photograph 49 per cent of the time compared to only 33 per cent in the 'weapon' case.

Spring Festival in Paotow A Chinese crowd watching American tourists and no doubt commenting that all Westerners look alike!

A single experiment of this sort is again rather slender evidence on which to base a firm conclusion. However, it does support evidence from elsewhere which indicates that fear may tend to narrow the attention on to what is seen as the most crucial feature of the situation, and hence to reduce the reliability of the witness.

Identifying people of other races

'Two women are walking to school one morning, one of them an Asian and the other white. Suddenly two men, one black and one white, jump into their path and attempt to grab their purses. Later, the women are shown photographs of known purse snatchers in the area. Which statement best describes your view of the women's ability to identify the purse snatchers?

(a) both the Asian and the white woman will find the white man harder to identify than the black man;
(b) the white woman will find the black man more difficult to identify than the white man;
(c) the Asian woman will have an easier time than the white woman making an accurate identification of both men;
(d) the white woman will find the black man easier to identify than the white man.'

Three cars passed Number 2 when it was already in the flames. What was the colour of the first car to pass? (Refer back to page 116.)

This is the scenario which Loftus used to investigate cross-racial identification. Which of the responses would you choose? Of the Washington students, 55 per cent chose (b) which is the correct answer. The remainder were approximately equally distributed across (a), (c) and (d). The evidence here is extensive and strong, and indicates that we are consistently poorer in remembering and recognizing faces of people from other racial groups. This seems to be the case even though a witness may have extensive experience of interacting with people from another race. It might also be thought that strong racial prejudice would exaggerate the effect, but the evidence available seems to suggest that this is not so.

Leading questions

'Suppose a person witnesses a car accident and he is later asked questions about it: 1. "Did you see a broken headlight?" or 2. "Did you see the broken headlight?" Would it make any difference which question the witness was asked?

(a) no, since the witness would know whether or not he had seen a broken headlight;
(b) no, since there is no difference between the two questions;
(c) yes, since question 2 assumes that there was a broken headlight;
(d) no, the witness would disregard the distinction between *a* and *the*.'

Given this particular scenario, 90 per cent of Loftus's subjects chose (c), with the remaining 10 per cent spread across the other three possibilities. No doubt you too chose (c), so it will come as no surprise to you that the exact nature of a question can strongly influence the testimony of a witness. What is perhaps surprising is the range and reliability of effects that can thus be produced.

Loftus herself has carried out a number of experiments on this point. In one study[9], people watched a film of a car crash and were subsequently asked: 'About how fast were the cars going when they hit each other?' All subjects were asked the same question except that the word *hit* was replaced with either *smashed, collided, bumped* or *contacted*. Speed estimates were highest (40.8 mph) when the word *smashed* was used, lower with *collided* (39.3 mph), and progressively lower with *bumped* (38.1 mph), *hit* (34.0 mph) and *contacted* (31.8 mph). Furthermore, when questioned a week later about whether there had been any broken glass about, those who had been tested using the word *smashed* were consistently more likely to report (incorrectly) that glass had been broken.

In another study[10], a film again represented a car accident: one version involved a broken headlight while the other did not. Subjects were asked either 'Did you see the broken headlight?' or 'Did you see a broken headlight?' When a headlight was in fact broken, the probability of saying 'yes' did not differ, but when no broken headlight was present, the subjects were more than twice as likely to falsely report a breakage when asked about 'the' broken headlight rather than 'a' broken headlight. There is however a suggestion in the results that some subjects may have been detecting the suggestion and responding negatively to it since when the question is posed using the definite article 'the' subjects are more likely to say 'no' than 'don't know'.

Another series of experiments carried out by Loftus[11] convincingly demonstrates that it is possible to change a witness's recollection of an incident by subtly introducing new information during questioning. In one study subjects were shown a series of slides representing a traffic accident in which a pedestrian was knocked down at a pedestrian crossing. A green car drove past the accident without stopping, a police car arrived and a passenger from one of the cars in the accident ran for help. Subjects were then asked 12 questions about the incident, of which question 10 referred to the *blue* car that drove past the accident. When asked 20 minutes later to indicate the colour of the car that drove by without stopping, subjects given the false information tended to choose a blue or bluish-green. In another experiment, Loftus managed to persuade her subjects to report a completely non-existent barn which had been 'inserted' into their memory during questioning.

If witnesses' reports of events can be changed, does that mean that what they actually *remember* has changed, or are they simply changing what they say? Are they just 'guessing' differently under social pressure? In order to probe this question, Loftus[12] conducted an experiment in which subjects saw a pedestrian accident which involved a car stopping at either a stop sign or a yield sign. Two days later subjects were asked a series of questions about the incident, one of which biased them away from what had actually occurred; if they had seen a stop sign, the biasing question referred to a yield sign, and vice versa. Their memory of the incident was then tested by showing them pairs of slides and asking them which sign they had seen. In the critical pair of slides, one showed a stop sign and the other a yield sign. Loftus argued that if her subjects genuinely remembered the correct version, but simply responded otherwise to

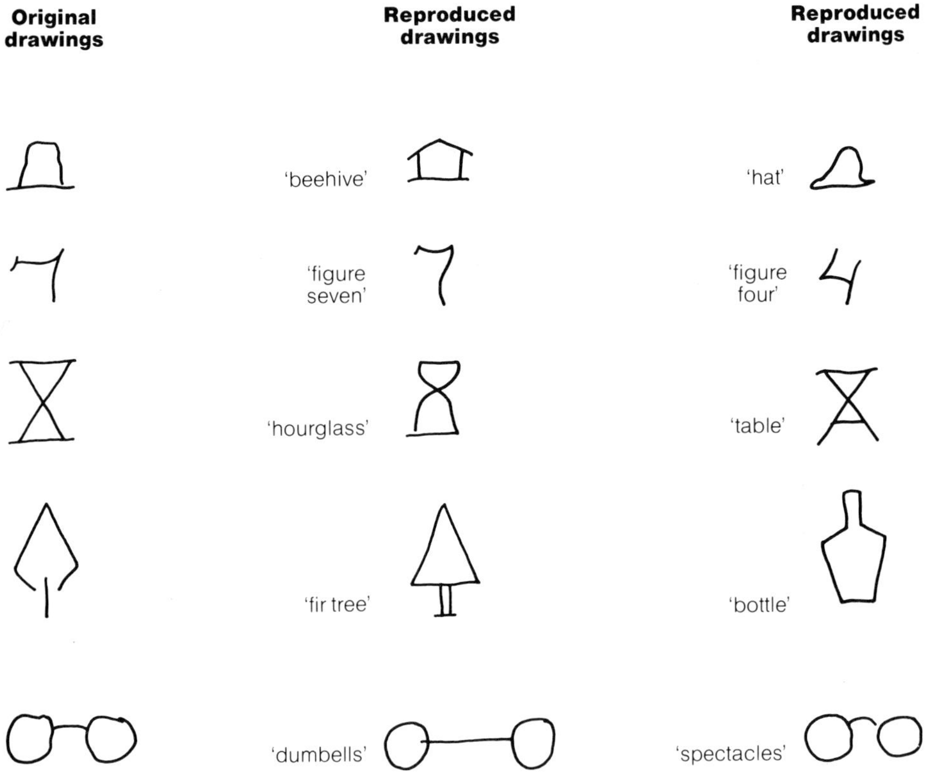

**Original
drawings**

**Reproduced
drawings**

**Reproduced
drawings**

'beehive'

'hat'

'figure
seven'

'figure
four'

'hourglass'

'table'

'fir tree'

'bottle'

'dumbells'

'spectacles'

More evidence for the
distorting power of
suggestion on memory.
Shown the ambiguous
drawings on the left and
asked to redraw them, you
too would misremember if
you were given such
suggestions as *hat, seven,
hourglass*, and so on.

please the experimenter, the bias could be overridden if she offered a high
enough pay-off for making a correct response. One group of subjects was
therefore given no reward, one was promised $1 each if they decided correctly, a
third group was offered $5, while the fourth was told that the person in the
experiment who scored the highest would receive $25. Despite this, 70 to 85
per cent of those tested selected the wrong response in accordance with the
bias; there was no tendency for higher reward to lead to greater accuracy.

Other experiments showed that subjects reacted just as rapidly and confidently when they were responding to the misleading information as they
would have done without biasing questions. Finally, Loftus was able to show
that the effect was not dependent on the subjects failing to notice the crucial
information in the first place. When they were asked immediately afterwards
to give a detailed account of what they had seen, the relevant information was
usually mentioned; but subjects who mentioned the crucial feature on immediate test showed the normal process of disruption by subsequent misleading questions.

From this Loftus argues that it is the actual memory trace which is changed
by subsequent information. While acknowledging that it is logically impossible ever to prove that a pure and undistorted memory trace still lurks
somewhere in the observer's brain, she points out with some justification that

all her efforts to get at such a trace have proved unsuccessful. It therefore does appear to be the case that what we remember is an amalgam of what we saw and what we subsequently thought. In this connection she quotes an intriguing personal reminiscence from the Swiss psychologist Jean Piaget.[13]

'One of my first memories would date, if it were true, from my second year. I can still see, most clearly, the following scene, in which I believed until I was about fifteen. I was sitting in my pram, which my nurse was pushing in the Champs Élysées, when a man tried to kidnap me. I was held in by the strap fastened round me while my nurse bravely tried to stand between me and the thief. She received various scratches, and I can still see vaguely those on her face. Then a crowd gathered, a policeman with a short cloak and a white baton came up and the man took to his heels. I can still see the whole scene, and can even place it near the tube station. When I was about fifteen, my parents received a letter from my former nurse saying that she had been converted to the Salvation Army. She wanted to confess her past faults, and in particular to return the watch she had been given on this occasion. She had made up the whole story, faking the scratches. I, therefore, must have heard, as a child, the account of this story, which my parents believed, and projected it into the past in the form of a visual memory.'

Try to memorize the markings on these three different species of butterfly. Now turn to page 129 and see which species you recognize.

Remembering faces

'I never forget a face!' We have no doubt all met people who make such claims, but how likely are they to be justified? Muriel Woodhead[14] was particularly interested in this issue and conducted an experiment in which about 100 Cambridge housewives were shown a series of unfamiliar faces on slides, and then required to recognize them when they were presented again together with a series of similar but new faces. They were also asked to rate themselves on how good they thought their memory for faces was. There were large differences in how well they performed on the recognition test, and considerable variation in how good they thought their memory was. There was however absolutely no relationship between their performance and their estimate of how good they thought their memory for faces was. Some women performed extremely well but made very modest claims, some claimed to have a remarkable memory for faces and performed very poorly, some were reasonably accurate, and most were somewhere in between. This could of course have meant that this was simply not a very good test, either because it was not related to face recognition ability outside a laboratory setting, or possibly because it was very unreliable, giving rise to different scores on different occasions.

Muriel Woodhead and I decided to follow up this experiment by investigating whether there were consistent differences among people's memory for faces, taking advantage of the fact that we had already tested a large number of subjects over a period of two years or more. We selected people who had performed particularly well or particularly badly in the previous experiments and brought them back for further testing. We found that subjects who had performed well on previous face-memory experiments did perform substantially better on re-test than those who had performed poorly. We also compared their memory for two other types of material, typewritten words and reproductions of paintings. The purpose of these further tests was to examine whether the enhanced performance of our good recognizers would apply to all memory, to all visual memory, or only to faces. Good face recognizers proved to be better at recognizing paintings, but did not differ from poor recognizers in their verbal memory score. This suggests that there is something special about visual memory which separates it from verbal memory; but it does not indicate a clear distinction within visual memory between remembering faces and remembering pictures of objects and scenes.

Can you recognize these buildings without turning the page upside down?

It has in fact sometimes been suggested that memory for faces depends on a particular system located in a special part of the brain. One piece of evidence that is sometimes held to support this comes from patients suffering from *prosopagnosia*, a rare neurological condition in which the patient is unable to recognize the faces of previously familiar people, despite having no difficulty in recognizing objects, and having no general visual impairment. A second argument in favour of the view that the perception and memory of faces is special stems from the observation that the angle from which faces are viewed is particularly important. An inverted face is much harder to recognize than an inverted building, it is also very difficult to perceive the emotional expression on a face that is inverted. Try it for yourself by looking at the items above and overleaf. The buildings are all well known and the faces are all of famous people.

One neuropsychological study[15] tested the memory of patients with right hemisphere damage for faces and buildings both the right way up and inverted. For upright faces the control patients, with other types of brain damage, made far fewer errors than those with right hemisphere damage. But when the faces were inverted the reverse was true; they did better than the controls. This pattern did not emerge in the case of pictures of houses, where the controls did

Buildings are, right to left Brighton Pavilion (Sussex, England), St. Mark's Cathedral (Venice, Italy), Taj Mahal (Agra, India) and Sacré Coeur (Paris, France).

slightly better under both conditions. While such results may be peculiar to faces, other evidence suggests that they are not; for example, one patient with right hemisphere damage was a very keen birdwatcher and in his case the recognition difficulty extended beyond faces; he found it very difficult to make the subtle discriminations necessary to tell one species or sub-species of bird from another. Even if face recognition proves not to be a separate function, it does appear to be the case that recognizing faces depends on detecting relatively subtle differences in the relationship between their component features.

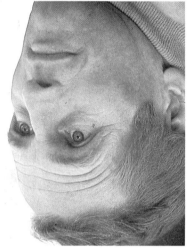  

Whose faces are these? Don't cheat! In general faces – features and expressions – seem to be harder to recognize upside down than buildings or other objects. Why do you think this is?

The faces are those of Paul Newman, Elizabeth Taylor and Woody Allen.

It is clear from the first section of this chapter that memory for faces is very fallible. Can it be improved? A few years ago Muriel Woodhead, Derek Simmonds and I[16] were invited to evaluate a course specifically aimed at improving a person's ability to recognize and to remember faces. It was based on an approach to face perception popularized by Jacques Penry[17], the inventor of the system called *Photo-fit*. Photo-fit comprises a box containing sets of features, such as a large number of chins, noses, eyes, types of hair and so on, all taken from actual photographs, which can be put together to construct a face. By putting together combinations of such features it is possible to produce a very large number of different faces, and it is claimed that, given a skilled operator, it is possible to reproduce any given face. Penry believed that in order to perceive and remember a human face it was necessary to abstract from it the various features and categorize these systematically. He talks of 'reading' a face, for example noting the nose and categorizing it in terms of size and shape, and then going on to perform a similar categorization of all the features that make up the human face. Such a view is not of course original to Penry. It goes back at least to Leonardo da Vinci who discusses memory for faces in his treatise on painting[18], advising the artist to divide the face into four parts: the forehead, the nose, the mouth and the chin. He suggests the artist study the possible forms that each of these features might take and, having learnt the range of categories, apply it to any face he sees. This, claims Leonardo, will allow the artist to retain a face at a single glance.

The course my colleagues and I evaluated was inspired by Penry's approach, and devoted a good deal of attention to his classification system. It was carried out with great enthusiasm and imagination, and involved lectures, film demonstrations, discussions, case histories and field exercises. Then, in order to see how effective the course was, we carried out three experiments. In the first, subjects were tested for their ability to commit faces to memory and subsequently recognize them. In the second and third studies subjects were allowed to refer to a set of photographs, just as if they were passport officials at an airport with photographs of wanted men. In all three studies we tested two groups of similar people: one group took the three-day course being evaluated, while the other went about its normal business. The first two studies were unable to show up any difference between the two groups. The third did show a small difference: the trainees were actually *worse* than those who had not taken the course.

Why was the course so ineffective? One possibility is that since we spend our whole lives remembering faces a two- or three-day course is unlikely to make much impression on the way we experience faces. Another possibility is that the training course was based on inappropriate principles. The Penry approach is very much concerned with analyzing a face into component features. It could be argued that perception of a face depends on processing the *pattern* of features, paying attention to the way in which each feature is related to another, so that isolating a feature is distracting. Expert chess players are very good at perceiving and remembering chess positions because the pattern of pieces is meaningful to them, not because they concentrate on the location of particular pieces. Such a view would be consistent with the 'levels of processing' approach to memory already discussed in Chapter 7. This theory claims that 'shallow' processing in terms of superficial features gives rise to poor memory, whereas 'deep' processing in terms of the meaning of the stimulus leads to much better memory.

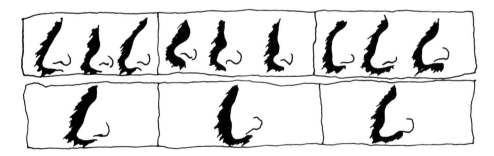

Types of noses (after Leonardo da Vinci).

Karalyn Patterson and I[19] decided to test this view by doing an experiment in which subjects were required to categorize photographs of unfamiliar people either on the basis of some of the physical dimensions advocated by Penry, or on the basis of several 'deeper' dimensions such as honesty, intelligence, or liveliness. We also included another factor, namely disguise. We reasoned that although it might be easier to remember a face for its honesty or intelligence than for its nose or ears, it might well be the case that a broad judgment of character would be much more easily misled by disguise. It may be much easier to make a person look more friendly or less intelligent than to change the shape of his face or size of his nose.

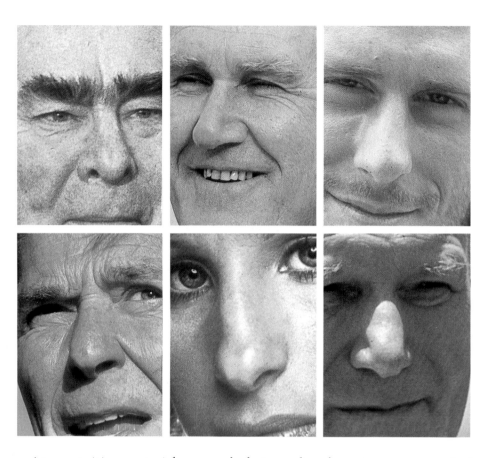

Identikit DIY-style: six sets of eyes, noses and mouths belonging to six famous faces. But whose? Answers on page 131.

As recognition material we used photographs of amateur actors and of colleagues, all of whom were photographed either undisguised or wearing a beard, wig, spectacles, or any combination of these. The photographs were taken either full face or profile; a colleague, Alan Copeman, suitably disguised, agreed to pose for them. Our subjects were familiarized with one photograph of each person in any one combination of disguised features. This was repeatedly presented until it was consistently recognized and the person's name given correctly. Our subjects were then presented with a set of photographs comprising the target people in all possible combinations of disguise, either in full frontal view or in profile, together with a number of similarly disguised but unfamiliar people. Their job was to detect and name the targets.

Our results had two interesting features. First, we found that under all conditions subjects were somewhat better at recognizing the faces they had categorized using the 'deep' dimensions of intelligence, liveliness and so forth. This effect was not particularly great, but there was no evidence to suggest that analyzing a face into its component features was helpful either with disguised or undisguised faces. Second, we found that the effect of the disguise was very dramatic. Each additional feature that was changed by adding or removing disguise reduced the probability of detecting the target. Performance ranged from extremely good when the face was presented in the same form as it had originally been learned to virtual guesswork when the maximum number of disguised features was changed.

Only the butterfly in the middle appeared on page 124. Did the wording of the question on page 124 predispose you to 'recognize' more than one?

There is no doubt that disguise can be very effective. Consider the case of the Cambridge Rapist. A few years ago great consternation was caused in the British university city of Cambridge by the activities of a rapist. He was clearly someone with considerable local knowledge, and hence someone who presumably lived locally. A number of his victims had had the opportunity of seeing him, but their descriptions were somewhat variable since he sometimes wore a wig, or even on one occasion a mask with 'RAPIST' written across it. Although by some standards he was probably rather insignificant, for Cambridge he was a major threat; thus various precautionary measures were taken, including the kind offer of a number of male students to sleep in girls' bedrooms! Not to be outdone, Oxford produced its own rapist, although he never achieved the press coverage of his Cambridge counterpart.

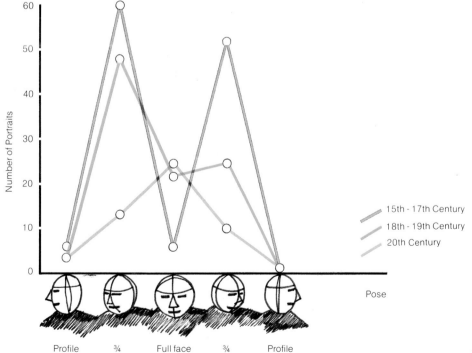

15th - 17th Century
18th - 19th Century
20th Century

An analysis of the poses favoured by the portrait painters represented in The National Portrait Gallery, London. Until this century, and the influence of photography, the most favoured pose was the three-quarters. Though this was partly for reasons of fashion, the three-quarters view probably gives more information about the sitter's character than other poses. (Adapted from Baddeley and Woodhead, 'Improving Face Recognition Ability', in Lloyd-Bostock and Clifford (eds.), *Evaluating Witness Evidence*, Wiley, 1983.)

Police notices usually show full-face or profile views, yet research shows that three-quarters views might be more helpful.

The main ways of conveying information about a wanted person are by verbal description, Photo-fit, or artist's drawing. Even when accurate, a verbal description is clearly a very unsatisfactory way of communicating someone's appearance. Try describing your own face. Do you think that you could be recognized from the description, even by your own mother? Photo-fit and similar systems such as Identikit have consequently been widely used by the police, in conjunction with drawings by police artists. How good are these systems at conveying a witness's recollection of a face? This question has been extensively explored by Graham Davis, Hadyn Ellis and John Shepherd[20] (a group of psychologists at the University of Aberdeen) with, on the whole, disappointing results. They found that even when the respondent attempts to reproduce a face that is actually in front of him, the average person has great difficulty in producing a likeness. When the efforts of their subjects were checked out by asking new subjects to match up a given Photo-fit with the appropriate original face, performance was above chance but not very decisively so. What evidence we have seems to suggest that the efforts of police artists are not very much better, but why should this be? It may be that the only way to draw or construct a Photo-fit face is in terms of individual features, whereas, as suggested earlier, we perceive faces in terms of meaningful patterns rather than features. No doubt the police will continue to use methods of this kind, simply because it is so desirable to be able to circulate a picture of the wanted person, but it is essential to recognize the limitations of the material that witnesses are likely to produce.

Consider the case of David Webb, who was sentenced to up to 50 years in prison in 1976 following a rape and an attempted rape and robbery carried out in two grocery stores in Everett, Washington, USA. Webb was identified on the basis of a composite picture built up by witnesses, who also identified him at the trial. He was convicted despite inconsistencies in the testimony of the prosecution witnesses and evidence from defence witnesses that he was elsewhere at the time of the crime. Several months later another man confessed to the crimes for which Webb had been sentenced. The confession was investigated and in 1978 Webb was released. Without the confession, he would probably still be in jail and likely to stay there.

Identity parades and line-ups

Clearly we are much better at recognizing faces than we are at recalling and representing our recall either by Photo-fit or description. For this reason, the identity parade or line-up procedure is an important component of the detective process. The suspect is presented together with a number of non-suspects of broadly similar characteristics and the witness asked if he recognizes any member of the line-up as the criminal. It is of course essential that the suspect is not distinguished from the other members of the line up (the 'distractors') if the evidence is to be at all valid. Loftus[21] describes simple techniques for ensuring that a given line-up is not biased. There have, however, been cases where bias has been introduced to an extreme degree: imagine placing one black-haired person in a group of fair-haired people, or a youth suspected of a crime known to have been committed by a young man in a line-up of men over

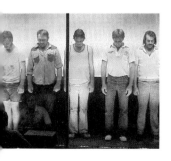

An identification parade, a useful source of evidence but liable to bias witnesses unless set up with scrupulous care.

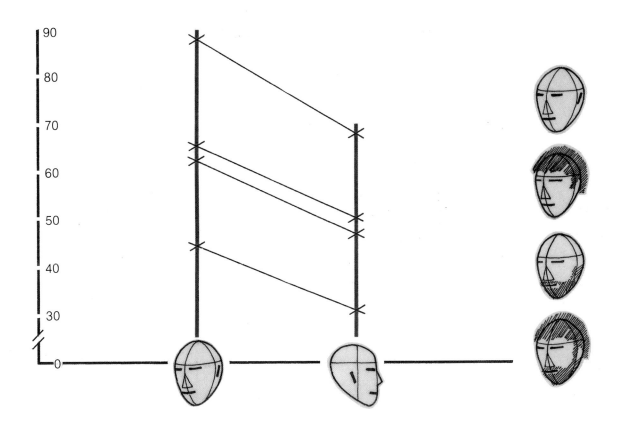

This graph shows how effective disguises are. With a wig and a beard you are only half as likely to be recognized. It also shows the greater recognizability of faces seen in the three-quarters view compared with faces seen in profile. (Based on Baddeley and Patterson, 1975)

The famous faces on page 138 are: on the top line Leonid Brezhnev, Malcolm Fraser and Bjorn Borg; and on the bottom line Ronald Reagan, Barbra Streisand and Pope John Paul.

forty. In one extreme case, where the suspect was known to be an Oriental, the line-up included only one Oriental!

Such cases are of course very rare and in any case should be picked up by the defendant's solicitor at the time of the line-up. But other more subtle influences can come into play. If for example a witness describes a criminal as good-looking, then it would be important to ensure that the line-up consists of people who are reasonably good-looking. Another source of bias is that which occurred in the case of George Davis, where a photograph of the accused was shown to the witness *before* the line-up. Under such circumstances the witness may be tempted to pick out the most familiar face in the line-up, the familiarity having come entirely from the photograph just seen.

One particularly powerful source of bias in recognition is the clothing worn by the culprit and the suspect. This issue has been extensively explored in Australia by Donald Thomson[22], who became interested in the question following a legal case in which the clothing worn by a criminal was a very important factor in causing someone else wearing similar garb to be identified as the perpetrator of the crime. Thomson was able to show that context, in terms of the location of the crime or the clothing of the criminal, had an extremely powerful effect on whether the person would be recognized or not. He went on to show that this effect was still present even with highly sophisticated subjects who were alert to the possibility of bias.

Thomson became actively involved in presenting the case for the unreliability of eyewitness evidence, and on one occasion took part in a television

This is the photograph of
the man in the four Photofit
pictures opposite. Would
you have recognized him?

Four Photofit pictures of the
same man. Can you find any
common features? Would
these pictures help you if
you were the detective on
the case?

discussion on the topic. Some time later he was picked up by the police, who
refused to explain why they were arresting him. He assumed he was being
unofficially harassed because of his strong views on eyewitness reliability. At
the police station he was placed in a line-up; a woman, clearly very distraught,

An 18th century tea room scene by a painter for the British School. For centuries European artists have favoured the three-quarters view of their sitters . . . and their pets.

identified him, and he was then told he was being charged with rape. When he asked for details it became clear that the rape had been committed at the same time as he had been taking part in the television discussion. He said he had a perfectly good alibi with a large number of witnesses, including an official of the Australian Civil Rights Committee and an Assistant Commissioner of Police. To this the policeman taking his statement replied: 'Yes, and I suppose you've also got Jesus Christ and the Queen of England too!' It transpired that the woman had in fact been raped while watching the program, and that Thomson was a victim of what is often termed *unconscious transference* whereby a witness correctly recognizes a face as being that of someone seen before but incorrectly assigns that face to the crime.

Thomson also drew attention to another important aspect of identification, namely the role of knowledge other than memory for the target event. He cites a case in which an accused person, having been identified in a line-up, swapped identities with another man in the remand cell. The accused thoroughly briefed his substitute, and it was the substitute who was interviewed by the defence lawyer. In court, all the witnesses identified the substitute as the offender. After all, he was the person in the dock, wasn't he? When the ruse was revealed the accused was aquitted. The witnesses unquestioningly believed that the person produced in court by the police was the person picked out from the line-up.

Chapter 9

Amnesia

The term *amnesia* refers to a failure of some part of the memory system. We have already discussed in Chapter 5 hysterical amnesia, where a person may be unable to remember a particularly stressful incident, or may suffer from fugue in which he forgets who he is. As we saw, hysterical amnesia is almost always associated with a need, conscious or unconscious, to escape from intolerable anxiety. It is usually temporary and the patient typically returns to a normal state of memory in due course. In this respect it differs from most other types of amnesia, where the memory defect results from brain damage of some kind.

The causes of such amnesia are various, ranging from a blow on the head, through brain damage due to alcohol or infection, to the effects of ageing. In all cases, loss of memory is more specific than occurs in hysterical amnesia: the patient rarely loses his sense of identity or awareness of the past, but usually has great difficulty in acquiring new information, a memory defect which can be extremely incapacitating. We shall begin by considering *traumatic amnesia*, the memory disruption that follows a severe blow to the head.

Traumatic amnesia

Four days before writing this I was sitting in my car in a line of traffic waiting to cross a busy seaside road. In front of me was a car, and in front of that a tractor and cart. Quite suddenly the body of a man wearing a blue crash helmet sailed high in the air across the front of the tractor, landed in the road, and lay motionless. It was a motorcyclist whose bike had apparently struck a car turning into our side road. A woman passenger in the car in front got out and began to weep hysterically, crying that it was someone's son, while a swarm of helpers gathered to render what first aid they could, call the ambulance and generally control the traffic. It was yet another head injury. What were the chances of survival for this young man? If he survived what was his likely quality of life?

The question of survival is a comparatively straightforward one. Of the 7500 serious head injury cases that are estimated to occur every year in Britain, about 97 per cent of those reaching hospital survive, though with varying degrees of disability. The unfortunate few are so intellectually impaired as to be virtually vegetables, but most make an almost complete recovery. However, even if an accident victim is fortunate enough to recover completely, he will have difficult months ahead. A severe blow to the head is likely to lead to loss of consciousness for a period lasting from a few seconds up to several months and, in the extreme, to failure ever to recover consciousness. The process of recovery is gradual, and depends on careful nursing and monitoring.

On emerging from coma, the patient is likely to go through a confused state known as *post-traumatic amnesia*. He will appear to be conscious and often able to converse relatively fluently. However, he is likely to be disoriented, not knowing where he is and not remembering when told. He may fail to recognize familiar objects and people, and may be incapable of building up a consistent, coherent picture of himself or his plight. This confused state may last from a few minutes to a matter of months, but it almost invariably passes. The state that follows is one in which the patient is likely to be able to build up an increasingly coherent picture of himself and his surroundings, but he is still

Is it possible to have an identity if you do not have a memory?

likely to have no memory of the accident, and indeed may have an amnesia extending back for several years. This state is known as *retrograde amnesia*. As the case history below indicates, this form of amnesia gradually recedes.

Beware, potential brain damage! Having your head punched regularly, as boxers do, entails significant risk of brain injury and associated memory problems.

Retrograde amnesia

A greenkeeper, aged 22, was thrown from his motorcycle in August 1933. There was a bruise in the left frontal region and slight bleeding from the left ear, but no fracture was seen on X-ray examination. A week after the accident he was able to converse sensibly, and the nursing staff considered that he had fully recovered consciousness. When questioned, however, he said that the date was February 1922, and that he was a schoolboy. He had no recollection of five years spent in Australia and two years in this country working on a golf course. Two weeks after the injury he remembered the five years spent in Australia, and remembered returning to this country; the past two years were a complete blank. Three weeks after the injury he returned to the village where he had been working for two years. Everything looked strange, and he had no recollection of ever having been there before. He lost his way on more than one occasion. Still feeling a stranger to the district, he returned to work; he was able to do his work satisfactorily, but he had difficulty in remembering what he had actually done during the day. About 10 weeks after the accident the events of the past two years were gradually recollected and finally he was able to remember everything up to within a few minutes of the accident.[1]

The consistent tendency for the period blanked out by retrograde amnesia to shrink over time is very characteristic, as is the failure ever to recover the last few seconds before the accident. Why should this be? Could it be that the accident victim represses the event, refusing to recall it because it is emotionally painful? This is not really a plausible explanation since head injuries resulting from penetrating bullet wounds or the crushing of the head which do not result in loss of consciousness do not produce this totally amnesic period, despite the fact that such events are clearly emotionally significant and very unpleasant. Could it then be that the person simply fails to take in the necessary information over the last few moments? This view is refuted by studies carried out by Yarnell and Lynch[2] on American football players who had been 'dinged' (concussed). The players were asked immediately they recovered consciousness the name of the particular play that had preceded the incident (for example 32 pop); immediately after the concussion they were able to answer the question, indicating that the information had certainly been registered. When asked again some 3 to 20 minutes later, however, they were quite unable to recall any of the relevant information. A subsequent study of the memory of football players taken off the field with other types of injury indicated that this very rapid forgetting was not simply a characteristic of the memory capacity of the average American football player! What appears to be the case is that a memory trace requires a certain amount of time to consolidate. A blow on the head, or possibly, as we shall see later, an electric current passed through the brain, probably prevents the physiological process of consolidation of the trace, and hence no permanent record is left of the event.

A few seconds of total amnesia is a small price to pay for recovery from a head injury, but is it the only price? Unfortunately not, since the process of recovery is typically a very gradual one often accompanied by cognitive and emotional problems. Most patients complain of difficulty in concentrating, of becoming tired very easily, and of memory difficulties. They may also experience irritability and sudden rages or periods of uninhibited and childlike behaviour which in more severe cases may reflect an apparently altered personality. It is these changes, rather than any physical disability, that the person's family is likely to find most difficult to accept. It is very hard to come to terms with the feeling that someone is not only handicapped but has become a different person.

Left: a skull X ray. A depressed fracture of the skull can exert pressure on the brain, but cranial fractures do not necessarily cause brain injury.

Right: many accident victims never manage to remember the last few moments before their accident.

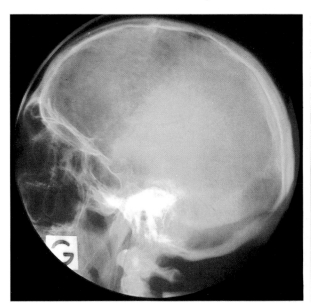

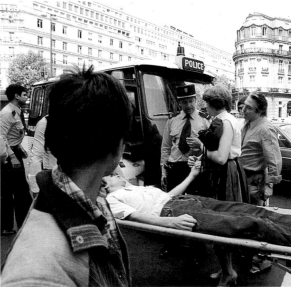

Amnesia following ECT

A second type of amnesia that resembles the post-traumatic amnesia following a blow on the head is that experienced by patients undergoing electro-convulsive therapy (ECT). In certain cases of acute depression, it is not uncommon to treat people by passing an electric current through the brain. This technique tends to produce a cerebral seizure and temporary loss of consciousness. When the patient recovers consciousness he is initially somewhat confused and is typically unable to recall events immediately preceding the shock, just as the head-injured patient is unable to remember the last few seconds before the accident, although his memory for much earlier events may be intact. This is illustrated in the graph below which shows the results of a recent study by Squire and Cohen[3] who administered a long-term memory questionnaire to patients before and after ECT. These people were asked to recognize the titles of one-season TV programs screened between 1957 and 1972. As the graph shows, ECT dramatically impaired memory for recent titles, but had no appreciable effect on memory for titles current several years previously.

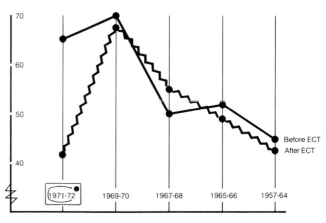

Percentage of program titles recalled correctly

Before ECT
After ECT

1971-72   1969-70   1967-68   1965-66   1957-64

Years in which TV programs were shown

Electroconvulsive therapy can severely impair memory for recent events but leave more distant recollections intact. (Adapted from Squire and Cohen, 1981)

There is evidence that in addition to the *retrograde amnesia* effect, patients given ECT may also experience absentmindedness and problems with new learning. There is furthermore evidence that the nature of the problem may depend on the position of the electrode on the patient's head. There is a great deal of evidence to suggest that the left side of the brain plays a particularly important role in the processing of speech and language, while the right side is more important in spatial processing. A number of experiments suggest that the memory deficit may be somewhat less if the standard procedure of shocking both hemispheres is modified, and only the right hemisphere is shocked.

As was mentioned earlier, it is usually argued that the period immediately before ECT fails to be remembered because the memory trace is not allowed to consolidate. On this assumption, a great deal of work has been carried out on animals with a view to studying the process of memory trace consolidation. In general, the results have been complex and sometimes contradictory, and it has more recently been argued that the electro-convulsive shock may simply be interfering with the retrieval of information rather than with its consolidation. Hence, although the amnesic side-effects of ECT are of obvious practical significance, their theoretical interpretation is problematic.

Aging and senile dementia

Most of us will be fortunate enough to escape having our memories affected by either head injury or ECT. Our memories are however very unlikely to escape the effects of a third cause of amnesia, normal aging. I recall a conversation with an older colleague who pointed out that one's ability to retrieve names at the appropriate moment deteriorated at a depressingly young age. However, he comfortingly pointed out that one does soon develop strategies to cope with the problem. I was 36 years old at the time of this conversation, and listened with interest; I still had no difficulty at all in pulling out from my memory information from journal articles that I had read years before, together with the name of the author and a pretty good guess at the date and place of publication. Depressingly soon after this conversation, however, I began to discover that he was right, at least about recalling names, or rather retrieving them at the crucial moment. I find it particularly difficult to retrieve rapidly the names of even quite close friends and colleagues whom I have known for many years, particularly when introducing them to visitors. This is a terrible confession for someone who is writing a book on memory to make. The best strategy I usually manage on the spur of the moment is to use the name of whichever of the two I can remember, saying to the other 'This is Dr Bloggs', and hoping the person will reply with his own name.

Taking a lively interest in things – one way to keep faculties sharper longer.

'When it all comes back to me, and I recall my youth and gaiety, it tickles me to the roots of my heart. To this day it does my heart good that in my time I've had my fling'

Although one's memory may lose its edge even by the early forties, the effects are far from dramatic at least up into the sixties. Indeed, on some tests, such as knowledge of vocabulary, one's performance improves over this period. While learning ability might be slightly less than in one's teens or twenties, immediate memory for things like telephone numbers is not very noticeably poorer. By one's sixties and seventies, however, memory really does start to become a problem. This shows up very clearly if elderly people are asked to remember lists of words, but more importantly it is reflected in their problems of coping in everyday life, in that it becomes harder to remember to do things, like taking pills or passing on messages. Although ability to repeat back a telephone number does not decline dramatically, working memory does seem to be impaired. It is very evident in the difficulty of keeping track of several things at the same time, and it can make following a conversation involving several people very problematic. Such difficulties can of course be made even worse by a failing sense of hearing. The same limitation in working memory capacity can present real problems in following a play on television or in understanding complex written material; this is certainly not taken sufficient account of when written material is prepared for the elderly.

In general, old people given the task of learning tend to use a more stereotyped and less rich set of learning and retrieval strategies. Even well-learned skills are often operated less efficiently because of the problem of encoding and keeping track of the situation. This point was illustrated particularly clearly in an experiment carried out in Oxford by Patrick Rabbitt[4] which studied the performance of old and young chess players playing against a computer. Computer programs can be set at a whole range of levels, and hence can be used to measure the overall standard of performance of the players. In Rabbitt's experiment, he carefully chose players of comparable standard and required them to talk through their various moves. A relatively common situation was one where a player would come to a difficult choice point, select and talk through a move and then reject it as being ultimately unsuitable.

Sometimes, having worked through and rejected two or three other moves, the initial move would come up again. In the case of the young players they would immediately reject it and move on, while the old players would often fail to recognize it, and go ahead to make the unsuitable move.

The future of our memories therefore seems somewhat gloomy. However it is important to bear in mind that at the same time that some of our memory faculties are losing their edge, we are gaining in experience; while a mathematician might be regarded as past his best by his mid-thirties, participants in professions such as the law, politics and perhaps music, where experience might be regarded as more important than flair, often operate at or near peak performance well past middle age. The sensible thing is to accept that although some aspects of our memory are not as good as they used to be, we can try to design our lives to take account of this.

While it is normal and inevitable that as we get older we become a little forgetful, it is unfortunately not uncommon for the aged to suffer from a much more extreme form of intellectual handicap, namely *senile dementia*. A serious deterioration in memory is one of the precursors of this disease. The deterioration might start in a relatively benign way, with an increased difficulty in remembering where objects have been left, and a tendency to forget apppointments. However, the memory problem can escalate to a point at which it makes the elderly person incapable of coping with the running of their own life. An old lady I know agreed to have a night nurse to stay with her, but then forgot all about it, so that when the nurse arrived, she was treated with extreme suspicion, locked out and the police telephoned.

While memory may be the first area in which deterioration is detected, intellectual impairment gradually becomes general, and the person increasingly disoriented. In the case of my 90-year-old grandfather, he was convinced shortly before he died that pigeons sitting on the roof opposite were eagles, and that various old friends, long dead, were calling to see him. Senile dementia is almost invariably progressive and typically occurs shortly before death. Riegel and Riegel,[5] who have carried out a series of studies of old people, testing their intellectual and physical competence over a period of several years, suggest that mental capacity declines at a relatively gradual rate through age up to a point about a year before death, when deterioration becomes rapid, a phenomenon sometimes known by the somewhat macabre title of the 'death drop'.

A small proportion of unfortunate individuals exhibit symptoms like those of senile dementia quite early in life. A number of different varieties of the illness have been identified, two of the commonest being Alzheimer's disease and Huntington's Chorea. There is some disagreement as to whether these represent a premature aging process or are of somewhat different origin, but the pattern of symptoms is very similar. Demented patients almost certainly do have a genuine amnesia, but this is typically made worse by their other intellectual impairments. For example, a demented patient asked to learn a list of words is unlikely to use a coherent strategy to organize the material; he is likely to pay little attention to the meaning of the words. With most subjects, including amnesic patients, giving more time for learning leads to better recall; not so with demented patients who apparently just sit passively waiting for the next item to appear.

Society in Western Europe and America is aging, so that the proportion of old people, and hence the proportion of those suffering from senile dementia, is likely to continue to rise. Such patients represent a major nursing burden to their families or hospitals, and there is thus a great deal of interest in the possibility of alleviating senile dementia. There is evidence that it is associated with changes in the structure of the brain, and in its biochemical balance. This has led to a very active interest in the possibility of drug treatment which will reinstate the biochemical balance.

A few years ago it was discovered that the brains of demented patients were deficient in choline, a neurotransmitter which may be important for the biochemistry of learning. Attempts were made to increase the amount of choline in the brain by simply feeding it to patients. Such a strategy has been somewhat unkindly likened to attempting to relieve a country's petrol shortage by flying over it and pouring petrol from the aeroplane. The analogy seems to have been all too appropriate, since the only effect of eating choline was to make the patients concerned smell of bad fish. Other treatments are now being explored, although without conspicuous success so far. In the long run, however, it does seem plausible that a thorough understanding of the complex neurochemistry underlying brain function will eventually allow us to slow down, if not reverse, the process of dementia.

Pure amnesia

In all the cases we have discussed so far, a memory problem has been only one of several symptoms of intellectual impairment. Consequently, it is often difficult to know to what extent a memory problem is primary, reflecting a basic inadequacy of the person's memory system, and to what extent it is a consequence of other problems. In the case of a head-injured person, the memory problem is probably compounded by difficulty in concentrating, and may be complicated by the presence of additional brain damage, possibly producing problems of perception or language comprehension or personality difficulties. The effects of ECT tend fortunately to be relatively short lived, but during the time they are present they are likely to be complicated by the fact that the person may be taking drugs, and will still be confused and generally disorientated. In the case of dementia, memory problems are only one of a whole constellation of signs of general intellectual blunting, so that by the time memory loss is really marked, it is likely to be accompanied by general intellectual deterioration. Because in all these cases the person's memory problems are mixed in with other difficulties, it is impossible to draw clear theoretical conclusions about the nature of memory from its breakdown.

There is however a small sub-set of patients who suffer from a truly dense amnesia, and yet show no general intellectual impairment. Although comparatively rare, such patients are of considerable interest because of the light they cast on our understanding of the normal and the amnesic memory.

The most celebrated case of a relatively pure amnesia[6] is provided by a patient, HM, who became amnesic after being treated surgically to alleviate incapacitating attacks of epilepsy. One source of epilepsy is scar tissue in the brain, and in some cases removal of this tissue can substantially reduce the number of seizures. These days such an operation might be performed, but it would be limited to one side of the brain, since most brain functions have some representation in both hemispheres. In HM's case however brain tissue was removed from both sides of the brain, with the drastic result that he became grossly amnesic. He was still able to talk quite normally and to remember his early life, but seemed unable to commit new material to memory. He was dismally bad at memorizing lists of words, or indeed becoming familiar with the faces of the people around him. He could still perform old skills like mowing the lawn, but could not remember where the lawnmower was kept. His amnesia did have some minor advantages – he could go on reading the same magazines repeatedly without apparently getting bored – but it also had some bizarre costs. While he was in hospital, a favourite uncle had died. On asking about the old man he was told of his death and exhibited considerable distress. On numerous occasions afterwards he would ask about his uncle and each time he appeared to show the distress appropriate to hearing the news for the first time. His memory problem was so crippling that he was quite unable to cope with his normal job.

Needless to say, neurosurgeons learnt from the case of HM that it was essential not to remove the equivalent tissue from both sides of the brain, so there have been no subsequent equivalent cases. There are however a number of conditions which can produce somewhat similar results. Sometimes infections may cause brain damage which can be limited to those areas which appear to be essential to long-term memory. Occasionally subjects suffering from a stroke may be unfortunate enough to suffer damage to both sides of the brain in areas that appear to mediate memory. Sometimes poisoning by coal gas may produce a relatively pure amnesia, but perhaps the commonest source of patients with a gross and relatively specific amnesia occurs in cases of Korsakoff's Syndrome. This occurs in alcoholic patients who over a considerable period of time have drunk too much and eaten too little, which results in a thiamine deficiency. The patient is initially confused and delirious, showing general signs of dementia and disorientation. Under careful nursing he may emerge from this, and once again become, superficially at least, normal. Nevertheless parts of the brain are likely to have deteriorated, producing at one extreme quite general intellectual deterioration, and at the other a relatively pure amnesia.

In all the cases described, the pure amnesic appears to have suffered damage to both sides of the brain involving the temporal lobes of the cortex, and/or the hippocampus, a subcortical structure, and/or the mammillary bodies, small but comparatively important structures deep in the brain. There is a good deal of controversy over the question of whether these different causes produce a single pattern of amnesia. It is comparatively rare to find an amnesia which is not associated with other aspects of intellectual impairment, and it is even rarer to have cases in which one knows both the detailed psychological nature of the impairment and the anatomical nature of the brain damage. There would however probably be agreement that such 'pure' amnesic patients do present a broadly unitary picture.

A pure amnesic patient is quite likely to appear entirely normal on first meeting. Speech and social manner are quite unimpaired, and typically he can talk about his early life without apparent difficulty. He may or may not be aware of his memory problem; if he is, it is quite possible that he may have developed strategies for hiding it. A Korsakoff patient I know is an absolute master at this, with a large repertoire of socially acceptable responses which keep the conversation going without actually revealing the fact that he can remember nothing about the topic in question. Hence if asked about how he thinks the government's economic policy is going, he will reply with 'Well of course politicians are all alike aren't they?' When asked who is likely to win a sports contest like the FA Cup, he is likely to come up with some phrase like 'They are both good sides and it should be a close game'. He previously ran a pub, and presumably had many years of practice in such conversational ploys with the customers.

In contrast with this apparent fluency, an amnesic patient is likely to be quite lost for an answer if one asks him what he had for breakfast or what day of the week it is, or indeed even the month or year. When asked the name of the Prime Minister, one patient came up with 'Winston Churchill', who had in fact died several years before. When told that this was not correct, he suggested 'Mr Attlee', even longer ago, and then said he simply was not very interested in politics. One can spend a whole morning with such a patient and in the afternoon he will completely fail to recognize you. For a patient who is intellectually otherwise intact, and who recognizes his problem, the situation is a very alarming one. It is sometimes described as like living in a dream, with no feeling of continuity or ability to reach out of the dream or plan for the future. Such a person, although perhaps physically fit and above average in intelligence, will not be able to cope with life in any other than a sheltered and carefully protected environment.

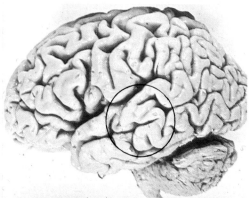

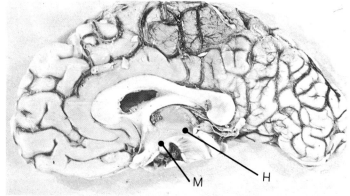

Left: the left hemisphere of the brain, showing the area of the temporal lobe involved in speech and verbal memory.

Right: a section through the mid-line of the brain showing the mammillary body (M) and hippocampus (H), two other areas vital for memory functions.

Fortunately such cases are rare, but because of their theoretical interest they have been studied extensively. What then are the characteristics of such a type of amnesia? Short-term memory may be quite normal, hence a typical amnesic patient will have a normal digit span and he could therefore repeat back a telephone number just as well as a person with normal memory. Performance may also be unimpaired on the Peterson Short-Term Forgetting Task (see page 154) which involves holding a small amount of information such as three letters in memory for twenty seconds or so, while counting backwards to prevent rehearsal. Some amnesic patients do appear to be impaired on this task, but it is possible, if not probable, that this stems from a rather more general intellectual impairment rather than from a short-term memory deficit. Given a string of words to remember, amnesics will show the normal tendency for the last few words to be very well recalled, but will do very poorly on the earlier items, whose retention it may be recalled is normally assumed to depend on long-term memory. The results of one experiment[7] in which amnesic patients and normal subjects were asked to perform this task are shown below.

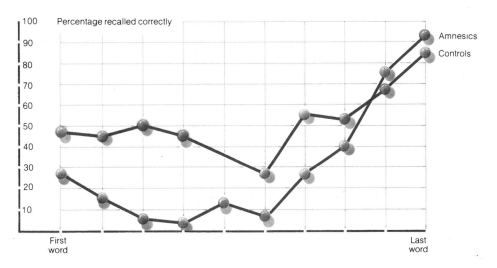

A clear discrepancy here between normal and amnesic subjects when asked to recall a string of ten words. The fact that the amnesics retained fewer of the early words suggests that their impairment has more to do with long-term than short-term memory. (Adapted from Baddeley and Warrington, 1970)

Amnesics also exhibit a gross impairment on a very wide range of long-term memory tests. While their ability to repeat back a string of digits is normal, once one exceeds the amount that can be recalled in one trial, performance declines catastrophically. Similarly, learning of pairs of words is very poor while the ability to repeat back a simple story is disastrous. They are also bad at learning lists of unrelated words and it does not seem to matter whether the testing is carried out by recall or recognition. Added to this, their ability to remember faces is very poor, as is their capacity for memorizing complex visual patterns, indicating that their deficit is not purely a verbal problem.

What aspects of amnesics' long-term memory are *not* impaired? As measured by their speed and accuracy in responding to simple statements about the world such as 'canaries have wings' or 'canaries have gills' (see Chapter 6), their semantic memory can be quite normal. In addition to this, performance on a number of other memory tasks appears to be relatively unaffected by amnesia.[8] The learning of perceptual-motor skills may be quite normal, both in the rate at which improvement occurs and also in the retention after an interval. One amnesic patient who was a pianist proved able to acquire a new tune and to play it some days later. Typically, however, the patient will be unaware of the incident during which he learned the skill, and declare that the experimental apparatus on which he has learned it is quite unfamiliar to him. While an amnesic patient's verbal learning is very poor, his performance is almost normal when memory is tested in certain ways. If for example he is taught a list of words and recall is measured by showing a degraded representation (fragments) of those words, an amnesic will appear to function quite effectively. A similar result will be achieved if memory is tested by cueing with the first two letters of a word (for example, *cy* . . . . . for *cyclone*). When the task involves doing a simple jigsaw puzzle, with performance scored in terms of time to complete, amnesics show normal learning and retention.

What is it about these latter tasks that differentiates them from the type of learning at which amnesics are so abysmally bad? Most of the memory situations require the amnesic patient to recall or recognize some episode or incident. He has for example to remember that a given word was presented to him some time ago, or must recognize that word as one which was presented at a particular time. The tasks in which performance is unimpaired all involve simply dealing with a situation that incidentally allows previous experience to help him cope. Consider the case of the fragmented words; here the amnesic is trying to come up with a solution which will allow him to read some word into the particular fragments; provided the word fits, he need not worry about whether it was a word which was presented previously or not. Similarly in the case of the jigsaw puzzle and the tasks involving acquiring particular skills; the ability to play a tune does not depend on being aware of when you learned it.

Amnesic patients therefore seem able to learn, but to have no conscious awareness of what they have learned. This particular feature of amnesia is perhaps best illustrated by an anecdote related many years ago by the Swiss psychiatrist, Claparède[9], who one morning secreted a pin in his hand before shaking hands with an amnesic patient. The following day the amnesic showed no evidence of remembering this, but nevertheless was reluctant to shake hands. When asked why, the patient was unable to come up with a convincing reason but speculated that sometimes pins were secreted in people's hands.

There have in recent years been a number of attempts to give an adequate

Many skills, once learned, are not easily forgotten, even by people who 'lose their memory'.

theoretical interpretation of pure amnesia. One suggestion was that amnesics simply do not encode information richly and deeply enough, and that, if only they could be induced to do so, their memory problems would be greatly alleviated. Alas, this proved not to be the case. Another possibility was that amnesic patients simply forget more rapidly than other people. This again proved not to be so; once he has learned something, an amnesic patient will retain it just as well as someone with normal memory. One interpretation which used to be very popular was that amnesic patients simply fail to consolidate their memory traces. The evidence for a wide range of things which amnesic patients can apparently learn makes this view less attractive, at least in its simple form. However the most likely interpretation of amnesia is that it is some form of retrieval deficit. A number of proposals have been made, including the suggestion that amnesics are particularly susceptible to interference from other material, and that they have a peculiar difficulty in relating material to its context. My own suspicion is that amnesia is indeed a retrieval deficit, but that we know too little about the processes of normal retrieval as yet to provide a convincing explanation of its breakdown in amnesia.

10 Short-term memory

How long is the present? A minute? A second? A millisecond? Or is it infinitesimally small? Suppose we hear the word 'bicycle' spoken. We do not have the sensation of needing to pull the initial syllable 'bi' out of memory when we come to the final syllable – the whole word appears to be present at the same time. The great American psychologist William James[1] referred to this sensation as 'the specious present', specious because it seems plausible, though is literally false, that the beginning and end of the word are present at the same time. Sir Frances Galton, the 19th-century British scientist gave the following description of a similar phenomenon: 'There seems to be a presence-chamber in my mind where full consciousness holds court, and where two or three ideas are at the same time in audience, and an ante-chamber full of more or less allied ideas, which is situated just beyond the ken of full consciousness. Out of this ante-chamber the ideas most nearly allied to those in the presence-chamber appear to be summoned in a mechanically logical way, and to have their turn of audience.'[2]

This concept of limited consciousness is closely related to but not identical with the concept of short-term memory, the system for storing information over brief intervals of time. The nature of consciousness is a fundamental and fascinating problem, but one which is beyond the scope of the present book. In considering short-term memory, however, we will be looking at one aspect of the problem, namely the characteristics of the system which allow it to hold and manipulate limited amounts of information. It is as if the system can grasp fleeting ideas which would otherwise slip into oblivion, hold them, relate them and manipulate them for its own purposes. The number of items or ideas that can be grasped is limited, but it can be supplemented in various ways.

A video mixer combining information from different TV cameras. Similar mixing and selecting operations occur in short-term memory.

Inside a modern telephone exchange. Even the most up to date exchange processors – which route calls, clock up accounts, monitor traffic and check that the exchange is working properly – are limited and cumbersome by comparison with the human brain.

Digit span

The question of the capacity of immediate memory was one which preoccupied a number of philosophers during the 19th century. Sir William Hamilton[3], for example, observed that if one flung a handful of marbles on the ground, the maximum number that could be perceived reasonably accurately would be about seven. The first systematic experimental work to be done on this problem was carried out in 1887 by a London schoolteacher, J. Jacobs[4], who was interested in measuring the mental capacity of his pupils. He devised a technique, the *digit span*, which has played an important role in psychology ever since. The procedure is as follows: the subject is presented with a sequence of digits and required to repeat them back in the same order. The length of the sequence is steadily increased until a point is reached at which the subject always fails. The sequence length at which he is right half the time is defined as his digit span. Try it for yourself. Read out loud each of the digit sequences listed below. After each sequence, close your eyes and try to repeat it in the correct order. Note in each case whether you get the sequence completely correct or not. Try to read each sequence at a relatively steady rate (about two digits per second) and continue testing yourself until you reach a span at which you are always incorrect.

```
9 7 5 4
3 8 2 5
6 5 1 4
9 4 3 1 8
6 8 2 5 9
3 8 1 4 7
9 1 3 8 2 5
6 4 8 3 7 1
5 9 6 3 8 2
7 9 5 8 4 2 3
5 3 1 6 8 4 2
7 9 1 8 5 4 6
8 6 9 5 1 3 7 2
5 1 7 3 9 8 2 6
5 1 3 9 8 2 4 7
7 1 9 3 8 4 2 6 1
1 6 3 8 7 4 9 5 2
6 1 5 9 4 3 8 2 6
9 1 5 2 4 3 8 1 6 2
7 1 5 4 8 5 6 1 9 3
1 5 2 8 4 6 7 3 1 8
```

Most people can manage six or seven digits, but there is quite a large range of capacity, with some people managing only four or five and others getting up to ten or more. Needless to say, tests would normally be carried out in much more controlled conditions than this!

If you spoke them aloud, then you would probably do somewhat better than if you simply read them to yourself. The reason for this is that hearing the digits registers them in a brief auditory memory store which will be discussed later on.

The first 200 decimal places of *pi*. How about applying the chunking principle to memorizing them!

1415926535 8979323846 2643383279 5028841971 6939937510 5820974944 5923078164 0628620899 8628034825 3421170679
8214808651 3282306647 0938446095 5058223172 5359408128 4811174502 8410270193 0521105559 6446229489 5493038196
4428810975 6659334461 2847564823 3786703165 2712019091 4564856692 3460348610 4543266482 1339360726 0249141273
7245870066 0631558817 4881520920 9628292540 9171536436 7892590360 0113305305 4882046652 1384146951 9415116094

Such is the fragility of short-term memory traces that even the few milliseconds one saves by push-button dialling reduce dialling errors.

The most accessible calculating aid in the world: fingers.

Another way of improving performance is to group the digits rhythmically. This technique appears to help reduce the tendency to recall them in the wrong order. Studies comparing different modes of grouping seem to come up with the conclusion that grouping in threes is best[5] and even a tiny gap between successive groups will be helpful, provided the listener can hear it. So, if you are telling someone your telephone number and you want to ensure that he writes it down correctly, group it in threes, or if it is not divisible by three, in threes and twos. Having done so, you would be wise to check it, since there is a surprisingly high error rate in reproducing telephone numbers, even when one is simply remembering the number for the brief period needed to copy it from one sheet of paper to another.

The role of rhythm in memory is one which we rather tend to neglect, possibly because it is associated with 19th-century ideas of memory drill which emphasized the parrot-like repetition of often useless information. It is probably the rhythm which makes poetry particularly easy to commit to memory, and it certainly played an important role in the memory of the late Professor A. C. Aitken of Edinburgh University. Aitken was a very talented mathematician who was also a lightning calculator and someone with remarkable memory abilities. He has been described in some detail by Ian Hunter[6], a psychologist who knew him and studied his remarkable talents. Hunter gives the following account of one of Aitken's mnemonic feats, the recall of the first thousand decimal places of the value of π or pi (the symbol of the ratio of the circumference of a circle to its diameter), a demonstration which Aitken himself regarded as 'a reprehensibly useless feat had it not been so easy.' Aitken discovered that by arranging the digits in rows of 50, of which each row contained 10 groups of 5, and reading them over in a particular rhythm, they were very easy to memorize: 'the learning was rather like learning a Bach fugue.' Hunter tape-recorded Aitken's recall and gives the following description: 'Sitting relaxed and still he speaks the first 500 digits without error or hesitation. He then pauses, almost literally for breath. The total time taken is 150 seconds. The rhythm and tempo of speech is obvious; about five digits per second separated by a pause of about half a second.'

When tested using the standard digit span procedure of one digit per second, Aitken's performance was unremarkable, but he complained that the presentation rate was far too slow, 'like learning to ride a bicycle slowly.' When the digits were read at a rate of five per second he had no difficulty in repeating back 15 in the order of presentation, or indeed in reverse order. Recalling in reverse order is much more difficult than normal auditory recall. Try it for yourself using a sequence length from the digit span list opposite.

Aitken's amazing memory capacity was not however limited to remembering numbers. In 1937 he had been tested using a passage of prose and a list of 25 words. Some 27 years later Hunter asked him to recall this material. Not only did he recall all 25 words correctly and in the right order, but the passage of prose was recalled virtually word-perfect. Aitken also had a remarkable memory for events and conversations, and on committees could always be relied on to give an accurate detailed account of what had occurred at previous meetings. He himself however took little pleasure in being used as a walking minute-book, was distinctly unimpressed by his abilities as a lightning calculator, and ceased to practice many of his calculative skills as soon as automatic calculators became available.

Chunking

A crucial element of the success of Aitken was his ability to integrate several digits into a single chunk. The capacity of immediate memory is determined by the number of chunks rather than by the number of digits, a point made more obviously if we move on to memory span for letters instead of remembering sequences of digits. Try reading off and repeating back the following sequence of letters: *I A R F T S K B G N I*. Were you able to repeat it correctly? If you were, you have a remarkably good immediate memory. Now try the next sequence which in fact comprises exactly the same letters: *F R I K B A S T I N G*. No prizes for getting that one correct. What is the difference between the two? The first comprised 11 unrelated letters, and although one might be able to chunk a few of them together into a single sound, *ARF* for example, in general the number of chunks remaining would be likely to exceed the six or seven that our short-term memories can hold. The second sequence could very easily be chunked into three speech sounds, or possibly even two if you were to regard *BASTING* as a single word. The task would of course have been even easier had the 11 letters made up an already existing word such as *intelligent*.

Chunking is something which the memorizer himself does with the material presented, but obviously some sequences lend themselves to this process much more readily than others. One factor that assists chunking is the redundancy or predictability of the material (see page 34). Consider the structure of the English language: certain letters occur much more frequently than others. If I were playing a guessing game and trying to determine what the first letter in a sequence was, I would be much more sensible to guess *S* or *T* than *X* or *Z*. Similarly, certain combinations of letters occur particularly frequently; there is a general tendency for vowels and consonants to alternate, and for certain letters to follow others; if I told you that the first letter in the word was a *Q* then it would not take great foresight to guess that the letter following would be a *U*. Such relationships are not limited to adjoining letters; if I tell you that the first two letters are *T* and *H*, you would be more likely to guess *E* than *U* as the following letter, and more likely to choose either of these than another consonant such as *S*.

The longest name in Britain belongs to a village on the island of Anglesey. A suitable case for chunking? A 19th century clergyman is said to have invented the name with a view to boosting the tourist trade.

These various probabilities can be calculated quite simply by feeding a sample of normal English into a computer and simply asking it to count the frequency with which individual letters occur on their own, and in association with preceding letters or pairs of letters. My colleagues, R. Conrad and W. E. Thomson, and I[7] performed such an analysis a few years ago using as our two samples of material leading articles from *The Times* newspaper, written in a rather formal kind of English, and scripts from a BBC soap opera, *Mrs Dale's Diary*, which used a much more popular English. The computer gave us information on the frequency of individual letters, pairs of letters, and triplets. Using the results we were able to produce letter sequences that ranged from completely random through so-called first order approximations where letters occurred with the frequency with which they would in English, second order approximations, where pairwise associations were mimicked, third order approximations based on triplets, and real words. Samples of the various types of material are shown overleaf. Try testing yourself on some of the sequences by simply reading them aloud, then closing your eyes and trying to repeat them back. If you would like to plot your performance more systematically, simply count how many times you get the sequence right for each order of approximation. Then compare your results with what our subjects achieved, as shown in the graph below.

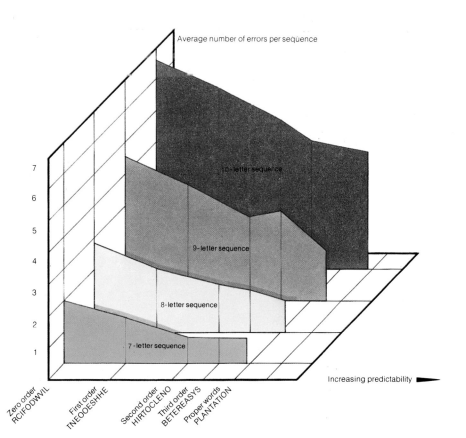

This graph shows the effects of two factors, predictability and sequence length, on recall of pseudo words and real words. The more word-like sequences are, the easier they are to remember. (Adapted from Baddeley and Conrad, 1960)

Why did we go to this trouble? We were interested in the design of codes in connection with the British Post Office's plans to introduce postal codes. Using the structure of English allowed us to create a series of codes related to letter sequences, producing the most memorable based on real words first, before moving on to slightly less memorable pseudo-words, and working down eventually to sequences which bore no relationship to English whatsoever. In fact the code that was adopted was very different from this, largely because of operational and engineering constraints.

Random sequences	First order (frequency of individual letters the same as in English)	Second order (pairs of letters equivalent to English)	Third order (letter triplets equivalent to English)	English words
RCIFODWVIL	TNEOOESHHE	HIRTOCLENO	BETEREASYS	PLANTATION
GKTODKPENF	INOLGGOLVN	DOVEECOFOF	CRAGETTERS	FLASHLIGHT
TZXKHAWCCF	PDOASLOTPP	SESERAICCG	TOWERSIBLE	UNCOMMONLY
NGORHQIYWB	AEOCAOIAON	AREDAGORIZ	DEEMEREANY	ALIENATION
BVNJSYZXUA	IRCRENFCTN	CUNSIGOSUR	THERSERCHE	PICKPOCKET

Short-term forgetting

So far we have concentrated on one technique, that of memory span. However, although memory span has been used steadily over the last 60 or 70 years, an intensive interest in short-term memory only developed in the late 1950s following two studies, one by John Brown[8] in England and one by the Petersons[9] in the United States, which showed that even sequences within the memory span would show clear forgetting, provided the subject was prevented from thinking about the item or rehearsing it in any way. Peterson and Peterson presented their subjects with sequences of three unrelated consonants. Immediately the subject had read them he was shown a three-figure number and asked to start counting backwards from it in threes. After an interval ranging from between 3 and 18 seconds he was asked to recall the original three consonants before going on to the next three, which would again be followed by the backward counting task, and then recall. Try it for yourself with the material at the top of page 155. As you can see, it is arranged in six columns. Beginning with the far left-hand column, cover up the figures with a sheet of paper and read out the three consonants B, K, Q. As soon as you have read them out, cover them up and do the simple arithmetical sum below them. Cover up the whole column and move on to the next, and so on. Now, working from memory, write down the consonants for each column, together with the total for the sum. When you have completed this task, you can read on to the next paragraph.

The results obtained by Peterson and Peterson and their subjects are shown opposite. Also illustrated are the results from an experiment by Murdock[10]

B	L	Q	F	P	D
K	Z	X	J	K	L
Q	M	C	V	H	X
7	8	5	9	6	8
+9	−2	+8	−4	+3	−5
+3	+6	−2	+5	−4	+9
−6	+3	+9	−7	+9	−4
+8	−9	−7	+3	+2	−6
−3	+7	−3	+6	−7	+7
−5	−5	+9	−2	−8	+2
+4	−2	−7	+8	+5	−4
Total?	**Total?**	**Total?**	**Total?**	**Total?**	**Total?**
Recall	**Recall**	**Recall**	**Recall**	**Recall**	**Recall**

using three unrelated words. As you will see, the forgetting curve is the same for both three letters and three words, indicating that, as with memory span, the important fact is the number of chunks remembered rather than the number of letters.

What about your own results? Clearly our attempted version of the experiment was a very rough-and-ready one. We did not for example systematically vary the length of time for which you had to remember each item. Furthermore not all triplets of letters are equally difficult. However, I suspect that you probably got the first item right, and possibly the second, but did rather worse on the later ones. This is the normal pattern of results and it has an important implication for the explanation of the Peterson effect.

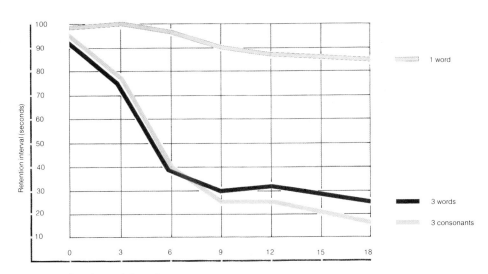

These are the forgetting curves found by Murdoch and the Petersons when they prevented their subjects from rehearsing the items they were asked to recall. (Adapted from Peterson and Peterson, 1959, and Murdoch, 1961)

Retention interval (seconds)

Percentage recalled correctly

1 word

3 words

3 consonants

It was initially thought that the sort of curve yielded by the Murdock and Peterson experiments indicated that the memory trace left by the three letters was becoming more and more faded and decayed as time elapsed, making it less and less likely that it could be accurately recalled. However, it was subsequently pointed out that on the first trial of such an experiment very little forgetting occurred; it is only later items that show the dramatic forgetting that is so characteristic of this procedure. The reason for this seems to be that the subject has difficulty discriminating between the three letters he has just been shown and the various triplets that have previously been presented; the greater the interval the greater the confusion. The Peterson task is not of course limited to use with letters; very frequently it is used with word threesomes, and if you are prepared to try another eight trials it should be possible to demonstrate another characteristic of the procedure. Move on to the lists below and carry out the task as before. The only difference is that this time you are being asked to remember triplets of words rather than triplets of letters. As before, concentrate entirely on the line you are working on and blank out the lines above with a piece of paper or card. Once again you should read out the three items and then go on to the arithmetic task, writing down the three items in the order in which they were presented at the end. Move straight on to the next item and so forth until you have completed the set. Then go back and mark how many you got right.

bear	horse	zebra	dog	grape	banana	cherry	coppe
cow	sheep	fox	camel	plum	orange	lemon	zinc
lion	tiger	cat	mouse	apple	strawberry	tangerine	lead
5	7	8	6	4	9	7	6
+9	−4	−7	+3	+9	−5	−4	+7
−7	+9	+3	−8	−5	+7	+6	−2
+4	−3	+9	+6	+8	−2	−3	+9
−8	+6	−4	+9	−2	+7	+5	−3
+3	−5	+6	−4	−4	−8	+2	−5
+2	−7	−8	−5	−7	+6	−9	+4
−5	+8	+6	+6	+2	+5	+8	−9
Total?	**Total?**	**Total?**	**Total?**	**Total?**	**Total?**	**Total?**	**Total?**
Recall	**Recall**	**Recall**	**Recall**	**Recall**	**Recall**	**Recall**	**Recall**

As you no doubt noticed, the words were not selected at random but came from within particular categories. You should again have observed the tendency for the first item to be well recalled, and for subsequent recall to decline, with one exception; when you changed from the category comprising animals to that comprising fruits, performance should have improved dramatically, before falling away again.

Why does performance improve? The reason is that by changing the category of item presented, you have been given a way of avoiding being misled by items presented on earlier trials since these were of a different category and hence could be ignored. This is termed *release from proactive inhibition*. However, having once moved on to a new category, by the second trial there are already previous items from that category to get in the way of recall. The release from PI technique was developed by the American psychologist Delos Wickens[11], who has shown that the effect can be produced by changing any of a wide range of different dimensions, including switching from letters to numbers, from large to small items or from dark to light backgrounds, although these effects tend not to be as dramatic as those obtained when a switch in meaning is used.

Rote learning of the Koran in a traditional Islamic school. Contrary to popular belief, learning things by heart does not have a beneficial effect on the rest of one's memory.

Free recall

Another technique popularly used to study short-term memory is *free recall*, so named because the subject is presented with a string of items to remember, which can then be recalled in any order, in contrast to *serial recall* where the items must be recalled in the order in which they were presented. In free recall it is usual to present the subject with considerably more items than he is likely to remember. Once again, the best way of getting the flavour of such a task is to try it for yourself.

Look at the six lists on page 158 and work your way through the examples. Simply read through them at a comfortable pace, covering up each word with a piece of card as you go. When you get to the bottom of each list you will find either the instruction 'Recall', in which case you should write down the words in any order you like on a piece of paper, or you will find some simple arithmetic; in this case do the sums and then try to recall the words previously read through. Allow yourself about one minute to do the recalling – you will find that most of the words you are likely to remember will be recalled in this time. One or two additional items may pop up later; if they do, ignore them. I suggest that you go right through all six lists before scoring for recall. Remember that you are allowed to recall the items *in any order you like*. Now score your recall by comparing the words you have written down with the lists below. Start by scoring Lists 1 to 3, adding up the number of times you got the first word right, the second, the third and so forth up to the sixth. Then score Lists 4 to 6 in the same way.

List 1	List 2	List 3	List 4	List 5	List 6
barricade	armchair	icicle	proud	parchment	sepulchre
children	glow-worm	instructor	stirrup	gold	gnome
diet	outhouse	kidney	villain	baroness	stage
gourd	troll	lapel	zodiac	lever	patriarch
folio	handshake	crooner	deer	manservant	diploma
meter	hoarfrost	funnel	arbitrator	divan	minstrel
journey	elephant	carpet	beginner	emporium	mayonnaise
mohair	pumpkin	haystack	courtroom	wood	portcullis
phoenix	graveyard	hopper	hobby	gorge	dyke
crossbow	capsule	chancery	measles	windscreen	effigy
alligator	file	simpleton	ogre	armada	tiger
doorbell	package	theatre	nosegay	beverage	wage
muffler	playhouse	stencil	film	flowerpot	yacht
menu	ferry	urn	peg	lotion	maggot
nebula	dumpling	slug	flagon	archer	inspector
	overcoat		head-dress	pharmacy	deformity
Recall	**Recall**	**Recall**	3	9	6
			+7	−5	−3
			−6	+6	+7
			+5	+3	−2
			−4	−1	+9
			−1	+4	+5
			+2	−8	−8
			+9	−2	+4
			−8	+7	−1
			Recall	**Recall**	**Recall**

You probably found that on the first three lists you did only moderately on the earlier and middle items but rather better on the last one or two items. With the last three lists this tendency probably disappeared. Clearly under such uncontrolled conditions you are unlikely to get a very clear result. But the results that would have been obtained if a large number of people had been tested, each with a large number of lists, is shown opposite. The curve relating presentation position to the likelihood that the word will be recalled is known as the *serial position curve*. Free recall without any intervening task gives rise to a very clear and characteristic curve, with the first one or two items moderately well recalled, a very flat middle portion to the curve and excellent recall of the last one or two items. Such a curve is obtained across an amazingly wide range of conditions, whether the list is long or short, whether it contains words or nonsense material, whether it is presented rapidly or slowly, and indeed whether the subject is drunk or sober. The curve is not limited to Western culture; students of an Islamic village school in Morocco whose education consisted of learning by rote sections of the Koran also showed just such a curve when presented with unrelated material.[12]

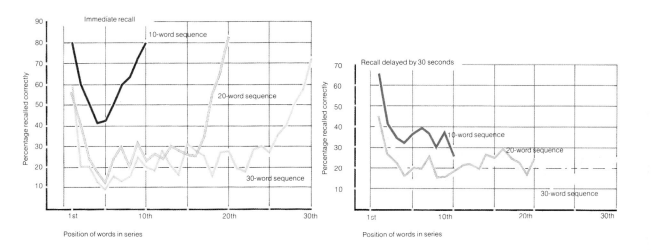

The graph above illustrates the tendency for the last items in lists of items to be recalled fairly accurately. But this effect, the recency effect, disappears if recall is delayed, as in the right hand graph; after a 30-second delay recall of later items drops dramatically. (Adapted from Postman and Phillips, 1965)

As should be clear from your own last three trials, and from the curve on the right, the picture changes dramatically when the subject is not allowed to recall immediately. Even a very brief interruption is enough to abolish the tendency of the last few items to be well recalled. This tendency is known as the *recency effect* because it reflects the recall of the most recent items – the last few presented – and it appears to behave very differently from performance on the rest of the curve, and to be unaffected by many other factors which influence performance. For example, familiar words are generally better recalled than rare words, but show no greater recency effect; presenting words slowly increases overall performance but leaves the recency effect unaffected; presenting words that refer to concrete objects rather than to abstract concepts increases performance on the earlier part of the curve, but again leaves the recency effect intact. And yet the recency effect can be abolished very simply by interpolating a small amount of distraction, such as requiring the subject to add five single digits. Because of the apparent difference between the recency effect and the rest of the curve it has often been suggested that it depends on short-term memory, while the rest reflects a longer-term aspect of memory.

Are short-term and long-term memory separate?

A major controversy within experimental psychology during the 1960s was whether long- and short-term memory involved two separate systems, or whether they were simply different aspects of one unitary system. Until the 1960s there was virtually no discussion of this point, at least in part because those people who were working on long-term memory did not work on short-term memory and vice versa. During this period, long-term memory work was carried out largely in North America by a close-knit group who used mainly nonsense material and who were much more concerned with plotting the relationship between variables than with producing theories. What theories they did produce were based on the simple concept of association and on interference between associations. Work on short-term memory was particularly strong during the same period in Britain where it had its roots in applied problems such as designing telephone numbers and codes. People working on short-term memory, both in Britain and North America, were very interested in explanatory models, often using concepts derived from the digital computer which was developing rapidly at that time. It was the development by Peterson and Peterson of an experimental technique which appeared to allow one to plot short-term forgetting simply and elegantly that focused the attention of both groups on a common problem. This was whether it was necessary to assume that there were two separate kinds of memory, short-term and long-term, or whether all the effects observed could in fact be explained in terms of the principles then assumed to govern long-term memory. This latter view was put forward by a highly-respected advocate of the traditional North American approach to memory, Arthur Melton[13], in an influential paper which triggered off a whole series of attempts to argue for or against a separation.

The issue is still a controversial one, and I should therefore state that I myself believe that the data are far too complex to fit into a single unitary theory. There are indeed problems with the view that there are two systems, but here again I think that they stem from over-simplification; there are in fact probably *more* than two memory systems. Short-term memory is not a single unitary system; rather it is an amalgam or alliance of several temporary memory systems working together. It is however an issue too complex to be

Completing a jigsaw puzzle. Unless you hold an image of the total pattern in your head, your efforts will be hit-and-miss.

discussed in detail here, though it is perhaps worth describing some of the evidence that was used to argue for two memory systems rather than one, before going on to discuss the need for a more complex theory.

The first source of evidence has already been discussed; it concerns the fact that a number of memory tasks appear to have two components which behave in quite different ways. The clearest example is free recall where, as you may remember, the recency effect was very fragile, disappearing after a brief interval which has no effect on the retention of earlier items. On the other hand, performance on earlier items is sensitive to a wide range of factors that are known to influence long-term learning. These include: rate of presentation, with slow presentation leading to better performance; familiarity of the words, with familiar words being better remembered; distraction arising from the request to do another task at the same time, thus impairing performance on the words being remembered; and factors such as the age of the subject, with elderly subjects remembering fewer words than younger subjects. But none of these variables affects the recency component. One simple explanation of this is that they influence long-term memory but not short-term memory.

A second source of evidence comes from brain-damaged subjects, who occasionally have very specific memory problems. Certain amnesic patients, described in more detail in Chapter 9, have great difficulty learning new material. Their ability to remember a free recall list, such as the one presented earlier, is abysmal, and their everyday life performance is quite appallingly bad. They have great difficulty remembering where they are, what day of the week it is or what they had for breakfast; you could spend all morning with such a patient who would then fail to recognize you in the afternoon. Nonetheless, despite their dramatically impaired performance on the early part of the free recall list, such patients show normal recency. They also show good performance on memory span, and can in certain cases be quite normal on the Peterson task. In

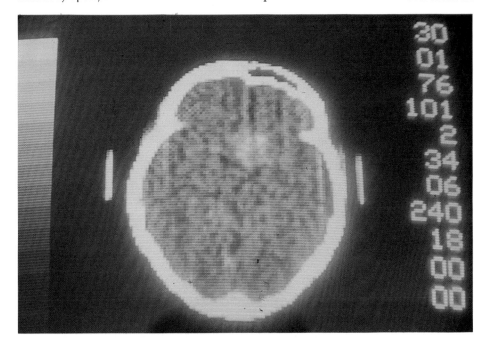

Mapping the brain slice by slice: a CAT (computerized axial tomography) brain scan. Impairment of short-term memory is often associated with damage to the left hemisphere.

contrast, there are occasional amnesic patients who appear to have exactly the opposite set of symptoms. Their memory span may be limited to two or three items, their recency effect limited to one and their Peterson performance extremely poor, particularly with auditory presentation. Despite this they may have quite normal learning ability.

These two types of brain-damaged patient do of course have damage to different parts of the brain. The short-term memory problem is associated with damage to the left cerebral hemisphere in an area close to that involved in speech, and such patients may, but need not, have language problems. Amnesic patients who show defective long-term memory tend to have damage to both sides of the brain, normally the temporal lobes of the cortex and deeper structures such as the hippocampus and the mammillary bodies. The fact that tasks associated with long-term memory may be very badly impaired while those associated with short-term memory are intact, and vice versa, speaks strongly for the view that different memory systems are involved.

A third source of evidence for separating long- and short-term memory comes from experiments which suggest that material in our short-term memory is processed largely in terms of speech sounds, while our long-term memory depends primarily on meaning. In the early 1960s, experiments on memory for letter codes carried out by Conrad[14] in connection with work for the British Post Office threw up an interesting phenomenon. Conrad's subjects were presented with sequences of unrelated consonants and were required to write them down immediately afterwards as accurately as possible in their right order. He noted that the short-term memory errors made were not random, and more particularly that these errors tended to be similar in sound to the correct item, despite the fact that items were presented visually. Hence *B* was more likely to be remembered as *V* than as *R*. Conrad went on to show that sequences containing letters that sounded alike were much more likely to be erroneously remembered than sequences made up from letters that sounded different; hence a sequence like *P D G C V B* (*pee, dee, gee, see, vee, bee*) was much more subject to error than a sequence like *K X R Y L F*. He showed that similar effects could be produced using words that sounded alike, again indicating that they were remembered in terms of their sound rather than their visual appearance.

Acoustic cues

Conrad's data suggested that short-term memory relied on some form of acoustic, or at least speech-based, code. It was however still possible to argue that any form of similarity would cause confusion, and that it simply happened to be the case that letters are more similar in sound than they are visually or in any other dimension. I decided to explore this possibility by using words and comparing the effect of similarity of sound with that of similarity of meaning.

The experiment I carried out[15] was a very simple one which involved presenting subjects with sequences of five words and asking them to write them down in the order presented – basically a memory span task. You may like to look at the word lists below and try the test for yourself. Read off the top row of words, look away, write them down in the correct sequence, and then move down to the second row and so forth. When you have finished, check how many you got right in each of the four categories described below.

List A

mad	mat	can	map	cap
ap	can	cat	cad	map
at	map	map	man	mat
nap	mad	man	mad	man
ad	cat	cap	can	can
Recall	**Recall**	**Recall**	**Recall**	**Recall**

List C

big	long	tall	broad	wide
wide	tall	broad	tall	large
high	wide	high	long	long
broad	large	large	big	great
tall	great	long	large	high
Recall	**Recall**	**Recall**	**Recall**	**Recall**

List B

en	few	sup	day	cow
ow	sup	day	sup	pit
ar	cow	bar	few	few
day	pit	pit	pen	hot
up	hot	few	pit	bar
Recall	**Recall**	**Recall**	**Recall**	**Recall**

List D

foul	late	thin	old	strong
strong	thin	hot	deep	old
hot	old	late	safe	late
old	foul	safe	foul	safe
deep	hot	strong	thin	thin
Recall	**Recall**	**Recall**	**Recall**	**Recall**

The words in the lists above, as you may have noticed, belong to several different categories. Those in List A are all words similar in sound – *man, mad, mat, map, can, cat, cap, cad*; those in List B are equally common words in English but they have distinctive sounds – *pen, day, few, cow, pit, bar, hot, sup*; those in List C are all adjectives with approximately similar meanings – *high, great, big, long, tall, broad, large, wide*; and those in List D are adjectives with distinctive meaning – *old, foul, late, strong, thin, deep, hot, safe*. Was there a noticeable difference in your performance on the basis of these four categories? The bar chart on page 164 shows the percentage of sequences that my subjects recalled entirely correctly in the experiment. Two things are clear. First, I successfully repeated Conrad's finding; my subjects found the words that sounded alike very much harder to remember than those which did not. Secondly, I found that similarity of meaning had only a very slight influence on the subjects' performance. It appeared therefore that they were relying much more on the sound of the words than on their meaning. Thus it seems that Conrad was right in assuming that short-term memory is particularly closely associated with speech. But what of long-term memory?

In order to look at long-term learning I used the same experiment but extended the length of the lists from five to ten, preventing the subjects from relying on rote rehearsal by interrupting them after each presentation. To ensure that learning occurred I presented the lists four times and then tested recall after a 20-minute delay. Under these conditions the effects of similarity of sound disappeared; the words that gave subjects the most trouble were the adjectives with similar meanings. Or to put it another way, this particular long-term memory task appeared to depend on the meaning of the words, not on their acoustic characteristics.

Similar effects were observed in other experiments conducted at about the same time[16]. Again it appeared to be the case that short-term memory was sensitive to the surface or sound characteristics of the text, while long-term memory discarded such information, retaining only its meaning.

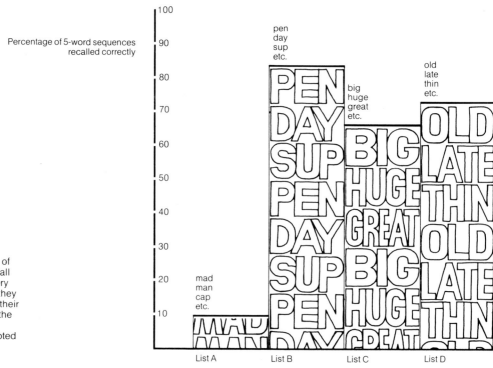

Percentage of 5-word sequences recalled correctly

Word categories

A clear demonstration of how difficult it is to recall words which sound very similar. The less alike they sound, whether or not their meanings are similar, the more likely you are to remember them. (Adapted from Baddeley, 1966)

Short-term memory store

By 1970 opinion favoured the view that long- and short-term memory involved two quite separate systems. There were many divergent opinions on the exact nature of and relationship between the two, but most conformed more or less to a model of memory put forward in 1968 by two American psychologists, Richard Atkinson and Richard Shiffrin.[17]

Atkinson and Shiffrin considered memory to have three major constituents. The long-term memory system was concerned with storing information over extensive periods of time and was fed by a short-term memory that acted as a controller, feeding in new information and selecting particular processes for pulling information out of the long-term memory. The short-term memory system was itself fed by a series of *sensory registers* which were essentially micro-memories associated with perception. These registers acted as a system for selecting and collating sensory information, and could be viewed as an essential component of perception. This concept of memory is visualized opposite. A diagram like this is not a literal representation of what happens in the brain but it does help to make Atkinson and Shiffrin's theory more comprehensible. The same model could equally well be expressed mathematically, or in purely verbal terms.

The heart of Atkinson and Shiffrin's system was the *short-term memory store*. It is important to note that they drew a distinction between short-term *memory*, which they used to refer to performance of a range of tasks in which small amounts of material need to be remembered for short periods of time, and the short-term *store*. This is a theoretical concept used to explain results obtained in short-term memory experiments. Any experiment which tries to probe temporary working memory is likely to give results which are influenced not only by the performance of the short-term store but by other factors as well, in particular long-term memory. To take an extreme example, suppose I gave you the sequence *1234567890* to remember in a memory span test; you would almost certainly remember it correctly, though I doubt if you have a memory span of 10 items. If I were to ask you to repeat it five minutes later you would still get it right, indicating that performance was in this case relying heavily on long-term storage. Many short-term memory tasks clearly do have a long-term component, and this inevitably makes theoretical interpretation difficult. The *release from PI* techniques (page 157) where subjects remember words from one category and are then switched to another is a case in point. Although recall is typically requested after only a few seconds, this does not prevent the items being stored in long-term memory; indeed, unpublished experiments of my own have shown that subjects, when tested after a week, are able to recall many of the words presented in this type of experiment.

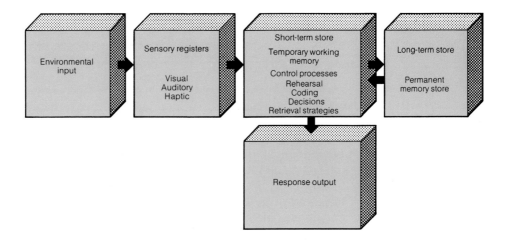

The links between long-term and short-term memory according to Atkinson and Shiffrin.

Levels of processing

Despite the fact that the Atkinson and Shiffrin model, or some variant of it, was extremely popular in the early 1970s, it has been overshadowed in recent years by the *levels of processing* approach put forward by Fergus Craik and Robert Lockhart[18] and already referred to in Chapter 7.

A central characteristic of the Atkinson and Shiffrin view of memory was that the only way to learn new material and commit it to long-term memory was via the short-term store, which was capable of processing information in a wide range of different ways. The method most extensively studied by Atkinson and Shiffrin was that of *subvocal rehearsal*, whereby an item is repeated again and again. It was assumed that the longer an item was held in the short-term store, the greater the probability that it would go into long-term memory.

Such a view ran into problems. As we saw earlier, brain-damaged patients may have very poor short-term memory yet unimpaired long-term learning ability. If the only route into long-term memory is the limited capacity short-term store, then logically someone whose short-term store is almost nonexistent should have enormous difficulties. However, such patients clearly do not have this handicap; not only can they learn normally but they also appear to have remarkably few problems in coping with everyday life. This evidence, which clearly undermines the Atkinson and Shiffrin viewpoint, has not been taken quite as seriously as I myself believe it should have been, possibly because such patients are rare and the nature of their deficit poorly understood.

However, a related problem, based on experimental evidence from normal subjects, has probably had more influence. The evidence came from a study carried out by Craik and Watkins[19] when they were trying to assess to what extent keeping an item in short-term memory might increase the probability of its passing into long-term memory. They required their subjects to hold a series of words in short-term memory for either long or short periods; after presenting many words they asked their subjects, without prior warning, to recall as many of the previously presented and tested words as possible. Would holding a particular word for a long period increase the chances of its passing into long-term memory and being remembered subsequently, as Atkinson and Shiffrin's model suggested? There was no evidence that this was the case. Words held over a long period were no more likely to be recalled than those held only briefly.

Craik and Lockhart argued that the previous view of a short-term memory store, relying on speech coding, feeding a long-term memory store was inappropriate. They proposed instead a view that assumed a short-term or primary memory system that could process material in a variety of ways, ranging from simply taking note of the visual characteristics of a printed word, through rehearsing it or paying attention to its sound, up to elaborate coding in terms of its meaning. They argued that all of these processes would lead to some long-term learning, but that the amount of learning depended on the type of processing, with 'deep' processing in terms of meaning leading to much better retention than 'shallow' processing.

The levels of processing approach is essentially concerned with the role of coding in learning, the relationship between the manner in which material is processed, and the probability that it will be subsequently remembered. As such, it is primarily a theory of long-term memory; it does assume a primary or short-term memory system that actually does the coding, but details of it are left unspecified. Indeed, so little emphasis is placed on the short-term component that the levels approach has often mistakenly been assumed to represent a unitary approach to memory, and any success it has had in relating coding to

Morse telegraphy (from
A. Ganet, *Natural
Philosophy,* London, 1887).
A Morse code operator, like
a typist or a pianist,
performs a short-term
memory task but draws
heavily on information in
long-term storage.

long-term memory has sometimes been interpreted as evidence against the idea that long- and short-term memory involve separate systems. In fact the preoccupation with levels has represented rather a reversion to the 1950s position of separate and parallel research on long- and short-term memory. The work stemming from levels has tended to go more and more in the direction of studying the factors governing retrieval from long-term memory, while short-term memory studies have tended to become more closely associated with problems of attention, and the role of short-term memory in other tasks such as reading and mental arithmetic.

11   Working memory

In this chapter I shall take the liberty of talking in somewhat greater detail than elsewhere about my own principal research interest. Underlying my approach is the assumption that a model or theory is useful if it helps one to come to grips with a problem. From this standpoint, a working memory approach to problems of short-term memory is not 'truer' than a simple dichotomy into long- and short-term memory, but its greater flexibility allows one to capture much more of the richness of the remarkable cognitive skills that we all display.

In the early 1970s a colleague, Graham Hitch, and I were about to start a three-year research project. We had been given funds by the Medical Research Council to carry out work on the relationship between long- and short-term memory. One lunchtime, over coffee, we fell to discussing some of our misgivings about the general field of short-term memory at the time. It was just passing through a peak of popularity, and the psychological journals were full of short-term memory experiments using a bewilderingly broad range of techniques, and coming up with a disconcertingly large set of explanatory models. One single book published in 1970 for example had 13 different contributors, each presenting a different model of short-term memory[1]; surely not all of them could be right! Of course the models had much in common with each other. Nevertheless we felt uncomfortably like those medieval scholastic philosophers who spent their time discussing how many angels could perch on the point of a pin.

We decided to step back from the complexity and ask a single basic question. What is short-term memory for? The patient with a memory span of only two digits seems to cope with life effectively. Perhaps short-term memory had no function other than to keep experimental psychologists amused? If that were so, we decided, we would rather amuse ourselves in other ways.

There had already been a good deal of discussion as to the probable role of short-term memory, and there was fairly general agreement that its function was to serve as a *working memory*, a system that allowed several pieces of information to be held in mind at the same time and interrelated. This kind of system is clearly useful if you are trying to understand a spoken sentence where it may not be possible to process the beginning of the sentence fully until you have reached the end. Take the following sentence: 'He strode across the court and protested vigorously to the judge that his opponent was infringing the rules by using (an illegally strung tennis racquet) (inadmissible evidence).' It is of course not possible to tell until the last phrase whether the court is a tennis court or a court of law.

Some form of temporary storage is also necessary for a wide range of tasks such as mental arithmetic, reasoning and problem solving, and it is surely not accidental that virtually all attempts to simulate complex human behaviour by computer have ended up requiring some type of working memory, a subcomponent of the overall system which holds and manipulates material that is being processed. If the short-term store does fulfil this role, then it is clearly a very important component of human behaviour. Unfortunately however, although many people had suggested this possibility, there was virtually no direct evidence. So Graham Hitch and myself decided that we would attempt to collect some[2].

The auditory imagery you use to conjure up the sound of the wind in the trees is part of your working memory system.

Capacity and limitations

One of the first problems in trying to decide whether short-term memory functioned as a working memory derived from the lack of agreement as to what the characteristics of short-term memory were. It was clearly likely to prove rather a long job if we were to take all available models of short-term memory and test them one after the other. Fortunately there were two features common to all, namely that short-term memory has a limited storage and processing capacity and that the memory span task relies quite heavily on short-term memory.

We reasoned therefore that if short-term memory does function as a working memory, and we were to use up the available capacity of our subjects by requiring them to remember strings of digits, they should have great difficulty in simultaneously performing other information processing tasks, such as reasoning or comprehending, even though these are not usually thought of as tasks involving memory. This approach assumes that the short-term memory system is like the control tower of a major airport, responsible for scheduling and co-ordinating all the incoming and outgoing flights. Our experimental procedure was analogous to jamming the control room with additional high-priority demands which had to be met before the routine functioning of the airport could be continued. The outcome should be a dramatic disruption of performance.

The task that we chose to inflict on our subjects at the same time as they were remembering strings of digits was a verbal reasoning task, which is itself worth explaining briefly. During the 1960s both psychologists and linguists became very interested in grammar, and in the way in which syntax is processed. A number of experiments were run to show that active sentences such as 'The boy kicked the ball' were more rapidly processed than passive sentences like 'The ball was kicked by the boy', or negative sentences such as 'The boy did not kick the ball'[3]. At about that time I myself was interested in the effect on deep-sea divers of nitrogen narcosis, the drunkenness that appears if one breathes air at pressures exceeding that experienced at depths around 100 feet (30 m). To demonstrate the effect of nitrogen narcosis I needed a simple reasoning task that could be performed by my divers under water; it had to be one which could be administered very quickly since bottom time was strictly limited, and I wanted it to be a task which required very little learning. I therefore borrowed the techniques being developed by the psycholinguists and produced a grammatical reasoning test. This involved presenting subjects with a series of sentences, each describing the order of presentation of the two letters A and B. Each sentence was followed by the pair *AB* or *BA*, and the subject's job was to decide whether the sentence correctly described the attached letter pair. The sentences used varied from simple active sentences such as 'A follows B – *AB*', to which the correct answer is obviously 'False', passive sentences such as 'B is followed by A – *BA*', to which the correct answer is obviously 'True', to more complex versions such as 'A is not preceded by B – *BA*', to which the answer would be 'False', and so on. It proved a very successful test for the purpose and could be carried out after a very small amount of practise by virtually all the subjects I tested. By counting how many sentences my divers could complete correctly in three minutes I was able to get a very rapid measure of their mental capability at depth. It also proved to be reasonably sensitive, picking up impairment even at 100 feet (30 m), about the shallowest depth at which one can reliably detect impaired performance.

Now if short-term memory is indeed required for reasoning, one should have difficulty doing a sentence-checking test of the kind just described while remembering telephone numbers! We were anxious not to overload our subjects, so we began by giving them just one or two items to remember while doing the test. We found absolutely no effect, and so progressed to giving them strings of six numbers to remember; you will recall that six numbers approaches the average digit span, and so ought to occupy a great deal of one's short-term memory system.

Wim Klein, the 'Human Computer', a specialist in lightning mental arithmetic. The number on the blackboard tallies exactly with the answer given by a computer.

We ran the experiment as follows: each subject was given a six-digit number such as 731928; he was then required to say it aloud, and to continue saying it. Meanwhile a sentence such as 'A precedes B – BA' was shown to him and he was required to press a key marked 'True' or one marked 'False', as appropriate, while continuing to rehearse the telephone number. Our subjects were initially rather horrified at being asked to do these two things at the same time, but somewhat to their surprise, they discovered that they could do so with very few errors on either the digit span or sentence-checking task. With six-digit numbers, however, there was a consistent tendency for reasoning to be slowed, though the magnitude of the disruption was much less than we had expected. Was this slowing-down evidence that short-term memory acts as a working memory system?

All things considered, our results seemed to be telling us that the short-term store is involved in the system used for reasoning, comprehending and learning, but that this involvement is by no means total; the two systems appeared to have some overlapping components but were by no means entirely dependent on the same limited capacity system. As a result we began to reformulate our concept of short-term memory, and to attempt to sort out some of the sub-components.

Starting from the premiss that working memory was likely to be a complex and flexible system, we decided that our best strategy was probably to isolate certain sub-components and attempt to understand them. We therefore began by assuming the existence of a core system, a system responsible for controlling the overall system, and termed this the *central executive*. We postulated that the central executive was assisted by a number of slave systems which would allow it to offload some of its short-term storage functions, thereby freeing a portion of its own capacity for performing more demanding information processing tasks. An analogy can be drawn with a business executive who, if he is to avoid becoming overloaded, must delegate the more routine aspects of his job to subordinates, leaving himself free to give full attention to novel problems and dilemmas.

The articulatory loop system

You may recall that one characteristic frequently assigned to short-term memory is its reliance on speech coding – most models of short-term memory involve some process of rehearsal, usually via sub-vocal speech, to maintain the memory trace. Separating this aspect of memory from the rest, we postulated a slave system which we called the *articulatory loop*. The assumption that such a slave system existed was supported by three clusters of evidence. The first of these was the *acoustic* or *phonemic similarity effect,* shown by the tendency for subjects' errors to be phonemically similar to the correct item (*F* for *S* and *B* for *G*) and for sequences of items that have similar speech sounds to be particularly hard to remember in the appropriate order (for example *D B C T P G* is harder to remember than *K W Y L R Q*).

The second source of evidence came from studying the effects of *articulatory suppression.* This technique involves preventing the subject from rehearsing particular material by requiring him to articulate repeatedly some irrelevant item such as the word *the.* Suppression substantially reduces the subject's digit span, and in addition abolishes the phonemic similarity effect, provided he is remembering visually presented material. These two facts suggest, first, that memory span relies at least to some extent on the subject's ability to rehearse the material sub-vocally, and second that the phonemic similarity effect is crucially dependent on this process of rehearsal. This indicates that the effect is probably based on the *spoken* similarity of the material rather than on its similarity of sound. For this reason the original term 'acoustic' similarity is now rarely used, being replaced by the term 'phonemic' which refers to the speech-based characteristic of the effect.

Other evidence that the so-called acoustic similarity effect is not in fact acoustic came from experiments by Conrad[4] using congenitally deaf children. When such children were required to remember sequences of letters, Conrad observed that some of them made phonemic intrusion errors, while others did not. Since none of the subjects had ever been able to hear, the effect could

The relationship between word length and recall, and word length and reading speed, is fairly similar. This suggests that longer words are more difficult to recall because they take longer to articulate. It seems that our working memory can only retain about 1.5 seconds' worth of information with any degree of reliability. (Adapted from Baddeley, Thomson and Buchanan, 1975)

presumably not be acoustic. However, when the speaking ability of the deaf children was independently rated by their teachers, it proved to be the case that phonemic confusion errors were produced only by those who spoke reasonably well; presumably they found it useful to rehearse sub-vocally, while those with poor speech couldn't and didn't.

A third source of information about the articulatory loop came from other experiments we were carrying out on the effect of word length on memory span[5]. We found a very clear tendency for the length to decline as the span increased. You can demonstrate this for yourself by using the columns of words below. Read down each one silently, then look away and write down the words, or the first two or three letters of each word. Each correct word scores 1.

some	twice	yield	bond	hate
harm	harm	worst	harm	bond
bond	worst	harm	worst	some
yield	wit	twice	yield	twice
hate	some	hate	twice	yield
Recall	**Recall**	**Recall**	**Recall**	**Recall**
association	considerable	university	considerable	immediately
considerable	representative	representative	opportunity	considerable
representative	individual	association	organization	individual
individual	association	individual	university	association
immediately	opportunity	immediately	representative	opportunity
Recall	**Recall**	**Recall**	**Recall**	**Recall**

Your score on the shorter words was almost certainly better than on the longer words. We also had our subjects remember sequences like *Malta, Chad, Kenya, Burma, Chile* as compared with *Czechoslovakia, Switzerland, Ethiopia, Australia, Afghanistan* to reassure ourselves that this effect had nothing to do with English monosyllabic words being of generally Anglo-Saxon origin and polysyllables of Latin origin. It didn't. But when our subjects were prevented from sub-vocal rehearsal by being asked to mumble *the* over and over again the effect disappeared. Like the phonemic similarity effect it clearly depended on the process of rehearsal.

The concept of the articulatory loop quite neatly tied together this cluster of findings. We assumed that a process of sub-vocal rehearsal is used, probably to refresh a fading memory trace before it decays into inaccessibility. The process seems to involve sub-vocal speech and can be hindered if the subject's speech system is kept busy uttering irrelevancies. It appears to be this speech process that not only introduces phonemic errors, but also hinders memory span for long words. Long words represent increased demand on the system. Is it simply that long words take longer to articulate than short ones, or does the effect stem from their greater complexity, comprising more speech sounds, and hence perhaps overloading some part of the speech system? We were in fact able to investigate this point relatively simply by comparing memory span performance on two sets of words, both of which had the same number of syllables, letters and phonemes, but differed in the time they took to utter.

We required our subjects to remember either sequences of words with long vowel sounds, such as *harpoon* and *Friday*, or sequences of words containing the same number of syllables, but which are spoken relatively rapidly, such as *bishop* and *wicket*. We found a clear tendency for slowly spoken words to be

Dr. R. Conrad testing the memory of a child. By varying the pictures he shows her he can judge whether she is helping her memory by subvocalizing the names of the objects in the pictures. Inner speech is very important to intellectual development.

remembered less well, implying that the articulatory loop's limitation is purely one of time. Consistent with this, we found that there was a clear relationship between the speed with which an individual could read out sequences of words and his memory span; fast talkers were good rememberers, on this task at least. The relationship between the time it took to speak words of particular lengths and memory span for them was very orderly, as the graph on page 173 shows. On the basis of this, memory span can be redefined: what is constant is not the number of items but the amount of time. Our subjects could only remember as much as they could say in just 1.5 seconds.

A number of intelligence tests incorporate digit span as one of their measures, and it is very noticeable that memory span develops with age. There has been a great deal of discussion as to why this should be, but a recent study by Nicholson[6] tested the possibility that it may be simply because children cannot rehearse as rapidly as adults. Nicholson therefore measured both the digit span and the articulation rate of children of ages ranging from 8 to 12. He found that the older children had longer digit spans, as expected; he also found that their articulation rate was greater. But was the increase in speaking rate enough to account for the increased memory span? Nicholson's results are shown on page 176; clearly, development in span is very closely associated with increased rate of articulation. Of course a correlation between two variables does not necessarily mean that one is the cause or result of the other; both might depend on a third variable. However, at the very least, the articulatory loop idea does appear to offer a possible explanation as to why children's memory spans increase as they mature.

Another spin-off from our work on the articulatory loop was provided by a colleague, Nick Ellis[7], working in the University of Bangor in North Wales. Bangor is in a strongly Welsh-speaking area, and so when an educational psychologist wants to test a child whose first language is Welsh the standard psychometric tests are given in Welsh. Nick Ellis noted that the norms which indicated the expected level for an average child of a given age showed a curious discrepancy; in the case of digit span, Welsh-speaking children appeared to lag consistently behind the norms based on English-speaking American children. Was there some mysterious genetic deficiency in the Welsh, compensated for of course by a superabundance of genes related to choral singing and passing rugby balls? Perish the thought. Actually, numbers in Welsh all tend to contain relatively long speech sounds, and so are likely to be spoken more slowly even though they have just the same number of syllables as English digits. Ellis and a colleague, R. A. Hennelly, decided to explore this factor to try and account for the lower spans of Welsh-speakers. They did so by taking a number of students who were bilingual in English and Welsh, but who spoke Welsh for preference.

First of all they showed that their students had a greater digit span in their non-preferred language, English, thus supporting their view that the difference was based on the language, not on the individual. They then showed that the time required to read out Welsh digits was indeed longer than that taken to read out a similar number of English digits, and that when digit span was adjusted on account of this, the difference between English and Welsh disappeared. In other words, the span was determined not by the number of items but by the amount of speaking time a sequence took. In a further experiment

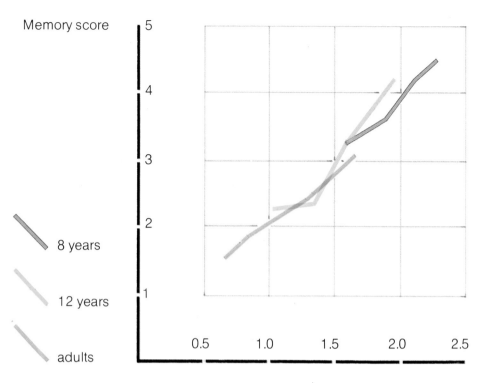

Memory score

5

4

3

2

1

8 years

12 years

adults

0.5   1.0   1.5   2.0   2.5

Rate of speaking (words per second)

Our memory span increases as we mature, as does the maximum rate at which we can speak. The relationship between memory span and articulation rate is remarkably uniform, whether one is an adult or a child. (Adapted from Nicholson, 1981)

they showed, as one would expect, that when their subjects were prevented from using the articulatory loop by being asked to repeat irrelevant speech sounds, the difference between their English and Welsh digit span vanished.

Suppose then we accept as a useful working hypothesis the concept of an articulatory loop. What purpose does it serve? It seems somewhat unlikely that evolution has specifically equipped us to remember telephone numbers. We have however begun to explore a range of tasks which might utilize the articulatory loop. These tend of course to be cognitive tasks with a speech component. Counting is an obvious example. Try counting the number of letters in the next line, while at the same time repeatedly and rapidly saying the word *the*. Time yourself, and then repeat the procedure without articulatory suppression. I think you will find that sub-vocalization plays an important part in normal counting, at least in our culture.

Nevertheless, people are quite ingenious at finding ways around the problem of not being allowed to sub-vocalize. Indeed there are many cultures which do not use sub-vocal counting, relying on something analogous to counting on the fingers, but often using many more parts of the body—hence allowing them to count well above 10. Arithmetic in general probably uses the articulatory loop. Graham Hitch[8] has begun to analyze the processes underlying simple arithmetic from a working memory viewpoint, and Ellis and Hennelly[9] have shown that their bilingual subjects are particularly prone to error when doing arithmetic in Welsh.

A task in which sub-vocalization might be assumed to play an important role is that of reading. People commonly 'hear' what they are reading spoken in some form of inner voice, and it is tempting to attribute this to the articulatory loop. However, although it may possibly be important in learning to read, it seems to play a much less crucial role in the fluent adult reader. If you remain to be convinced, try reading the next couple of sentences while repeating the word *the* under your breath. It may be a little uncomfortable, but you should have no great difficulty understanding what has been written. We have conducted a number of experiments along these lines, and find that people appear to read just as rapidly and have no difficulty in understanding the gist of what is written while suppressing sub-vocalization. They are however less good at picking up deliberate errors in prose passages. If for example I had reversed the order of two of the words of a sentence, you would have been much less likely to notice it while suppressing.

The articulatory loop appears then to be a checking mechanism that is particularly good at preserving the order of information. You probably use it when reading difficult prose – a legal document for example – where accurate understanding is essential, but I suspect that you do not sub-vocalize very much when reading a novel. You might well argue that, although you do not sub-vocalize, you still think you hear a voice when you read; I suspect that this 'voice' is based on another system, an *auditory imagery system*, related to but different from the articulatory loop.

Auditory imagery

We clearly do have some form of auditory imagery which allows us to imagine the voice of a great singer, or the sound of waves crashing on the beach, or a symphony orchestra tuning up. These are all sounds which we ourselves cannot possibly reproduce. It is therefore unlikely that our imagery is based on sub-vocalization. Experiments have shown that if people are shown a series of words they are capable of imagining themselves saying them in either a male or female voice[10]. If they have imagined a given word in a female voice they are more likely to recognize it later if it is spoken by a female rather than by a male voice, and vice versa. Curiously but conveniently, one's own voice appears to be hermaphrodite! One recognizes words that have been rehearsed in one's own voice equally well regardless of whether they are presented by a male or female voice.

How good is your imagination for sounds? Can you hear the sounds implied by each of these pictures? In what sense do you 'hear' them? To what extent are you trying to convert them into subvocal sounds? Do you think you have a non-verbal auditory imagery system?

Returning to the question of reading, one might imagine that judging the spoken sound of written words would require some form of sub-vocalization. We tested this recently[11] by having our subjects judge whether pairs of words were similar in sound or not, choosing words which were sometimes spelt irregularly; hence *dough* and *doe* should be given 'same' response, *dough* and *rough* a 'not same' response. Our subjects made these judgements either unimpeded or while suppressing articulation by repeatedly counting from one to six.

Another way of making the same point would be to ask you to read a series of 'nonwords' which, when pronounced, sound the same as real words, *cote* for *coat* and *eeggl* for *eagle*, for example. Try reading Sentence 1 below, and when you have completed that, begin suppressing and attempt to read Sentence 2.

1 *Iff yue sowned owt thiss sentans tew yoreselph, yoo wil komprehenned it.*

Now begin repeating the word 'the' under your breath and read Sentence 2.

2 *Moast peepul seem tue bee aybul tue heer thuh wirds eevan wen thay arr surpresing artikulashun.*

I suspect you had little difficulty in understanding either sentence, although the laborious nature of the process indicates, I think, that we probably do not normally read by sounding out the words in a text and listening to the sound, although we may well have gone through a process of sounding and listening when we were learning to read. The role of the sound or phonological compo-nent in fluent adult reading is still a controversial one, but it is by now I think fairly generally accepted that it is not necessary to be able to produce the sound of a word in order to understand it.

A classic test of spatial manipulative ability: the common deckchair. Frustrating for the unwary and a boon to the comedian.

Of particular interest in this connection is a rare group of patients whose reading performance has been disturbed by brain damage, often following a stroke. A sub-group of such dyslexic patients, known as 'deep dyslexics', have great difficulty in reading words aloud and are quite incapable of reading out pronounceable 'nonwords' such as *fleep* or *spart*[12]. They experience further problems in reading abstract words such as *hope* or *justice*, but find imageable words such as *castle* and *trombone* much easier. One such patient for example could read the concrete noun *inn* but not the much more common preposition *in*, and the word *bee* but not *be*. Their errors are also often very interesting in that they suggest it is possible approximately to understand a word but not be able to access its spoken sound: for example, *pray* might be read aloud as *chapel* and *sepulchre* as *tomb*. This problem does not stem from an inability to pronounce the words, since the subject can repeat them with no difficulty; it is simply that the written version of a word appears to access certain aspects of its meaning but does not access its spoken form.

However, we really know very little of the role of auditory imagery in the working memory system. In contrast, there has recently been a great deal of investigation into the role of *visual imagery*.

The visuo-spatial scratch pad

A great deal of interest has been focussed on the topic of visual imagery in recent years, partly because it plays such an important role in learning verbal material. Visual imagery mnemonics are an extremely effective way of re-membering random sequences and words which are imageable are more easily memorized than those which aren't. In particular, there has been a great deal of controversy as to whether images are in some sense stored directly in the brain, or created from some more abstract representation. Supporters of the former view have tended to look for similarities between the process of reading information from a mental image and the process of perceiving, and they have met with a good deal of success.

Imagine folding the two flat pieces of paper (left and centre) into a cube. Would the arrowheads meet as in the cube on the right? (Answer: page 180)

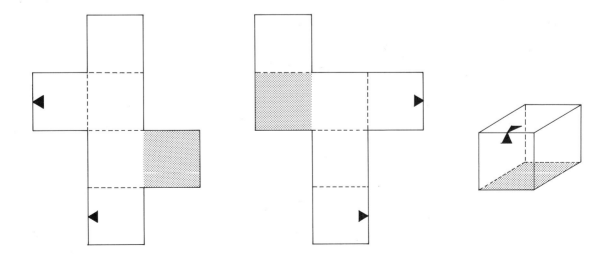

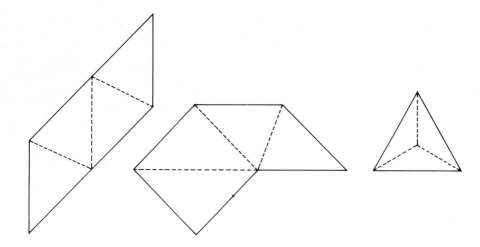

Can either of these flat
pieces of paper be folded
into a pyramid?

The one on the left can't but
the one on the right can.

The person most strongly associated with this approach is Roger Shepard[13] of Stanford University in California. Shepard has carried out a range of experiments which explore the similarity between imaging and perceiving. One of his early experiments is shown on page 179. Both the shapes depicted could, if they were made out of paper, be folded to create a solid, with the shaded area being the base. Your task is to imagine folding the shapes and to decide whether the arrows would meet head on. Shepard found that the time it took his subjects to come to a solution was systematically related to the number of folds that would have been required had they actually been doing the folding. It was as if they were folding the cube in their heads.

A similar effect was demonstrated even more elegantly[14] using the clusters of two-dimensional cubes shown opposite. Subjects were shown pairs of these pictures and asked to decide whether the clusters were the same but seen from a different angle, or were built up quite differently. The angular difference between the orientation of the two figures was varied systematically.

See how good you are at mentally rotating! Figures A and B are two drawings of the same cluster of cubes seen from different angles. If you rotated Figure B it would be exactly the same as Figure A.

Figure A   Figure B

Although we seldom see
such bizarre distortions in
real life, we see them easily
with our inner eye.

(From page 179): Both
figures can form the
illustrated cube

Figures C and D however are two drawings of two different clusters of cubes. You will find that no matter how you rotate them they will never match each other.

S Ⓓ

Figure C   Figure D

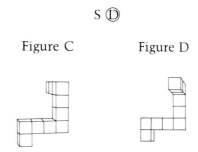

Mentally rotate the pairs of cube clusters below and decide whether the pairs are identical but seen from a different angle, or whether they are non-matching however you rotate them. Circle S if you decide they are the same and D if you decide they are different.

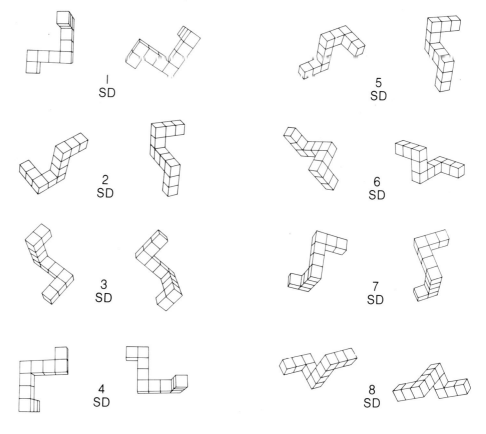

1
SD

2
SD

3
SD

4
SD

5
SD

6
SD

7
SD

8
SD

The correct answers are: Ⓢ Nos. 2, 3, 6, 7 and 8, and Ⓓ Nos. 1, 4 and 5.

Shepard's subjects showed a linear relation between time to make the comparison and degree of angular difference between the two clusters, as if they were rotating one cluster in their hand at a constant rate until it was in line with the second, then making their judgement.

Stephen Kosslyn[15] of Harvard University produced a related set of demonstrations. In one experiment he had his subjects memorize a series of pictures, such as the drawing of the boat opposite. He then asked them to scan their image of the boat in order to report on a particular detail. Kosslyn showed that a subject who had just responded to a question about the stern of the boat took longer to respond to a question about the bow then one who had just responded to a question about the porthole. It was as if the subject were taking time to scan across the boat, and the greater the distance that had to be scanned the longer it took to respond.

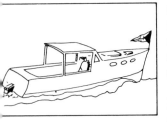

One characteristic of our visual images is that we appear to be able to manipulate their apparent sizes. We can for example consider a cat as a whole or 'zoom in' on its whiskers or the tip of its tail. When imaging two different sized animals together, say an elephant and a rabbit, Kosslyn[16] showed that it took longer to answer a question about the rabbit's ears, a relatively small detail in relation to the elephant, than it took if the subject were imaging a rabbit next to a fly for example the rabbit's ears being large in relation to the size of the fly. However, since our imagery system is conveniently flexible, it is also possible to reverse the effect by imaging a giant fly towering over a rabbit, or a tiny elephant overshadowed by it.

All these effects show that in some respects at least visual images do behave like visual percepts. It is important however not to regard them simply as pictures stored in the head. Consider the cat just mentioned; if our mental image of a cat had to contain all the information necessary to specify every whisker and piece of fur, it would be enormously costly in terms of information storage. There is considerable evidence to suggest that we simply do not have this degree of information about items that we image.

What has visual imagery to do with working memory? Our own approach is to suggest that spatial information is probably stored in some abstract code in long-term memory, but that one method of displaying and manipulating such information is via a spatial slave system. Such a system uses some of the same equipment as is used in perception, and depends for its functioning on the central executive component of the working memory system. What is our evidence for such a view?

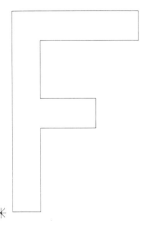

As with our other research on working memory, we have relied heavily on the technique of selectively interfering with some aspect of processing. In the case of our work on imagery, we were heavily influenced by some ingenious work by a Canadian psychologist, Lee Brooks[17]. In one of the tasks Brooks devised subjects were shown a block capital letter such as the *F* shown on the left. They were asked to hold it in their mind's eye and, starting at the bottom

This time Alice waited quietly until it chose to speak again in a few minutes the caterpillar took the hookah out of its mouth, and got down off the mushroom, and crawled away into the grass, merely remarking as it went: "the top will make you grow taller, and the stalk will make you grow shorter."

"The top of <u>what</u>? the stalk of <u>what</u>" thought Alice.

"Of the mushroom," said the caterpillar, just as if she had asked it aloud, and in another moment it was out of sight.

Alice remained looking thoughtfully at the mushroom for a minute, and then picked it and carefully broke it in two, taking the stalk in one hand, and the top in the other. "Which does the stalk do?" she said, and nibbled a little bit of it to try the next mo-ment she felt a violent blow on her chin: it had struck her foot!

A page of the original manuscript of *Alice in Wonderland* by Lewis Carroll, together with his original drawing. *Alice in Wonderland* makes full use of the exciting possibilities of visual imagery – one moment Alice is huge, and the next she is tiny enough to peep over the edge of a mushroom and talk to a caterpillar.

left, to classify each corner as a 'yes' if it involved the bottom or top line of the letter and a 'no' if it did not. In this case the correct sequence of responses would be 'yes, yes, yes, no, no, no, no, no, no, yes.' Subjects performed this task and responded either verbally or by pointing to the word 'yes' or 'no' located at different points down the page. His subjects found much more difficulty in responding by pointing than by speaking, as if the act of pointing interfered with the process of imagery. Brooks contrasted this task with a second in which the subject was given a sentence such as 'A bird in the hand is not in the bush' to remember and required to classify each word in the sentence as a noun or as a non-noun; in this case the correct sequence of responses is 'no, yes, no, no, yes, no, no, no, no, yes,'. With this task, performance was much better when the responses were made by pointing rather than by speaking. The reason is obvious. In a visual imagery test a visuo-spatial task like pointing appears to use some of the capacity of the imaging equipment, leaving less capacity available for mental imagery; but the same sort of task does not interfere with heavily verbal tasks such as classifying nouns, remembering sentences or making judgements based on knowledge of syntax.

Our first experiment[18] was somewhat similar to that of Brooks, but it was

The Piazza del Duomo in Milan. Patients suffering from damage to the right hemisphere of the brain were able to imagine this scene viewed from the Cathedral but left out most of the detail from the left hand side of the square.

derived, at least in part, from a rather disconcerting personal experience. While spending a year in the United States I became very interested in American football, and on one occasion decided to listen to a game while driving along a Californian freeway. In order to understand the progress of the game it was necessary to form a fairly clear and detailed image of the proceedings, and I observed as I did so that my car began to drift out of lane and back again. I rapidly switched to music, but remembered the experience and decided to explore it in the laboratory. In order to do so I used a task somewhat similar to the one just described. I had my subjects perform it either on its own, or at the same time as they were doing a simple tracking task which had some of the characteristics of steering a car. The task involved a spot of light that moved along a circular path; subjects had to try to keep a pointer in contact with the spot of light, their success being measured by how much of the time they were on target. We began by checking that this task would disrupt imagery in the same way as the pointing task used by Brooks. In one experiment we gave our subjects one of several blocked letters and asked them to perform the Brooks task, saying 'yes' for a top or bottom corner and 'no' for others while keeping the pointer in contact with the moving spot of light. We found that our subjects had great difficulty tracking the light spot while visualizing letters. A second experiment confirmed that an immediate memory task relying on imagery was disrupted by tracking, while one based on verbal coding was not.

We then proceeded to ask whether the imagery system is indeed a visual system or whether it is more generally spatial. The distinction between visual and spatial is not as odd as it sounds. A blind person who has never seen nevertheless has, as a result of touch and movement, a concept of space. Conversely, someone with their eyes closed could probably tell from the light passing through their eyelids whether they were in bright sunshine or pitch darkness; this would be visual discrimination arrived at independently of spatial information.

How many windows do you have in your house? Most people have to take an imaginary walk through their house to answer this question.

Our experiment depended on devising a tracking task which was performed using sound information rather than vision. To achieve this we blindfolded our subjects and seated them in front of a pendulum which swung from left to right. On the end of the pendulum was a sound source which gave out a tone as the pendulum swung. We gave our subjects a flashlight and demonstrated that when the light was shone on the pendulum, it would be detected by a photoelectric cell and the sound emitted would change. Hence our subjects, although blindfold, had the spatial task of following the pendulum, and knew when they were on target by the sound change – all of them managed to master this somewhat Gothic task after a little practice. Their performance on this task was then contrasted with that on a second task, this time a visual one in which they had to judge the brightness of a field of light and press a key whenever a particularly bright stimulus was presented. We then studied the effect of both these tasks on performance of a visual imagery task. The results were clear-cut: the spatial pendulum task disrupted performance on the visual imagery task to a much greater extent than it did on the verbal memory task, despite the fact that there was no visual input since the subject was blindfold. For the brightness judging task this difference was reversed, with the verbal memory task being more affected than the imagery task[19].

In short, it appears that our imagery system is spatial in nature rather than purely visual. It has subsequently been shown that non-visual disruption of imagery can be obtained without needing to go to the somewhat bizarre lengths of our pit-and-pendulum experiment. Disruption is just as effectively achieved by asking people to press a series of hidden keys. If you have a typewriter or pocket calculator you can produce a similar result by placing it out of sight behind a book and pressing the keys systematically from left to right and top to bottom while attempting the letter-visualization task on page 182.

Experiments by Bill Phillips and his colleagues[20] at the University of Stirling have shown that visual imagery can be disrupted without placing heavy visual spatial demands on the subject, provided he is given a task which places a heavy load on his general processing capacity. Hence a task like mental arithmetic interferes with visualization, presumably because it makes heavy demands on the central executive component of working memory. Without the full support of our general processing capacity our visual imagery system apparently cannot function at full efficiency.

All the experiments described in this section are consistent with the idea that there is some separate process or mechanism in the human brain which displays and manipulates spatial information. Presumably the system is fed from long-term memory and depends on the central executive for its operation. Some of its components also appear to be used in spatial perception, with the result that imagery and perception can sometimes interfere with each other. We know relatively little about the neuropsychological basis of the system, but some interesting possibilities are raised by a series of cases reported recently by two Italian neuropsychologists, Bisiach and Luzzatti[21].

The patients studied by Bisiach and Luzzatti had all suffered damage to the right hemisphere of the brain following a stroke (right-sided rather than left-sided stroke patients were studied because damage to the left side of the brain often interferes with language, making it difficult to.converse with patients). All of these patients had had an initial tendency to neglect the left side of their body, the side controlled by the damaged right hemisphere of the brain. A patient suffering from visual neglect in its most extreme form will even deny that a part of his body actually belongs to him and accuse the doctor of inflicting someone else's arm on him. Much more commonly, there is a tendency to ignore what goes on in that part of the visual field despite the fact that it can be perceived if requested.

Bisiach and Luzzatti's patients all came from the Milan region. Accordingly one of their tasks was to imagine themselves standing outside Milan cathedral and to describe the scene. The general tendency was to describe the right-hand side of the cathedral square in excellent detail, saying virtually nothing about the left. The patients were then asked to imagine that they had walked to the other side of the square. Again they were asked to describe the scene. This time that part of the square which had previously been ignored would be on their imagined right. Under these circumstances the other half of the square was described very adequately, though the scene to the left of their imaginary field of vision, the scene previously described in detail, was largely ignored. It was as if these patients' images were being projected on a screen, the left-hand part of which had been damaged. The process of conjuring up and projecting images was intact, but the mechanism for representing or reading them off was faulty. Bisiach now appears to have studied this phenomenon in quite a large number of patients, but fortunately for them it is rather transitory, clearing up during the process of general recovery. Though relatively unexplored, the phenomenon of visual neglect may eventually yield interesting insights into the process underlying visual imagery.

Imagery and long-term learning

So far we have been concerned almost entirely with the process of representing and manipulating images. However, as we have mentioned in several other chapters, imagery may play a prominent role in long-term memory. This prominence can be inferred from two pieces of evidence: first, there is a strong relationship between the imageability of a word and the ease with which it can be memorized; and second, imaging plays an important part in mnemonic strategies. Is there a relationship between our proposed visuo-spatial scratch pad system and imagery in long-term memory?

If the scratch pad system is used for displaying imageable words and for manipulating images in mnemonic schemes, performing the light-tracking task during learning ought to disrupt both these processes. If, on the other hand, our scratch pad system is quite unrelated to imagery in long-term memory, a visual tracking task would disrupt non-imageable material just as much as imageable, and would interfere with simple rote learning just as much as with learning based on an imagery mnemonic.

In our first experiment we tried to abolish the effect of imageability by testing peoples' memory for pairs of abstract and concrete words. The abstract pairs we used were noun-adjectives such as *mood-cheerful, idea-original* and *gratitude-infinite*; the concrete pairs were noun-adjective combinations such as *strawberry-ripe, bullet-grey, table-square* and so on – highly imageable. With half the pairs of words on our abstract and concrete lists subjects were free to devote their attention entirely to learning; with the other half they were required to perform a tracking task which again involved keeping a pointer in contact with a spot of light moving along a circular path. Our results were very straightforward: we obtained the usual massive effect of imageability (the concrete pairs being remembered better than the abstract), the tracking task impaired performance slightly, but the impairment was just as great for the abstract pairs as it was for the imageable ones. Whatever the mechanism whereby imageability has an effect, it does not appear to depend very crucially

Reading braille. Practised braille readers 'see' the words their fingertips feel.

on the visuo-spatial scratch pad.

What about the process of using imagery mnemonics? Do these make demands on the visuo-spatial scratch pad, or are all the long-term memory effects of imagery quite separate from the working memory system we have been describing? In order to test this we selected a mnemonic with a strong spatial component; we taught our subjects a series of locations and instructed them to imagine each of a series of objects in one of these locations[22]. The experiment was run using University of Stirling students and we taught a route through the university campus which involved ten landmarks. Subjects were taught the sequence and then encouraged to use it in remembering lists of ten words. Suppose the first landmark was the university entrance, and the second the entrance to the student bar, while the first two objects were, let us say, a pig and a lilac. They were instructed to imagine a pig at the entrance to the university and a lilac tree blocking the entrance to the student bar, etc.

Once again we relied on our light tracking task as our interference method. The results were again straightforward; under normal conditions subjects performed consistently better when they were using the mnemonic, but the advantage disappeared completely when they were required to perform the spatial tracking task as well. It seems then that the kind of manipulation and location of images used when applying a mnemonic does depend on the scratch pad. We noted incidentally that our subjects were able to use the scratch pad perfectly effectively whether the words they were using were imageable and concrete (*pig*) or abstract (*virtue, justice*). Presumably in the case of the abstract words, they created some serviceable form of representation.

The concreteness of a word, however, appears to have a quite different relationship to long-term memory. First, it does not seem to be mediated by the visuo-spatial scratch pad system, and second it is not affected by whether a person is instructed to conjure up images. The concrete/abstract difference probably has something to do with the way word characteristics are stored in semantic memory, with concrete words being either more easily accessible or more distinctive than abstract ones. At the moment we know too little about how meaning is stored in semantic memory to do more than speculate.

The central executive

Some of the peripheral slave systems of working memory have now been covered but little has been said about the all-important central executive. This is partly because we know even less about it than the slave systems. The strategy we have adopted is to take a complex system and attempt to separate out some of its simpler functions. The result of this is that we are left with a central core which we treat as a unitary system, only because we have not yet devised ways of breaking it down into components. We are at present busily trying to do so, and if I had to speculate, I would suggest that the component we have so far referred to as the central executive almost certainly has at least two sub-systems itself, one of which is devoted to memory, the other being largely concerned with conscious attention; it is this latter system that is probably responsible for controlling both the central processes of memory and the other slave systems. But our techniques for teasing out the components of systems as complex as this are still very much in their infancy, and by no means all my colleagues would agree that this approach is the most fruitful.

12

Improving your memory

We all tend to complain about our memories. Despite the elegance of the human memory system, it is not infallible, and we have to learn to live with its fallibility. It seems to be socially much more acceptable to complain of a poor memory, and it is somehow much more acceptable to blame a social lapse on 'a terrible memory', than to attribute it to stupidity or insensitivity. But how much do we know about our own memories? Obviously we need to remember our memory lapses in order to know just how bad our memories are. Indeed one of the most amnesic patients I have ever tested was a lady suffering from Korsakoff's syndrome, memory loss following chronic alcoholism. The test involved presenting her with lists of words; after each list she would comment with surprise on her inability to recall the words, saying: 'I pride myself on my memory!' She appeared to have forgotten just how bad her memory was[1].

One of the main problems in trying to evaluate one's own memory is that in doing so one is implicitly comparing it with the memories of other people. Typically we simply do not have real evidence of how good or bad other people's memories are, and hence it is very easy to obtain a distorted view of our own powers of memory.

Everyday remembering

However, memory for faces is only a minor aspect of day-to-day memory. In recent years there has been a considerable growth of interest in the problem of assessing everyday memory as a whole. Clearly it is very difficult to obtain an objective measure of memory in everyday life since it pervades so many tasks and depends so much on the lifestyle of the person concerned. However, there have been attempts to make assessments using memory questionnaires. One such questionnaire, designed by my colleagues John Harris and Alan Sunderland[2], appears in adapted form on page 22. I suggest you attempt to complete it, scoring yourself on each question in the boxes provided. When you have finished ask a close friend, preferably someone who lives with you, to give his or her estimate of your memory, using the same questionnaire. How does your estimate compare with that of your friend, and with the average scores obtained by Harris and Sunderland?

Let us suppose that there are discrepancies between your estimate of your memory and that given by your companion. Whose estimate is likely to be correct? Clearly the answer to this depends on the particular item being judged. You yourself are likely to have a much better idea of whether you have difficulty following the plots of plays and films since, unless you complain about such a difficulty, others are unlikely to be aware of it. However, forgetting appointments and losing things around the house may well be something that is as obvious to your companion as it is to you.

Some light is thrown on this problem by a series of studies recently carried out by John Harris, Alan Sunderland and myself[3] on the memory problems suffered by the victims of traffic accidents. We selected patients who had experienced at least 24 hours of PTA (post-traumatic amnesia, the confused state which follows a severe blow to the head), and who would therefore be regarded as moderate-to-severe cases. We studied three groups of patients: one group who had suffered their head injuries at least two years previously; a

Graffiti, mnemonic aids for telephone users?

A cribbage board for remembering the score. All sorts of games, from darts to bridge, use external memory aids for scoring.

second, more acute, group who were tested shortly after returning home from hospital; and a third group who had also been in road traffic accidents but who had suffered a broken limb rather than a head injury. This third group was used to give an indication of the overall level of performance of patients who would be expected to have normal memory. All three groups of patients were interviewed and required to answer questions resembling the ones in the questionnaire on page 22. They were then required to keep a diary over a one-week period, reporting each evening the occurrence or non-occurrence of the various memory lapses listed. These diaries were collected and analyzed. Each patient was also given a battery of memory tests, probing a range of memory abilities, verbal and visual, long- and short-term and semantic.

We found, as expected, that the performance of both head-injured groups was worse on most of the memory tests than that of the third group. What, however, of the questionnaire? Here we found that the head-injured patients did not report significantly more everyday memory problems than the broken limb patients. On the other hand, when relatives were asked to fill up a questionnaire describing the memory problems of the head-injured patients, a difference did appear. Similarly, when diary information was used, both the head-injured patients and their relatives reported more memory problems than the broken limb group. Apparently the former were aware that they were having memory problems, and could report them in a diary on a same-day basis, but were not able to give an overall accurate estimate when questioned about lapses farther back in time. Their relatives were much better judges of their memory.

Demands on memory

Another complicating factor in evaluating people's estimates of their own memory powers stems from the fact that people lead very different lives. One person might lead an extremely structured and sheltered life, making few demands on memory, while another may live a very active and stressful existence. Given an equal memory capacity, the second person is clearly likely to experience far more memory lapses than the first. We found very poor correlations between objective memory test scores and reports of memory lapses by either patients or relatives in our group of acute head-injured patients immediately after their discharge from hospital. The reason for this is probably that these acute patients were at different stages of recovery and adaptation to everyday life. Some of the more serious cases, who would be likely to perform most poorly on our memory tests, were still living very sheltered existences, being nursed and protected by a caring relative. They would have little need to rely on their memory. Other, less badly injured, patients would already be venturing out and returning to work, and putting themselves into situations where memory lapses were much more likely to occur.

A similar explanation probably applies to the observation made by a number of researchers, including ourselves, that the elderly often report fewer memory lapses than the young. This is probably because older people tend to live more structured and ordered lives than the young. Within a family, for example, the mother often acts as a memory not only for her own activities but for those of her husband and children as well. To do this she is likely to have to make more extensive use of memory aids such as calendars or diaries than they do, and is likely to make fewer errors as a result. Such organized habits are likely to continue into old age.

Choosing a memory. Diaries are, on the whole, a very efficient way of reducing demands on memory. One reason why older people report fewer lapses is probably that they tend to be more systematic users of such memory aids.

John Harris[4] recently carried out a survey to find out what sort of mnemonic aids people use most frequently. He tested a group of university students and a sample of housewives. His questionnaire, in modified form, appears on page 194. Perhaps you would like to try if for yourself and see how your use of mnemonic aids compares with that of Harris' test groups. The figures given for the students and housewives are the most frequently chosen categories (in descending order where not equal). Overall, Harris found, the two groups had a similar pattern of mnemonic use, but there were some minor differences; for example, housewives seemed less inclined to write on their hands and more inclined than students to write on calendars!

Virtually everyone in this study showed some use of mnemonic aids, but these were overwhelmingly external aids such as diaries, calendars, lists and timers. Very few internal mnemonics of the kind advocated by memory training courses were used. I am referring here to courses of the kind devised by Lorayne and Lucas and described by *Time* magazine as a 'never-fail system to help you remember everything'. What do such systems involve? While the present book does not aim to be a primer for memory training, it would perhaps be appropriate to outline at least some of the more popular mnemonic systems before going on to say a little about the general principles of improving your memory.

Rating scale

0	Never used
1	Used less than three times in last 6 months
2	Used less than three times in last 4 weeks
3	Used less than three times in last 2 weeks
4	Used three to five times in last 2 weeks
5	Used six to ten times in last 2 weeks
6	Used eleven or more times in last 2 weeks

How often do you use memory aids?

1 **Shopping lists**
2 **First-letter memory aids** For example, the first letters of 'Richard of York Gave Battle In Vain' give the first letters of the colours of the rainbow.
3 **Diary**
4 **Rhymes** For example, 'In fourteen hundred and ninety-two Columbus sailed the ocean blue' helps you to remember the date 1492.
5 **The place method** Items to be remembered are imagined in a series of familiar places. When recall is required one 'looks' at the familiar places.
6 **Writing on hand** (or any other part of your anatomy or clothing).
7 **The story method** Making up a story which connects items to be remembered in the correct order.
8 **Mentally retracing a sequence of events or actions** in order to jog your memory; useful for remembering where you lost or left something, or at what stage something significant happened.
9 **Alarm clock** (or other alarm device) for waking up only.
10 **Cooker timer with alarm** for cooking only.
11 **Alarm clock** (or other alarm devices such as watches, radios, timers, telephones, calculators) used for purposes other than waking up or cooking.
12 **The pegword method** 'One is a bun, two is a shoe, three is a tree', etc. as a method of remembering lists of items in correct order (see page 42).
13 **Turning numbers into letters** For remembering telephone numbers for example.
14 **Memos** For example, writing notes and 'To do' lists for yourself.
15 **Face-name associations** Changing people's names into something meaningful and matching them with something unusual about their face. For example, red-bearded Mr Hiles might be imagined with hills growing out of his beard.
16 **Alphabetical searching** Going through the alphabet letter by letter to find the initial letter of a name. For example, does a particular person's name begin with A . . . B . . . ah yes, C! C for Clark . . .
17 **Calendars: wall charts: year planners: display boards, etc.**
18 **Asking other people to remember things for you.**
19 **Leaving objects in special or unusual places** so that they act as reminders

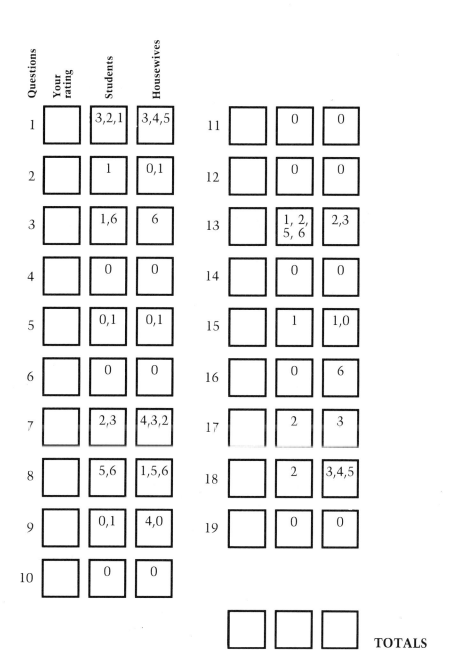

Questions	Your rating	Students	Housewives
1		3,2,1	3,4,5
2		1	0,1
3		1,6	6
4		0	0
5		0,1	0,1
6		0	0
7		2,3	4,3,2
8		5,6	1,5,6
9		0,1	4,0
10		0	0

Questions	Your rating	Students	Housewives
11		0	0
12		0	0
13		1, 2, 5, 6	2,3
14		0	0
15		1	1,0
16		0	6
17		2	3
18		2	3,4,5
19		0	0

TOTALS

Visual imagery mnemonics

Mnemonics based on visual imagery have been common at least since classical times. According to Cicero, writing in the first century BC, the first such mnemonic was devised by the Greek poet, Simonides, in about 500 BC. It appears that a Greek who had won a wrestling victory at the Olympic Games gave a banquet at his house to celebrate. Simonides was invited to attend and to give a recitation in honour of the victor. Shortly after completing his eulogy Simonides was called away . . . luckily for him, because just after he left the floor of the banqueting hall collapsed, killing and mutilating the guests. Many of the bodies were unrecognizable. How were the victims' relatives to identify them and give them a decent burial? Simonides found that he could quite easily remember where most of the guests had been at the time he left, and so was able to identify the bodies. This set him thinking: if his visual memory was so good, could he not use it to help himself recall other material? He therefore devised a system in which he visualized a room in great detail, and then imagined various items in special places in the room. Whenever he needed to remember what these items were he would 'look' at the appropriate location in his mind's eye. The system became popular with classical orators such as Cicero and has continued in use to the present day. The Russian mnemonist Shereshevski used this system (see page 44). As you will realize if you give it a serious trial, it operates very effectively and easily.

First of all, think of ten locations in your home, choosing them so that the sequence of moving from one to the other is an obvious one – for example, front door to entrance hall, to kitchen, to bedroom, and so on. Check that you can imagine moving through your ten locations in a consistent order without difficulty. Now think of ten items and imagine them in those locations. If the first item is a pipe, you might imagine it poking out of the letter box in your front door and great clouds of smoke billowing into the street. If the second is a cabbage, you might imagine your hall obstructed by an enormous cabbage, and so on.

Now try to create similarly striking images for the following in the ten locations:

shirt
eagle
paperclip
rose
camera
mushroom
crocodile
handkerchief
sausage
mayor

I have used this particular mnemonic very often in student laboratory classes and it almost invariably works very well. Although it is easier to perform with concrete words, such as the names of objects, it is still effective in remembering abstract words such as 'truth', 'hope' and so on, provided one manages to come up with a representative image. The use of imagery can be prevented either by presenting material very rapidly or, as we saw in the chapter on working memory, by introducing an interfering spatial task, so do not try to use the locations method while driving your car!

The same set of locations can be used repeatedly, as long as only the last item in a particular location is remembered; earlier items in that location will suffer from the usual interference effects, unless of course one deliberately links them into a coherent chain. Clearly one can create a system which has many more than ten locations; this is certainly true of classical mnemonic systems and of the complex and somewhat mystical systems developed during the Middle Ages. I suggest you now try to recall the ten items listed two paragraphs ago. No, don't look. Rely on the images you created at various points around your home or office.

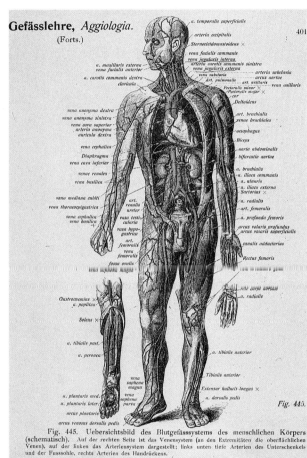

Fig. 445. Uebersichtsbild des Blutgefässsystems des menschlichen Körpers (schematisch). Auf der rechten Seite ist das Venensystem (an den Extremitäten die oberflächlichen Venen), auf der linken das Arteriensystem dargestellt; links unten tiefe Arterien des Unterschenkels und der Fusssohle, rechts Arterien des Handrückens.

Above: Peter Ramus, 1515-1572, mathematician and inventor of an abstract mnemonic system.

Right: the vascular system. Small wonder that medical students use special mnemonics!

There are obvious similarities between the locations method and the peg-word method described on page 42. The main difference is that the pegword system uses numbers rather than locations, and bridges the gap between number and image by means of a rhyme: *one is a bun, two is a shoe*, and so on. An intermediate system, developed in Cambridge during the 17th century by Henry Herdson[5], relied on a series of visual images of objects whose shape resembled that of various numbers. Hence 1 might be represented by a candle or a tower, 2 by a swan, 3 by a trident, and so on. The first object would then be imagined interacting with a candle in some way, the second with a swan . . . An elaboration of this system, combining it with a location mnemonic, was used by the late 18th-century mnemonist Gregor von Feinaigle[6].

Verbal mnemonics

Although classical mnemonics relied mainly on visual imagery, this was by no means the case in later times. In the 16th century, for example, Peter Ramus[7] devised a system in which information was represented in a hierarchical tree, with abstract concepts branching into progressively more concrete instances. Supporters of the Ramist system argued that it had the advantage of not requiring the persons to remember as much additional irrelevant information as the location and pegword systems did. The Puritans favoured verbal systems for an additional rather curious reason: they regarded images as wicked and liable to give rise to 'depraved carnal affections'!

Verbal mnemonics fitted in well with the Victorian educational tradition of rote learning, with its requirement that the unfortunate pupil should memorize vast numbers of facts, such as the dates of accession of kings and queens. A Yorkshire headmaster, the Reverend Brayshaw, published a book in 1849 entitled *Metrical Mnemonics* containing a selection of rhymes incorporating over 2000 dates and numerical facts drawn from physics, astronomy, history and geography.

The system underlying Brayshaw's mnemonics was a fairly old one, or certainly extant since the 17th century. It involved substituting consonants for particular numbers and then using the consonants to create words. This was the code used by Brayshaw:

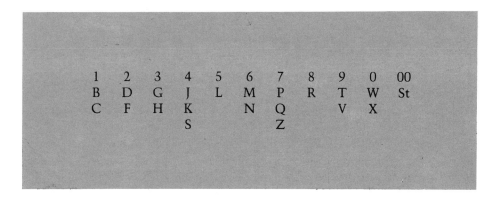

1	2	3	4	5	6	7	8	9	0	00
B	D	G	J	L	M	P	R	T	W	St
C	F	H	K		N	Q	V	X		
			S			Z				

To turn a number sequence into a word one simply selects one of the appropriate consonants, inserting vowels where necessary. Hence, to represent the year the First World War broke out, 1914, one could use the consonants *CTBS*, which could be turned into the words *CAT BASE*. In fact, since all Brayshaw's dates were later than 1000 AD he used to ignore the initial 1000. Here are some examples of his rhymes, which give the dates of English kings.

By MeN, *near Hastings, William gains the crown.* – 1066
A RaP *in Forest New brings Rufus down.* – 1087
Gaul's CoaSt *first Henry hates, whose son is drowned.* – 1100
Like BeaGLE *Stephen fights with Maud renoun'd.* – 1135

The vital information about a date is always given in the second or second and third word in the line, and the line is completed by incorporating the name of the monarch and some striking feature about him. Fortunately, rote memorization of dates is no longer a central part of history teaching. However, the system can be used effectively for what is perhaps the modern equivalent, learning telephone numbers or zip codes. If you have difficulty learning this kind of information it might well be worth while memorizing Brayshaw's system and using it consistently for a period of time to see if it helps.

There are many other situations in which mnemonics are useful and still widely used. Take, for example, the colours of the spectrum, where a whole range of mnemonics can be created from the simple acronym *ROYGBIV* (*red, orange, yellow, green, blue, indigo, violet*) to pieces of Brayshaw-like doggerel, such as *Richard Of York Gains Battles In Vain*. Medical students learning anatomy sometimes seem to be required to perform as much rote learning as Brayshaw's pupils, and still buy books of mnemonics to help them. One of the best-known anatomy mnemonics refers to the names of the cranial nerves: *On Old Olympia's Towering Top A Finn And German Vault And Hop* (olfactory, optic, oculomotor, trochlear, trigeminal, abducens, facial, auditory, glossopharyngeal, vagus, accessory and hypoglossal). The assumption is that one knows the particular names but cannot reliably retrieve them, or retrieve them in the appropriate order; the rhythmic and relatively meaningful verse, with its first letter retrieval cues, is quite easily remembered.

A well-known mnemonic of a different kind, which I have never been able to dispense with, is that for remembering the number of days in a month. It starts: *Thirty days hath September, April, June and November, all the rest have thirty-one . . .* I always forget the rest but remember that it has something to do with February and Leap Year.

This problem of remembering how many days there are in each month and how different cultures tackle it is excellently discussed by Hunter[8]. It appears that Italy, France and The Netherlands have a rhyme which is similar in form and function to the English verse. Greece, Finland, Russia, China, Tibet and most of South America apparently use a system based on knuckle counting. Clench your fist and count off the months alternately on the knuckles and on the hollows between the knuckles. January is on a knuckle and is therefore long, February is on a gap between knuckles and is therefore short, March is long, April short, May long, June short and July long. This takes you to the end of one set of knuckles. Continue by returning to the beginning of the fist again. This gives you August as long, September short, and so forth.

Other cultures have yet other ways of solving the problem. The Iranian calendar has 31 days for each of the first six months of the year and 30 days for the next five, with the last month of the year having 29 days except in leap years. Thailand has a calendar similar to our own, but the months have suffixes which indicate the number of days; months with 31 days end in *om* (January is *Magarakom*, March is *Minakom*, etc.), and months with 30 end in *on* (September is *Kanyayon*, November *Prusjikayon*, etc.), while February has the special suffix *-an*, *Kumpapan*. In short, the months are a problem in many cultures and mnemonics are routinely used as a way of remembering their unequal lengths.

Before moving away from verbal mnemonics, it is perhaps worth citing one cautionary tale. While writing about mnemonics in a previous book[9], I remembered a mnemonic told to me by an old friend which enables one to perform the rather useless task of remembering the value of *pi* to the first 20 decimal places.

Pie
I wish I could remember pi
Eureka cried the great inventor
Christmas pudding Christmas pie
Is the problem's very centre

Unfortunately, I simply could not remember how on earth one got from the rhyme to the appropriate numbers! I rang my friend, and he explained that one simply counts the number of letters in each word to give 3.14159265358979323846. When the book was duly published I pointed out the section to him, only to be told that I had got it wrong – the second line should be 'I wish I could *determine* pi', making the fifth decimal place 9, not 8. As he pointed out, psychologists remember (or misremember) but mathematicians determine!

Two cities, one remembering the other.

Ritual and oral tradition

While mnemonics are certainly useful in contemporary Western society, the role they play is comparatively minor. The reason is simple: important information is usually written down, or indeed recorded on film or magnetic tape. In non-literate societies, however, tradition is crucially dependent on memory, and hence devices to preserve and communicate traditions assume vital importance. One means of achieving this preservation is to use ritual. Hunter describes the ritual involved in making a traditional Japanese ceremonial sword; each step in the complex process is marked by a ritual act. Religious ritual often has a similar purpose; it reminds the participants of some aspect of their faith. Here is a description of the Jewish Passover feast by Paul Levy, writing in the *Observer* (19 April 1981).

'The table (and the stage for the re-telling of the Passover story) is set with three *matzot* ... They represent not only the unleavened bread of the Israelites'

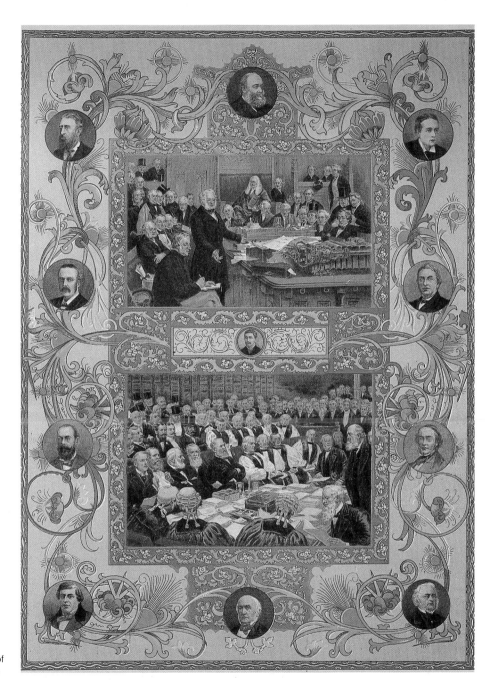

Commemoration of a reign and of an institution: a page from the Jubilee edition of the *London Illustrated News*, 1897, commemorating 60 years of parliamentary government.

journey but also "the poverty they suffered both in Egypt and in the desert".

'A roasted lamb bone is on the table "to commemorate the paschal sacrifice which every family brought to the Temple in ancient times". Boiled eggs are on the table as "symbolic of the festival sacrifice which was always additional to the paschal lamb".

'Bitter herbs, usually horseradish, are eaten to remind the *Seder* participants that the lives of the slaves in Egypt were bitter. A mixture of nuts, apples, sweet wine and spices, *charoset*, commemorates the mortar used by Jews at forced labour to build the Egyptian "treasure cities".

'Green herbs such as parsley and watercress are eaten to symbolize the return of spring and the renewal of life; but they are dipped into salt water in memory of the tears shed by the enslaved Hebrews.

'The best part of the evening is the compulsory four glasses of wine – of which even the youngest member of the party takes a sip. An extra place is laid at the table for the Prophet Elijah, who is supposed to visit every Jewish home during the *Seder*. And his glass of wine is always poured out too.

'In addition to ensuring that the feast is a jolly one, the wine plays its symbolic part in the proceedings. At one point in the ceremony ten drops of wine are poured out to represent the Ten Plagues suffered by the Egyptians before they would agree to Moses leading away the children of Israel. I well remember the look of malicious pleasure on my grandfather's face as he conducted the ceremony, and visited locusts and boils on the Egyptians. It was just after the war, and even the children knew that the "Egyptians" he had in mind were German.'

Non-literate societies depend heavily on oral tradition, enshrining important or significant information in some form of verse or song which is passed down from father to son. Such societies often have a specific person who is responsible for remembering such information. The Rwanda of Central Africa, for example, have four specialized remembrancers[10]. The task of the first (*Abacurabwenge*) is to remember the lists of kings and queen mothers; the second (*Abateekerezi*) is required to remember the most important events in the various reigns; the third (*Abasizi*) celebrates the deeds and qualities of the kings, and the fourth (*Abiiru*) must preserve the secrets of the dynasty.

This kind of information is highly important to a society, and there is evidence to suggest that when a society changes, remembered legend changes with it. Goody and Watt[11] give a good example of a changed legend in the State of Gonja in Northern Ghana, which was ruled by several chieftains. It was the custom that certain of these chieftains took turns to rule the whole State. The precedent for this is contained in a legend which tells how the State was founded by a man who had seven sons. He allocated a territory to each of his sons, and commanded them to rule the State in turn. This legend was initially recorded about the turn of the century. But since that time the number of territories has been reduced from seven to five; now the original founder is said to have had only five sons.

In communities which have a strong oral tradition, memory is frequently supplemented by rhythm and music. Drums are used as a mnemonic aid throughout most of Africa. In many African languages the pitch of speech sounds is an important feature, enabling much information to be conveyed using a set rhythm and tone. Hunter discusses at some length the use of singing and epic poetry as a means of preserving oral tradition. He points out however that the bard or poet does not rely on rote-learning alone; his art is much more sophisticated. Every time he tells a story or a legend he recreates it, but within a constrained yet flexible poetic system (Spanish flamenco and jazz share this characteristic). The storyteller adheres to a highly stylized set of characters and events, and to specific rhythms, but he is free to combine them somewhat differently on each occasion. In order to allow him to fit his theme to the appropriate rhythm, a number of stylistic devices are available. For example, in Homeric verse it was customary to refer to a ship as *equal, curved around* or *dark-prowed* but the exact choice of adjective depended entirely on whether the verse required two, two and a half, or two and three-quarter units of metre.

Most of the external memory aids listed in John Harris's questionnaire depend either on literacy (calendars, diaries, and so on) or on technology (watches or alarms for example), but there are many other possibilities. The Incas[12] used knotted cords (*quipu*) as memory aids, and I myself often use the related but more primitive mnemonic of tying a knot in my handkerchief.

Australian aborigines[13] used notched sticks or tallies to help them remember messages. Although they lived in small nomadic groups, an important part of their social and cultural identity depended on occasional intertribal ceremonies. The decision to hold a ceremony would be taken by the elders of the tribe, who would also decide which groups and which members of those groups should be invited. The actual invitation would be delivered by one of the younger men who would carry a message stick. He would look on while the head man of the group made marks on the stick, a notch at one end indicating the sender, and a large notch for each tribal group invited to attend. If all the people were invited, then the stick would be notched along the edge from end to end; if only a few were invited, then only a portion of the stick would be notched; if very few, then a notch would be made for each individual, who would be named to the messenger.

Ever forget where you parked your car? It's easy enough if you're thinking of something else at the time.

Once the head man had completed the message on the stick he would hand it to the elder nearest to him, who would inspect it and add any necessary further instructions before passing it to the other elders present. The messenger would then take the stick to the group to be invited and relate the message, referring as he did so to the marks on the stick. The marks do not represent a written language, in that the messenger would not be able to 'read' messages he had not heard, but they are retrieval cues for an oral message.

Memory aids

A society where few people can read and write must needs rely heavily on memory, and will rightly value the capacity to remember large amounts of information in great detail. But in a society such as our own, we are not obliged to commit everything to memory. Indeed in very important matters it would not be sensible to do so. That is why committees have minutes, companies company reports, and lawyers put agreements in writing. These are obvious precautions against the distortions and deletions to which human memory is heir. Even when shopping I must confess that once the list of items gets beyond three or four I do not imagine my house festooned with them but simply write a shopping list. It's more convenient, just as a diary is more convenient, and relieves one from worrying about whether one should be seeing someone today or tomorrow. There are however situations in which such obvious aids as diaries and shopping lists are inappropriate.

What the particular problems are will vary from person to person. Just as the problems will vary so will the solutions, and there is no alternative to tackling each problem in its own right, using as much good sense and ingenuity as you can bring to bear on it. Though there are no simple rules for improving your memory, there are a number of general principles that will help you make the most of your memory.

Improving your memory

As I hope the previous chapters have demonstrated, human memory is a remarkably effective system for storing and retrieving information. Nonetheless we all find that our memory lets us down, particularly as we get older. Our lapses are often rather trivial and easily remedied, for example describing an incident involving a mutual friend and forgetting his name. Other memory failures can be more serious however; a missed appointment may sour a potentially important working relationship or lose a valuable contract. If you are a student you need to remember information for exams, and if you have a job dealing with people you need to remember faces and names.

In one sense we cannot change our memory. By this I mean that I know of no way in which the neural systems underlying memory can be systematically enhanced. As we get older our brains inevitably get somewhat smaller and our brain cells apparently less efficient, and it is unrealistic to assume that techniques will be found in the foreseeable future for replacing ageing or defunct brain cells. What we can do however is use the system we have more effectively.

First of all it is important to accept that your memory is not a system like your heart and lungs for which simple 'fitness' exercises can be prescribed. This particular fallacy used to be common among 19th-century educationists and is still sneakingly believed today. For example, it is not uncommon for speech therapists to try to help patients with memory problems by giving them

The best way of remembering where you put something is always to keep it in the same place. Here's an original solution to the problem of storage and retrieval.

practice at Kim's Game (a trayful of objects is shown to a patient, and then covered while the patient tries to remember as many of the objects on the tray as possible). Well-meaning though this may be, the chances of it actually helping the patient are rather slight.

Ian Hunter, whose excellent book on memory has two very useful chapters on improving memory performance, cites an experiment published by W. G. Sleight[14] in 1911 in which 84 12-year-old schoolgirls were tested on their ability to memorize the dates of historical events, lists of nonsense syllables, verses of poetry, passages of prose, lists of names, the position of towns and rivers on a map, an array of visual forms and a sequence of letters of the alphabet. The girls were then split into four groups, three of which were given memory practice for half an hour a day, four days a week, over a six-week period, making 12 hours of practice in all. One group practised memorizing poetry, a second memorized quantitative facts such as scientific formulae and geographical distances, while the third was given passages of prose about geographical, historical and scientific subjects, and required to reproduce the content of these passages from memory. The fourth group acted as a control and had no practice. All four groups were then re-tested using material similar to that used at the beginning of the experiment. Did practice in memorizing a particular type of material enhance later performance on the same type of material? Sleight's results were unequivocal: the control group who were given no training performed just as well as the three other groups, who showed virtually no difference in performance as a result of their intervening training.

Similar negative results have emerged from a number of other studies. One of the most interesting of these is a recent one by Daniel Wagner[15] of the memory capacity of rural Moroccan students attending a Koranic school. Although a great deal of their training involved memorizing verses from the Koran, their performance on memory tests involving other material was relatively poor compared with that of other Moroccans or American students. They also showed little use of mnemonics.

In contrast to this Hunter cites an experiment by Woodrow, published in 1927 involving 182 university students. They were tested initially on a range of memory tasks involving remembering poetry and prose, learning the English meaning of Turkish words, the dates of historical events and a memory span test using consonants. One group spent a total of three hours distributed over a four-week period memorizing poems and nonsense syllables. A second group spent the same amount of time being instructed in memorization techniques of poetry and nonsense syllables. A third group served as a control and was given no memory training. When re-tested at the end of the four-week period, the first group performed no better or worse than the control group. The second group, the memory training group, however, did consistently better than either of the other groups on all the tests, including some which were quite different from those used during the training period; the techniques they had learned stood them in good stead.

That's all very well, you may be thinking to yourself, but learning poems off by heart is not my particular problem; the amount of English/Turkish vocabulary you have to master is probably not enormous either. Will Woodrow's principles help you? The answer is that they, and other principles like them, will help you to help yourself, provided you are prepared to tackle the task of improving your memory with initiative and persistence. You will have to develop new habits, and these cannot be acquired without a fair amount of effort, so the first question to ask is whether you have a serious need to improve your memory, and if so, which aspect of it.

If you are worried about your memory keep a diary and jot down your memory lapses. This has two advantages: first it usually reveals that your memory problem is not nearly as dramatic as imagined, and second it pinpoints those situations which are giving most trouble.

Attention and interest

It should be clear from previous chapters that nothing is likely to get into long-term memory unless you attend to it. As we saw in the case of the BBC saturation advertising campaign, even presenting the same information a thousand times over will not make it stick if the listener does not pay attention and process it actively. This is almost certainly the failing which underlies the common difficulty of remembering people's names on first meeting. On being introduced to someone new, one's attention tends to be concentrated on looking at them and making whatever initial remarks are appropriate, with the result that the name often 'goes in one ear and out of the other'. If you want to improve your memory for people's names on first meeting, you have no option but to make sure you consciously attend to them, if necessary asking for them to be repeated. Socially it is much less embarrassing to ask for someone's name to be repeated immediately you are introduced to them than to have to confess to having forgotten it later; asking for a repetition implies interest, whereas forgetting implies that perhaps you were not sufficiently interested in the other person to notice or retain this name. Similarly, it makes sense to look directly at the person when you are being introduced; to show interest in the appearance of someone you have just met is likely to seem much more flattering than staring at them on a subsequent meeting, racking your brains to think whether you really have met them before, and if so, what their name is. Having learned their name, check from time to time that you can recall it. Check after a short delay at first, gradually increasing the interval between checks. The process of recall will of itself help you learn the name.

The same principle applies if you want to remember the contents of a book you are reading. If you skim through with one eye on the book and the other on the television, you cannot expect to absorb very much of the content of either. One reason why top chess players have a phenomenal memory for chess games, or football fans for the teams of yesteryear, is that they have an intense interest in the topic and avidly attend to incoming information about it.

The relationship between interest, expertise and memory is of course not limited to Western culture. Sir Frederick Bartlett[16] reports an attempt he made to check out a claim that the Swazi of South Africa had remarkable memory capacities. He began by asking a Swazi boy to take a message to the other end of the village. The message contained ten elements and the journey took about two minutes. The boy made two major errors – what one might expect from an English boy of the same age. A similar conclusion followed the testing of Swazi adults on a range of memory tests. Then a white farmer suggested that one of his herdsmen should be tested on his memory for cattle. The man was sent for and asked to give a list of the cattle bought by a former employer a year previously, together with any details he could remember. He squatted on the ground and rapidly recited a list of nine transactions, of which the following two are typical: 'From Mbimbimaseko, one young black ox with a white bush to its tail, for £2; from Ndoda Kedeli, one young red heifer, the calf of a red cow, and with a white belly, for £1'. The nine transactions were checked against the sales list from the farmer's records and all nine were found to be accurate, with small exceptions – one price was out by 10 shillings and the colour of one animal was discrepant. The reason for this remarkable memory for stock transactions, none of which the herdsman had conducted himself, lies in the fact that cattle are of enormous interest to the Swazi, since they play a very important role in their social structure.

In the case of new material (sets of facts, a foreign language), the way in which it can best be organized for learning is obviously crucially dependent on the material itself and on the level of interest of the learner. In general, it helps to relate new material to yourself and to your own circumstances as richly and elaborately as possible in the time available. A good example of this comes from a recent study by Chase and Ericsson[17] in which an individual was given repeated practice at the digit span task; in all he practised for more than 200 hours, spread over a period of 18 months, and was simply encouraged to do whatever he could to increase his capacity for repeating back a sequence of digits, each time a different sequence, presented at a rate of one digit per second. By the end of 18 months he was able to repeat back sequences of no fewer than 70 digits (as you will recall most people can manage six or seven digits, but ten or more is rather exceptional). How did he do it?

For the first four hours of practice Chase and Ericsson's subject, SF, showed very little improvement, but on the fifth day his span jumped from eight to ten digits. From then on his span continued to increase at the rate of about one digit per week; I understand that his span has now passed the 80-digit mark, and is still climbing. What happened on the crucial fifth session was that SF hit on a strategy for coding the digits he was presented with. He was, as it happened, a keen and accomplished middle- and long-distance runner, with a detailed knowledge of times for various distances and standards. What he did was to recode number sequences as running times: hence 3 4 9 2 would become *3 min 49.2 sec, a near world record for the mile.* He has 11 major categories of running times at his disposal, ranging from the half-mile to the marathon, and within each category he has lots of sub-categories. Numbers greater than six occasionally present problems – there are only 60 seconds in a minute – so he

Left and right: two approaches to flight simulation, 1930s and 1980s style. In-the-air training for a commercial pilot today is about 13 times as costly as simulator training. No matter what skills you set out to learn, nothing can take the place of practice (see page 211).

deals with these by using other coding strategies, ages for example; 8 9 3 would be recoded as *89.3 years old, a very old man*. Running times make up 62 per cent of his associations, ages 25 per cent and the next are mostly dates; for example, 1 9 4 6 becomes *one year after World War Two*.

While such associations are clearly helpful, it is obviously necessary to have some means of making them occur in the right order. SF does this by means of a hierarchical strategy, grouping digits into sequences of four and three.

Digit span is normally regarded as a manifestation of short-term memory. Does SF therefore have a quite out of the ordinary short-term memory capacity? Two features of his performance indicate that he does not. First of all, if he is asked to remember sequences of consonants instead of numbers, his span drops from over 70 to about six. As might be expected from his strategy, SF's amazing span is limited to numerical material. The second feature that differentiates his performance from normal digit span is that after a digit span session is over he is able to go back and recall about 65 per cent of the digit groups presented during the session. Normally, people who take part in digit span experiments can recall virtually nothing. In short, it appears that SF is primarily using long-term memory in order to perform this traditional short-term task. In this respect he resembles expert mental arithmeticians, many of whom display a remarkable memory for numbers. Digit sequences are usually highly meaningful to such people because of their numerical characteristics. To a person who is fascinated by numbers almost any string of numbers has rich associations.

The general conclusion to be drawn from SF's remarkable digit span is that good memory demands attention and organization, and this in turn depends on interest. This is all very well if you are reading a fascinating account of some new development in your favourite area, but what if you are a student following a set curriculum? What can you do to boost your attention to material which may be, by any standards, rather tedious and boring?

You should begin by selecting a working environment that does not have too many distractions. People vary in the kind of environment they find most conducive to work, some preferring complete seclusion and silence, others claiming to work best against a background of quite loud music. I myself find that if a task is very demanding, an atmosphere with occasional distractions is sometimes more productive than complete peace. Once you have found a good environment for your work, it is sensible to use it regularly; with practice, you will find that it is increasingly easy to adopt the habit of studying there.

Try to read whatever you are reading as *actively* as you can – not in the spirit of someone trying to commit it to memory, but of someone questioning the author; try to relate what he says to what you already know. If you find the material very unsympathetic, why not attempt to pinpoint your dissatisfaction, and imagine how the author might reply to your criticisms? You may well find that this gives you a greater understanding of what he is trying to say, even if you move no closer to his viewpoint.

This may be all very well if you are reading a text on history or biology, but what if you are learning a foreign language? Once again, the same broad principles apply. If you are learning the language so as to be able to converse when in a foreign country, then it is essential that you do not confine your attention to the rote-learning of grammar and vocabulary, but actively use the language as you acquire it. Imagine yourself in various situations and attempt to produce the necessary requests and conversation. It is obviously much easier if you have colleagues who are also learning the language, or better still have already acquired it. Some students find it helpful to use visual imagery mnemonics in trying to acquire some of the rote-learned aspects of a language, such as vocabulary, but remember that if you wish to use the language, there is no alternative to practising speaking it. Pay attention to the sound and rhythm of word sequences as well as to their meaning. Finally, try to bear in mind the range of tasks you will have to perform in the language; bear in mind your own purpose in learning the language and try to gear your practice to that purpose.

Organization

Back in 1891 the great American psychologist William James suggested that all improvement of memory consists in the improvement of one's habitual methods of recording facts.[19] Needless to say, this remains true. As mentioned earlier, long-term memory is like an enormous library, and unless the information stored in it is organized in a systematic way, it is unlikely to be retrievable when required. Organization helps in two ways: it structures what is being learnt so that recalling a fragment of information is likely to make the rest accessible; and it relates newly-learnt material to what has gone before, which means that the richer your existing knowledge structure the easier it is to comprehend and remember new material. A student beginning a new subject finds research papers extremely difficult to understand, but an experienced researcher in the field is likely to be able to skim the same papers very rapidly, extracting the essentials in a fraction of the time.

How should you organize new material? Obviously a lot depends on the nature of the material you are trying to commit to memory. In general however it helps to relate the new material to yourself and your own interests as richly and elaborately as possible in the available time. Suppose, for example, that I wanted to memorize my office postal code, *CB2 2EF*. What associations does it conjure up? The first two letters are easy, they are shorthand for CamBridge, the town where I live, or I might possibly have remembered them as the standard abbreviation for 'Confined to Barracks', imagining myself confined to my office. The 22 I might remember as the number of yards in a cricket pitch, so I could imagine myself confined to barracks and barred from playing cricket. As for the *EF*, I could perhaps remember that they are the fifth and sixth letters in the alphabet and also the fifth and sixth letters in the code.

Practice

But no matter how ingenious your techniques for committing information to memory, you cannot escape the effects of the total time hypothesis, which states that the amount you learn depends on the amount you practice. This is true whether you are trying to learn the name of someone you have just met, trying to commit a telephone number to memory, or trying to master a difficult concept in physics. Nevertheless it is important to organize your practice time sensibly. Massing all your practice together into a few marathon learning sessions is not an efficient way of learning. A little and often is a better strategy.

The novelist Arnold Bennett once wrote a short book entitled *How to Live on 24 Hours a Day* which I remember reading as a student. The main theme of the book, at least as I remember it, is that there are far more things to do, to read, to learn, and to think about than one can ever find time for. And yet most of our lives are filled with intervals – intervals waiting for a bus or washing up

Left and right: whether you are learning movements, facts, theories, or languages, nothing takes the place of practice.

or walking across town – when we simply let our mind freewheel. Bennett argued that these unoccupied interludes can and should be used productively to think about and plan new projects, work out solutions to current problems, or rehearse material we are trying to learn. As a student who did not want to give up too much of his social life to revising for exams, I adopted the policy of writing very brief but systematic summaries of the topics I needed to revise, and carrying them around with me in a small notebook. I found I could use the odd few minutes spent waiting for a train or bus very productively.

If you know you are going to need to use newly acquired material in a wide range of contexts, try varying the way in which you rehearse it. To use an

The fabric of memory, richer and more reliable the more tightly the threads are woven together.

academic example, an examiner often expects students to answer questions in ways which go beyond mere regurgitation of curriculum facts; he is looking for the rather rarer ability to apply concepts in different ways, or to cross-link concepts previously treated separately. If you concentrate on merely committing material to memory without thinking more deeply and widely about it, you are likely to find later manipulation of that material very difficult; all your new thinking will have to be done during the examination itself. But if, as you revised, you thought fairly broadly about the topics concerned, interrelated them, and imagined their application to problems you yourself have encountered, you are likely to make a much better job of the examination and also retain more of what you have learned.

This point is discussed in some detail by John Bransford[19] who lays great emphasis on what he calls *transfer-appropriate processes*. By this he means that you should ensure that what you do during learning will enable you to apply what you have learned when the time comes. He refers to the case of a graduate student learning statistics who was quite sure he understood each chapter and could do the exercises; however, once the order of the exercises was switched, he found great difficulty. This is not uncommon with statistics where it is easy to become preoccupied with the mechanics of performing a particular test while neglecting to learn which statistical test one should apply in what situation. It is important therefore to continue to monitor your learning, and be alert to the danger of being too easily satisfied. It is tempting to move on when you can *recognize* the right answer, but not *produce* it. It is often said that the best way to learn a subject is to teach it; to convey the necessary information to someone else, you must be able to produce it, not just recognize it when you read it.

Conclusion

The human memory system is remarkably efficient, but it is of course extremely fallible. That being so, it makes sense to take full advantage of memory aids to minimize the disruption caused by such lapses. If external aids are used, it is sensible to use them consistently and systematically – always put appointments in your diary, always add wanted items to a shopping list, and so on. If you use internal aids such as mnemonics, you must be prepared to invest a reasonable amount of time in mastering them and practising them. Mnemonics are like tools and cannot be used until forged. Overall, however, as William James pointed out (the italics are mine): 'Of two men with the same outward experiences and the same amount of mere native tenacity, *the one who thinks over his experiences most and weaves them into systematic relations with each other will be the one with the best memory.*'[20]

Introduction

1 Hunter, I. M. L., *Memory: Facts and Fallacies*. Baltimore: Penguin, 1957
2 Solso, R., *Cognitive Psychology*. New York: Harcourt, Brace and Jovanovich, 1979
3 Bransford, J. D., *Human Cognition: Learning, Understanding and Remembering*. Belmont, California: Wadsworth Publishing Company, 1979
4 Loftus, E. F., *Eyewitness Testimony*. Cambridge, Massachusetts: Harvard University Press, 1979
5 Baddeley, A. D., *The Psychology of Memory*. New York: Basic Books, 1976

Chapter 1

1 Tulving, E., *Organization of Memory*, E. Tulving and W. Donaldson (Eds.). New York: Academic Press, 1972, pp. 381–403
2 Galton, F., *Inquiries into Human Faculty and its Development*. London: Dent, Everyman Edition, 1883, pp. 57–78
3 Bartlett, F. *Remembering*. Cambridge: Cambridge University Press, 1968, pp. 59–61 reprinted 1972
4 Di Vesta, F. J., Ingersoll, G. and Sunshine, P., A factor analysis of imagery tests. *Journal of Verbal Learning and Verbal Behavior*, 1971, *10*, 471–479
5 Conrad, R. and Hull, A. J., Information, acoustic confusion and memory span. *British Journal of Psychology*, 1964, *55*, 429–432

Chapter 2

1 Ebbinghaus, H., *Über das Gedachtnis*. Leipzig: Dunker. Translation by H. Ruyer and C. E. Bussenius, *Memory*. New York: Teachers College, Columbia University, 1913
2 Baddeley, A. D. and Longman, D. J. A., The influence of length and frequency of training sessions on rate of learning to type. *Ergonomics*, 1978, *21*, 627–635
3 Landauer, T. K. and Bjork, R. A., Optimum rehearsal patterns and name learning. In: *Practical Aspects of Memory*, M. M. Gruneberg, P. E. Morris and R. N. Sykes (Eds.). London: Academic Press, 1978, pp. 625–632
4 Nilsson, L.-G. *Personal communication*
5 Bekerian, D. A. and Baddeley, A. D., Saturation advertising and the repetition effect. *Journal of Verbal Learning and Verbal Behavior*, 1980, *19*, 17–25
6 Baddeley, A. D., *The Psychology of Memory*. New York: Basic Books, 1976, p. 307
7 Taylor, W. L., 'Cloze procedure': a new tool for measuring readability. *Journalism Quarterly*, 1953, *30*, 415–433

Chapter 3

1 Bartlett, F. C., *Remembering*. Cambridge: Cambridge University Press, 1968, pp. 2–7
2 Bartlett, F. C., *Remembering*. Cambridge: Cambridge University Press, 1968, pp. 65, 70
3 Hastorf, A. H. and Cantrill, H., They saw a game: a case study. *Journal of Abnormal and Social Psychology*, 1954, *97*, 399–401
4 de Groot, A., Perception and memory versus thought: some old ideas and recent findings. In: *Problem Solving*. B. Kleinmontz (ed.) New York: Wiley, 1966
5 Lauria, A. R., *The Mind of a Mnemonist*. New York: Basic Books, 1968

Chapter 4

1 Ebbinghaus, H., *Über das Gedachtnis*. Leipzig: Dunker. Translation by H. Ruyer and C. E. Bussenius, *Memory*. New York: Teachers College, Columbia University, 1913
2 Warrington, E. K. and Sanders, H. I., The Fate of Old Memories. *Quarterly Journal of Experimental Psychology*, 1971, *23*, 432–442
3 Woodhead, M. M. and Baddeley, A. D., (in preparation)
4 Squire, L. R. and Slater, P. C., Forgetting in very long-term memory as assessed by an improved questionnaire technique. *Journal of Experimental Psychology: Human Learning and Memory*, 1975, *104*, 50–54
5 Bahrick, H. P., Bahrick, P. O. and Wittlinger, R. P., Fifty years of memory for names and faces: a cross-sectional approach. *Journal of Experimental Psychology: General*, 1975, *104*, 54–75
6 Gittins, D., Oral history, reliability and recollection. In: *The Recall Method in Social Surveys*, L. Moss and H. Goldstein (Eds.). London: University of London Institute of Education, Studies in Education (new series) 9, 1979, pp. 85–86
7 Linton, M., Real world memory after six years: an in vivo study of very long-term memory. In: *Practical Aspects of Memory*, M. M. Gruneberg, P. E. Morris and R. N. Sykes (Eds.). London: Academic Press, 1978, pp. 69–76
8 Baddeley, A. D. and Hitch, G. J., Recency re-examined. In: *Attention and Performance VI*, S. Dornic (Ed.). Hillsdale, New Jersey: Erlbaum, 1977, pp. 647–667
9 Minami, H. and Dallenbach, K. M., The effect of activity upon learning and retention in the cockroach. *American Journal of Psychology*, 1946, *59*, 1–58
10 Hockey, G. R. J., Davies, S. and Gray, M. M., Forgetting as a function of sleep at different times of day. *Quarterly Journal of Experimental Psychology*, 1972, *24*, 386–393
11 McGeoch, J. A. and MacDonald, W. T., Meaningful relation and retroactive inhibition. *American Journal of Psychology*, 1931, *43*, 579–588
12 Ausubel, D. P., Stager, M. and Gaite, A. J. H., Retroactive facilitation in meaningful verbal learning. *Journal of Educational Psychology*, 1968, *59*, 250–256
13 Crouse, J. H., Retroactive interference in reading prose materials. *Journal of Educational Psychology*, 1971, *62*, 39–44
14 Underwood, B. J., Interference and forgetting. *Psychological Review*, 1957, *64*, 49–60
15 Blakemore, C., The unsolved marvel of memory. *The New York Times Magazine*, 6 February 1977, p. 88. (Reprinted in *Readings in Psychology, 78/79*. Guildford, Connecticut: Annual Editions, Dushkin Publishing Group, 1979)

Chapter 5

1 Freud, S., *Psychopathology of everyday life*. In: *The Writings of Sigmund Freud*, A. A. Brill (Ed.). New York: Modern Library, 1938
2 Zeller, A. F., An experimental analogue of repression: III. The effect of induced failure and success on memory measured by recall. *Journal of Experimental Psychology*, 1951, *42*, 32–38
3 Levinger, G. and Clark, J., Emotional factors in the forgetting of word associations. *Journal of Abnormal and Social Psychology*, 1961, *62*, 99–105
4 Yerkes, R. M. and Dodson, J. D., the relation of strength of stimulus to

rapidity of habit-formation. *Journal of Comparative and Neurological Psychology*, 1908, *18*, 459–482

5 Kleinsmith, L. J. and Kaplan, S., Paired associated learning as a function of arousal and interpolated interval. *Journal of Experimental Psychology*, 1963, *65*, 190–193

6 Folkard, S., Monk, T. H., Bradbury, R. and Rosenthall, J., Time of day effects in school children's immediate and delayed recall of meaningful material. *British Journal of Psychology*, 1977, *68*, 45–50

7 Bradley, B. P. and Morris, B. J., Emotional factors in forgetting. Part II Research Project, Cambridge University Department of Experimental Psychology, 1976

8 Hunter, I. M. L., *Memory: Facts and Fallacies*. Baltimore: Penguin, 1957, p. 270

9 Robinson, J. O., Rosen, M., Revill, S. I., David, H. and Rus, G. A. D., Self-administered intravenous and intramuscular pethidine. *Anaesthesia*, 1980, *35*, 763–770

10 Hunter, M., Philips, C. and Rachman, S., Memory for pain. *Pain*, 1979, *6*, 35–46

11 Cited from Hunter, I. M. L., *Memory: Facts and Fallacies*. Baltimore: Penguin, 1957, pp. 233–234

12 Thigpen, C. H. and Cleckley, H., *The Three Faces of Eve*. London: Secker and Warburg, 1957

Chapter 6

1 Freedman, J. L. and Loftus, E. F., Retrieval of words from long-term memory. Journal of *Verbal Learning and Verbal Behavior*, 1971, *10*, 107–115

2 Loftus, E. F. and Loftus, G. R., Changes in memory structure and retrieval over the course of instruction. *Journal of Educational Psychology*, 1974, *66*, 315–318

3 Collins, A. M. and Quillian, M. R., Experiments on semantic memory and language comprehension. In *Cognition in Learning and Memory*, L. W. Gregg (Ed.). New York: Wiley, 1972

4 Rosch, E., Human categorisation. In: *Advances in Cross Cultural Psychology Volume 1*, N. Warren (Ed.). London: Academic Press, 1977

5 Bransford, J. D., *Human Cognition: Learning, Understanding and Remembering*. Belmont, California: Wadsworth Publishing Company, 1979, p. 197

6 Bransford, J. D. and Johnson, M. K.,

Contextual prerequisites for understanding: some investigations of comprehension and recall. *Journal of Verbal Learning and Verbal Behavior*, 1972, *11*, 717–726

7 Bruce, D. J., The effect of listeners' anticipations on the intelligibility of heard speech. *Language and Speech*, 1958, *1*, 79–97

8 Bartlett, F. C., *Remembering*. Cambridge: Cambridge University Press, 1968

9 Schank, R. C., *Scripts, Plans, Goals and Understanding: An Inquiry into Human Knowledge Structures*. Hillsdale, New Jersey: Erlbaum, 1977

10 Whorf, B. L., *Language, Thought and Reality*. Cambridge: Technology Press, 1956

11 Brown, R. W. and Lenneberg, E. H., A study in language and cognition. *Journal of Abnormal and Social Psychology*, 1954, *49*, 454–462

12 Rosch-Heider, E., Universals in color naming and memory. *Journal of Experimental Psychology*, 1972, *93*, 10–20

13 Moar, I. T., Mental triangulation and the nature of internal representations of space. Unpublished PhD thesis, University of Cambridge, 1978

14 Potter, M. C. and Faulconer, B. A., Time to understand pictures and words. *Nature*, 1975, *253*, 437–438

15 Heidbreder, E., The attainment of concepts: 1. Terminology and Methodology. *Journal of General Psychology*, 1946, *35*, 173–189

16 Bransford, J. D. and Nitsch, K. E., Coming to understand things we could not previously understand. In *Speech and Language in the Laboratory, School and Clinic*, J. F. Kavanagh and W. Strange (Eds.). Cambridge, Massachusetts: MIT Press, 1978

17 Bransford, J. D., *Human Cognition: Learning, Understanding and Remembering*. Belmont, California: Wadsworth Publishing Company, 1979

Chapter 7

1 Tulving, E., Subjective organization and effects of repetition in multi-trial free-recall learning. *Journal of Verbal Learning and Verbal Behavior*, 1966, *5*, 193–197

2 Brown, R. and McNeill, D., The 'tip of the tongue' phenomenon. *Journal of Verbal Learning and Verbal Behavior*, 1966, *5*, 325–337

3 Craik, F. I. M. and Lockhart, R. S., Levels of processing: a framework for memory research. *Journal of Verbal Learning and Verbal Behavior*, 1972, *11*, 671–684

4 Tulving, E. and Osler, S., Effectiveness of retrieval cues in memory for words. *Journal of Experimental Psychology*, 1968, *77*, 593–601

5 Tulving, E. and Thomson, D. M., Encoding specificity and retrieval processes in episodic memory. *Psychological Review*, 1973, *80*, 352–373

6 Engen, T., Kuisma, J. E. and Eimas, P. D., Short-term memory of odors. *Journal of Experimental Psychology*, 1973, *99*, 222–225

7 Engen, T. and Ross, B. M., Long-term memory of odors with and without verbal descriptions. *Journal of Experimental Psychology*, 1973, *100*, 221–227

8 Locke, J., *An Essay Concerning Human Understanding*. London: Dent, Everyman Edition, 1961

9 Godden, D. R. and Baddeley, A. D., Context-dependent memory in two natural environments: on land and underwater. *British Journal of Psychology*, 1975, *66*, 325–331

10 Baddeley, A. D., Cuccaro, W. J., Egstrom, G., Weltman, G. and Willis, M. A., Cognitive efficiency of divers working in cold water. *Human Factors*, 1975, *17*, 446–454

11 Godden, D. R. and Baddeley, A. D., When does context influence recognition memory? *British Journal of Psychology*, 1980, *71*, 99–104

12 Goodwin, D.W., Powell, B., Bremer, D., Hoine, H. and Stern, J., Alcohol and recall: state-dependent effects in man. *Science*, 1969, *163*, 1358

13 Eich, J. E., The cue-dependent nature of state-dependent retrieval. *Memory and Cognition*, 1980, *8*, 157–173

14 Brown, J., Lewis, V. J. and Monk, A. F., Memorability, word frequency and negative recognition. *Quarterly Journal of Experimental Psychology*, 1977, *29*, 461–474

15 Camp, J.C., Lachman, J.L. and Lachman, R. (1980). Evidence for object-access and inferential retrieval in question answering. *Journal of Verbal Learning and Verbal Behavior*, *19*, 583-596.

Chapter 8

1 Devlin, Lord Patrick (Chairman), Report to the Secretary of State for the Home Department Committee on Evidence of Identification in

Criminal Cases. London: HMSO, 1976

2 Loftus, E. F., *Eyewitness Testimony*. Cambridge, Massachusetts: Harvard University Press, 1979

3 Cattell, J. M., Measurement of the accuracy of recollection. *Science*, 1895, *20*, 761–776

4 Nickerson, R. S. and Adams, M. J., Long-term memory for a common object. *Cognitive Psychology*, 1979, *11*, 287–307

5 Loftus, E. F., *Eyewitness Testimony*. Cambridge, Massachusetts: Harvard University Press, 1979, pp. 171–177

6 Idzikowski, C. and Baddeley, A. D., Fear and performance in dangerous environments. To appear in: *Stress and Fatigue in Human Performance*, G. R. J. Hockey (Ed.). Chichester: Wiley, 1983, pp. 123–144

7 Clifford, B. R. and Scott, J., Individual and situational factors in eyewitness testimony. *Journal of Applied Psychology*, 1978, *63*, 342–359

8 Loftus, E. F., *Eyewitness Tesimony*, Cambridge, Massachusetts: Harvard University Press, 1979, pp. 35–36

9 Loftus, E. F. and Palmer, J. C., Reconstruction of automobile destruction: an example of the interaction between language and memory. *Journal of Verbal Learning and Verbal Behavior*, 1974, *13*, 585–589

10 Loftus, E. F. and Palmer, J. C., Reconstruction of automobile destruction: an example of the interaction between language and memory. *Journal of Verbal Learning and Verbal Behavior*, 1974, *13*, 585–589

11 Loftus, E. F., Shifting human color memory. *Memory and Cognition*, 1977, *5*, 696-699

12 Loftus, E. F., *Eyewitness Testimony*. Cambridge, Massachusetts: Harvard University Press, 1979, pp. 118–120

13 Loftus, E. F., *Eyewitness Tesimony*. Cambridge, Massachusetts: Harvard University Press, 1979, pp. 62–63

14 Woodhead, M. M. and Baddeley, A. D., in *Stress and Fatigue in Human Performance*, G. R. J. Hockey (Ed.). Chichester: Wiley

15 Yin, R., Face recognition by brain-injured patients: a dissociable ability? *Neuropsychologia*, 1979, *8*, 395–402

16 Woodhead, M. M., Baddeley, A. D. and Simmonds, D. C. V., On training people to recognise faces. *Ergonomics*, 1979, *22*, 333-343

17 Penry, J., *Looking at Faces and Remembering Them: A Guide to Facial Identification*. London: Elek

Books, 1971

18 da Vinci, L., *Trattato della Pittura*. After the edition by H. Ludwig, Vienna, 1882, cited in E. H. Gombrich, *Art and Illusion*. London: Phaidon Press, 1962, p. 294

19 Patterson, K. E. and Baddeley, A. D., When face recognition fails. *Journal of Experimental Psychology: Human Learning and Memory*, 1975, 3, 406–417

20 Davis, G., Ellis, H. and Shepherd, J., Face recognition accuracy as a function of mode of representation. *Journal of Applied Psychology*, 1978, *63*, 180–187

21 Loftus, E. F., *Eyewitness Tesimony*. Cambridge, Massachusetts: Harvard University Press, 1979, pp. 148–150

22 Thomson, D. M., Person identification: influencing the outcome. *Australian and New Zealand Journal of Criminology*, 1983

Chapter 9

1 Russell, W. R., *Brain, Memory, Learning: A Neurologist's View*. London: Oxford University Press, 1959

2 Yarnell, P. R. and Lynch, S., Retrograde memory immediately after conclusion. *Lancet*, 1970, *1*, 863–865

3 Squire, L. R. and Cohen, N. J., Remote memory, retrograde amnesia, and the neuropsychology of human memory. In *Human Memory and Amnesia*, L. S. Cermak (Ed.). Hillsdale, New Jersey: Erlbaum, 1982, pp. 275-304

4 Rabbitt, P., Human ageing and disturbances of memory control processes underlying 'intelligent' performance of some cognitive tasks. In: *Intelligence and Learning*, J. P. Das and N. O'Connor (Eds.). New York: Plenum Press, 1981, pp. 427–439

5 Riegel, K. F. and Riegel, R. M., Development, drop, and death. *Developmental Psychology*, 1972, *6*, 306–319

6 Milner, B., Amnesia following operation on the temporal lobes. In *Amnesia*, C. W. M. Whitty and O. L. Zangwill (Eds.). London: Butterworth, 1966

7 Baddeley, A. D. and Warrington, E. K. Amnesia and the distinction between long- and short-term memory. *Journal of Verbal Learning and Verbal Behavior*, 1970, *9*, 176–189

8 Baddeley, A. D., Amnesia: a minimal model. In: *Memory and Am-*

nesia, L. S. Cermak (Ed.). Hillsdale, New Jersey: Erlbaum (in press)

9 Claparède, E., Recognition and moiite. In: *Archives Psycologiques*, Genève, 1911, *11*, 79–90

Chapter 10

1 James W., *The Principles of Pschology*. New York: Holt, Rinehart and Winston, 1890

2 Galton, F., *Inquiries into Human Faculty and its Development*. Dent, Everyman Edition, London: 1883, p. 146

3 Hamilton, Sir William, *Lectures on Metaphysics*, *14*, 1859

4 Jacobs, J., Experiments in 'prehension'. *Mind*, 1887, Vol 12, 75–79

5 Wickelgren, W. A., Rehearsal grouping and hierarchical organization of serial position cues in short-term memory. *Quarterly Journal of Experimental Psychology*, 1967, *19*, 97–102

6 Hunter, I. M. L., An exceptional memory. *British Journal of Psychology*, 1977, *68*, 155–164

7 Baddeley, A. D., Conrad, R. and Thomson, W. E., Letter structure of the English language. *Nature*, 1960, *186*, 414–416

8 Brown, J., Some tests of the decay theory of immediate memory. *Quarterly Journal of Experimental Psychology*, 1958, *10*, 12–21

9 Peterson, L. R. and Peterson, M. J., Short-term retention of individual verbal items. *Journal of Experimental Psychology*, 1959, *58*, 193–198

10 Murdock, B. B. Jr., The retention of individual items. *Journal of Experimental Psychology*, 1961, *62*, 618–625

11 Wickens, D. D., Encoding categories of words: an empirical approach to meaning. *Psychological Review*, 1970, 77, 1–15

12 Wagner, D., Memories of Morocco: the influence of age, schooling and environment on memory. *Cognitive Psychology*, 1978, *10*, 1–28

13 Melton, A. W., Implications of short-term memory for a general theory of memory. *Journal of Verbal Learning and Verbal Behavior*, 1963, *2*, 1–21

14 Conrad, R., Acoustic confusion in immediate memory. *British Journal of Psychology*, 1964, *55*, 75–84

15 Baddeley, A. D., Short-term memory for word sequences as a function of acoustic, semantic and formal similarity. *Quarterly Journal of Ex-*

perimental Psychology, 1966, *18*, 362–365

16 Sachs, J. S., Recogintion memory for syntactic and semantic aspects of connected discourse. *Percpetion and Psychophysics*, 1967, *2*, 437–442

17 Atkinson, R. C. and Shiffrin, R. M., Human memory: a proposed system, and its control processes. In: *The Psychology of Learning and Motivation: Advances in Research and Theory*, vol. 2, K. W. Spence (Ed.). New York: Academic Press, 1968, pp. 89–195

18 Craik, F. I. M. and Lockhart, R. S., Levels of processing: a framework for memory research. *Journal of Verbal Learning and Verbal Behavior*, 1972, *11*, 671–684

19 Craik, F. I. M. and Watkins, M. J., The role of rehearsal in short-term memory. *Journal of Verbal Learning and Verbal Behavior*, 1973, *12*, 599–607

Chapter 11

1 Norman, D. A., *Models of Human Memory*. New York: Academic Press, 1970

2 Baddeley, A. D. and Hitch, G. J., Working memory. In: *The Psychology of Learning and Motivation*, Vol. 8, G. A. Bower (Ed.). New York: Academic Press, 1974, pp. 47–90

3 Wason, P. C. and Johnson-Laird, P. N., *Psychology of Reasoning: Structure and Content*. London: Batsford, 1972

4 Conrad, R., Short-term memory processes in the deaf. *British Journal of Psychology*, 1970, *61*, 179–195

5 Baddeley, A. D., Thomson, N. and Buchanan, M., Word length and the structure of short-term memory. *Journal of Verbal Learning and Verbal Behavior*, 1975, *14*, 575–589

6 Nicholson, R., The relationship between memory span and processing speed. In *Intelligence and Learning*, M. Friedman, J. P. Das and N. O'Connor (Eds.). New York: Plenum, 1981, pp. 179–184

7,9 Ellis, N. C. and Hennelley, R. A., A bilingual word-length effect: implications for intelligence testing and the relative ease of mental calculation in Welsh and English. *British Journal of Psychology*, 1980, *71*, 43–52

8 Hitch, G. J., The role of short-term working memory in mental arithmetic. *Cognitive Psychology*, 1978, *10*, 302-323

10 Geiselman, R. E. and Bjork, R. A.,

Primary versus secondary rehearsal in imagined voices: differential effects on recognition. *Cognitive Psychology*, 1980, *12*, 185–205

11 Baddeley, A. D. and Lewis, V. J., Inner active processes in reading: the inner voice, the inner ear and the inner eye. In: *Interactive Processes in Reading*, A. M. Lesgold and C. A. Perfetti (Eds.). Hillsdale, New Jersey: Erlbaum, 1981, pp. 107–129

12 Patterson, K. E., Neuropsychological approaches to the study of reading. *British Journal of Psychology*, 1981, *72*, 151-174

13 Shepard, R. N. and Feng, C., A chronometric study of mental paperfolding. *Cognitive Psychology*, 1972, *3*, 228–243

14 Shepard, R. N. and Metzler, J., Mental rotation of three-dimensional objects. *Science*, 1971, *171*, 701–703

15 Kosslyn, S. M. and Shwartz, S. P.,

16 Empirical constraints on theories of visual mental imagery. In: *Attention and Performance IX*, J. Long and A. Baddeley (Eds.). Hillsdale, New Jersey: Erlbaum, 1981, pp. 241–260

17 Brooks, L. R., Spatial and verbal components in the act of recall. *Canadian Journal of Psychology*, 1968, *22*, 349–368

18 Baddeley, A. D., Grant, S., Wight, E. and Thomson, N., Imagery and visual working memory. In: *Attention and Performance V*, P. M. A. Rabbitt and S. Dornic (Eds.). London: Academic Press, 1975, pp. 205–217

19 Baddeley, A. D. and Lieberman, K., Spatial working memory. In: *Attention and Performance VIII*, R. Nickerson (Ed.). Hillsdale, New Jersey: Erlbaum, 1980, pp. 521–539

20 Phillips, W. A. and Christie, D. F. M., Interference with visualization. *Quarterly Journal of Experimental Psychology*, 1977, *29*, 637–650

21 Bisiach, E. and Luzzatti, C., Unilateral neglect of representational space. *Cortex*, 1978, *14*, 129–133

22 Baddeley, A. D. and Lieberman, K., Spatial working memory. In: *Attention and Performance VIII*, R. Nickerson (Ed.). Hillsdale, New Jersey: Erlbaum, 1980, pp. 521–539

Chapter 12

1 Woodhead, M. M. and Baddeley, A. D. (in preparation)

2 Sunderland, A. H., Harris, J. E., and Baddeley, A. D. (1983) Do laboratory tests predict everyday memory?

Journal of Verbal Learning and Verbal Behavior, *22*, 341–357

3 Baddeley, A. D., Sunderland, A. and Harris, J. E., How well do laboratory-based tasks predict patients' performance outside the laboratory? To appear in: *Alzheimer's Disease: A Report of Progress in Research*, S. Corkin, K. L. Davis, J. H. Growdon, E. Usdin and R. J. Wurtman (Eds.). New York: Raven Press (in press)

4 Harris, J. E., Memory aids people use: two interview studies. *Memory and Cognition*, 1980, *8*, 31–38

5 Hunter, I. M. L., *Memory, Facts and Fallacies*. Baltimore: Penguin, 1957, pp. 295–297

6 Feinaigle, G. von., *The New Art of Memory* (third edition). London: Sherwood, Neely and Jones, 1813

7 Ramus, P. *Scholae Rhetoricae*. Bâle, 1578

8 Hunter, I. M. L., Memory in everyday life. In: *Applied Problems in Memory*, M. M. Gruneberg and P. E. Morris, (Eds.). London: Academic Press, 1979, pp. 1–24

9 Baddeley, A. D., *The Psychology of Memory*. New York: Basic Books, 1976

10 Vansina, J. *Oral Tradition*. Harmondsworth, England: Penguin University Books, 1973, pp. 32

11 Goody, J. and Watt, I., The consequences of literacy. In: J. Goody (Ed.)., *Literacy in Traditional Societies*. Cambridge: Cambridge University Press, 1968

12 Hunter, I. M. L., Memory in everyday life. In: *Applied Problems in Memory*, M. M. Gruneberg and P. E. Morris (Eds.). London: Academic Press, 1979

13 Hunter, I. M. L., *Memory: Facts and Fallacies*. Baltimore: Penguin, 1957, pp. 306–310

14

15 Wagner, D., Memories of Morocco: the influence of age, schooling and environment on memory. *Cognitive Psychology*, 1978, *10*, 1–28

16 Bartlett, F. C., *Remembering*. Cambridge: Cambridge University Press, 1968

17 Chase, W. G., Lyon, D. R. and Ericson, K. A., Individual differences in memory span. In: *Intelligence and Learning*, J. P. Das and N. O'Connor (Eds.). New York: Plenum, 1981, pp. 157–162

18 James, W., *The Principle of Psychology*. New York: Holt, Rinehart and Winston, 1980

19 Bransford, J. D., *Human Cognition: Learning, Understanding and Remembering*. Belmont, California:

Wadsworth Publishing Company, 1979, pp. 205–245

20 James, W., *Principles of Psychology*. New York: Holt, Rinehart and Winston, 1980

All Sport Tony Duffy 39 **Ardea Photographics** 177 centre left **Bob Bray** 151 bottom **British Museum** 77 **British Telecom** 151 top **British Tourist Authority** 106, Eric Powell 152 **Camera Press** Ralph Crane 171 **Dr R. Conrad** 174 **John Dawson** 24 **Ente Nazionale Italiano per il Turismo** 184 **Esso Petroleum Co. Ltd.** Tony Wingmore 32 top **Frank Spooner Pictures** Gamma 126 left and right, 128 bottom left, Michel Folco 130, Frank Fisher 66 Alain Voloch 36 **Guildhall Library, City of London** 201 **HAG** 134 **Alan Hutchinson Library** 84, 85 bottom, 205, A. Singer 157 **Keystone Press Agency Ltd** 48 **The Kobal Collection Ltd.** 73 **The Mansell Collection** 183 **Marshall Cavendish Picture Library** 16 **Mary Evans Picture Library** 10, 14 top, 53, 65, 108/109, 197 right **Molinare Ltd.** 149 left **MRC Applied Psychology Unit, Cambridge** 37, 131, 178 **Multimedia Publications Inc.** 100 140, 177 right, 193, 210, 211, Ron Isaak 14 bottom, 28 top right and bottom, 32 bottom, 41, 50 top right, 54, 62, 64, 67, 71 bottom, 72 left, 76 top, 94, 96 bottom 112, 130 top and middle, Israel Sun 12, 27, 50 top left, bottom left and right, 72 right, 137 left, M. Koren 15 top, 72 centre, 92, 95, 136, 139 left, 185, 190, 200, Arnon Orbach 60, 203, S. Trippodo 76 bottom **Novosti Press Agency** 48 **Korky Paul** 59 **Philips NV** 91 **Photri** 116 top **Popperfoto** 18 **Post Office** 149 right **Press Association Photos** 115 **Rediffusion Simulators Ltd.** 208 **Rex Features Ltd.** 7, 19 bottom, 97, 116 bottom, 128 centre top and right, 177 centre right, 192, Belg-Ingh 119, Champlong/Arepi 28 top left, A. Devaney 85 top left, 100 top, J. Barry Herron-Globe 104, Fotos International 128 centre bottom, Settimio Garritano 117, Sipa-Press 50 top centre, 71 top, 126 centre, Boccon/Gibod 128 top right and bottom left **John Rolfe Royal Air Force** 209, **Ann Ronan Picture Library** 167 **Science Photo Library** 85 left **Sheridan Photo-Library** 78, Ronald Sheridan 133 **Spectrum Colour Library** 15 bottom, 69 left, 85 centre **Sally Anne Thompson Animal Photography Ltd.** 68 left **Vision International** CNRI 137 left, 144, 161, Explorer (M. Cambazard) 188, (Duport) 100 centre, (V. Pascal) 31, (Perno) 139 right, (Roy) 148, Robin Fletcher 69 centre and right, 124, 129, Steve Herr 178 bottom, Simon Holledge 120, Angelo Hornak 125 left and centre left, Paolo Koch 30, 96 top, 100 right, Scala 57, 70, 125 centre right and right, Anthea Sieveking 160 **John Watney Photo Library** 19 top **Wellcome Institute for the History of Medicine** 25, 197 left **World Health Organization** T. Farkas 146 **Chris Yates** 46, 180/181, back cover **ZEFA** Philip Dowell 168, H. Grathwohl 212, H. Helmlinger 17 top, K. Kerth 21, A. Liesecke 13, J. F. Millies 68 centre and right, F. Paul 177 left, K. Rohrich 17 bottom, K. Scholz 74.